Lynette's HOPE

The Witness of Lynette Katherine Hoppe's Life and Death

Compiled and Edited by Fr. Luke A. Veronis

CONCILIAR PRESS MINISTRIES 🙐 BEN LOMOND, CALIFORNIA

Published by   Conciliar Press Ministries
                 P.O. Box 76
                 Ben Lomond, CA 95005-0076

Scripture quotations in the editorial portions of the book are from the New King James Version of the Bible, © 1982 by Thomas Nelson, Inc., Nashville, Tennessee, and are used by permission.

Printed in the United States of America

ISBN 10: 1-888212-99-3
ISBN 13: 978-1-888212-99-0

Cover design by Ninos Oshaana
Interior design by Katherine Hyde

Manufactured under the direction of Double Eagle Industries. For manufacturing details, call 888-824-4344

To Nathan, Tristan, and Katherine

"For me to live is Christ, and to die is gain."
(Philippians 1:21)

Contents

Acknowledgements

I WANT TO THANK, FIRST OF ALL, NATHAN HOPPE FOR ALLOWING ME TO put this book together. Obviously, this is Lynette's book. She wrote most of the pages, and she inspired countless people through her life and death. Precisely because of her witness, she has created a thirst in many people who want to know more about her life and source of inspiration. Nathan gave me the opportunity to read through her personal writings, combine them with her public epistles, and intermix my own experiences and interactions with Lynette, thus trying to create a fuller picture of who she was for the reader. The Hoppes have been dear co-workers and friends with my family, our children consider each other the best of friends, and we truly thank God for our special relationship with one another.

The idea for this book would have never taken root if not for the website www.prayforlynette.org, which George Russell and his internet team put together. George made Lynette's writings public domain to the world, and thus opened the door for countless people from six continents to feel connected to and blessed by Lynette. Thank you, George, for making that possible.

I truly appreciate the numerous people I approached to offer a reflection on their relationship with and perspective on Lynette. From His Beatitude Archbishop Anastasios to various friends and family, your contribution only added to the overall flavor of the book. I know that I could have asked many others, and for those who would have liked to add something, please forgive me for not asking you.

I appreciate the editorial support I have received from Conciliar Press, as well as suggestions from Chris Veronis. Also, I want to acknowledge the contribution of Helen Nicozisis and the Endowment Fund for Orthodox

Missions for helping to partially offset the cost of producing this book.

Finally, I want to thank my wife Faith, who acted as a sounding board throughout the entire process of editing this book. She offered many insightful suggestions, and remembered different stories and experiences about Lynette which only enhanced the final product. She is always my greatest encourager and support in whatever I do. I love you, Faith!

Foreword

I N THE ORTHODOX CHURCH'S FUNERAL SERVICE, WE HEAR OUR LORD
say, "Most assuredly, I say to you, he who hears My word and believes in
Him who sent Me has everlasting life, and shall not come into judgment,
but has passed from death into life" (John 5:24). This is surely the case
with our beloved Lynette Katherine Hoppe. She heard Christ's word. She
believed with all her heart in the Father who sent the Son. She gave witness to this truth through the Holy Spirit. Lynette was in divine communion with Christ, who is the Resurrection and the Life. She obeyed the last
commandment, "You shall receive power when the Holy Spirit has come
upon you; and you shall be witnesses to Me in Jerusalem, and in all Judea
and Samaria, and to the end of the earth" (Acts 1:8).

The last time I saw Lynette was at our church's summer girls' camp ten
days before her death. She was thin, smiling, and radiating a secret light—
the light of a martyr. Lynette had the seal of the Holy Spirit, knowing clearly
that the fruits of the Spirit are love, joy, peace, patience, kindness, goodness, faithfulness, gentleness, and self-control. With this power of the Holy
Spirit, Lynette confronted sickness and pain for twenty months.

I will always remember Lynette as a martyr ready to accept martyrdom
in a certain unknown process. She confronted death, face to face, for a very
long period. First, she met it with a strong faith in the crucified and resurrected Lord. Second, she handled it with a deep and abiding peace. Third,
she coped with her struggles emanating a sense of gratitude and authentic
joy. Finally, she dealt with her difficulties radiating divine love, which then
transmitted even more faith, more peace, and more love all around her.
Lynette became a model of love, and as we saw during her final days, even
created an atmosphere of love.

I could call Lynette a modern-day "secret martyr." In other ages, faithful Christians confronted lions and imprisonment, persecution and other threats. In our day and age, one of the great threats many face is cancer. As a brave, gentle, noble soul, Lynette confronted death singing, "Who shall separate us from the love of Christ? Shall tribulation, or distress . . . ? For I am persuaded that neither death nor life . . . nor any other created thing, shall be able to separate us from the love of God which is in Christ Jesus our Lord" (Romans 8:35–39).

Lynette had the seal of the Holy Spirit, knowing clearly that the fruits of the Spirit are love, joy, peace, patience, kindness, goodness, faithfulness, gentleness, and self-control. With this power of the Holy Spirit, Lynette confronted sickness and pain for twenty months.

By her life she underlined that whether we live or whether we die, we are God's (Romans 14:8). Lynette represents a special era in Orthodox missionary work, underlining the importance of people who can inspire others with their lives. Such a witness, of course, should not come only from clergy, but also from lay people, men and women alike.

I emphasize the importance of Lynette and her family to the Orthodox Church of Albania throughout their eight years of service. Although we experienced a great loss through Lynette's death, at the same time we received a precious treasure and asset. The witness and example of Lynette and Nathan's decision to come to Albania stands as a testimony of their love for Christ and their obedience to Him. Surely the decision to come as missionaries was not an easy one. As foreigners, they accepted many difficulties and risks. It was enough for them, though, to follow Christ and obey His final commandment, "Go therefore and make disciples of all the nations" (Matthew 28:19). This was their inspiration.

Lynette exemplifies a devoted spouse. Nathan remained near her, a person with a deep love, affection, and concern for all his family. Together with their two beloved children, Tristan and Katherine, they partook with us in all our troubles of life here in Albania over the past eight years. They came when many other people left after the chaos and anarchy of 1997, living with simplicity, humility, pure hearts, mercy and peace. They worked among the youth, edited different church publications, including Lynette's book, *The Resurrection of the Church in Albania*, and made many other important contributions.

In the final stages of her battle with cancer, Lynette and Nathan decided to return to Albania in order for her to die here, or rather to pass from death to life here. She wished to be buried in Albania as an everlasting symbol of the love of Christ, which is stronger than death. Through this act, she personified the secret treasure of the Orthodox Church, which is her universal character. We are thankful for Nathan, Lynette, and their children. We are thankful to her family, who raised our beloved Lynette with so much love, and then supported her decision not only to come to Albania as a missionary, but to return to Albania for her final journey. Too often I see families who create obstacles and try to hinder their loved ones from coming here. Lynette will now be an ambassador in heaven with the other holy women from Albania, who also offered their own powerful witness over the past decades.

I pray our Church in Albania, as well as all those who read this book and delve into Lynette's spirit, will always remain in this atmosphere of our Lord's Resurrection. Lynette's life and writings offer a significant witness to all those who face sickness and troubles. I hope that especially the youth, whom Lynette loved and with whom she toiled so much, will find inspiration in this modern-day example. St. John Chrysostom says, "We honor a martyr when we begin to imitate him." If we want to honor Lynette, we need to try to imitate her—imitate her deep faith in the Holy Trinity, her infinite love for our Christ, her affection and goodness toward everyone, the calm and humble way she served the Church, her joyful spirit, her courage and patience during the most difficult hours of her life. May the Lord inspire more and more people to follow Lynette in her obedience to Christ and become partners with Him in Jerusalem, in Albania, and to the ends of the earth, or wherever He may call us.

I began with the verse, "Most assuredly, I say to you, he who hears My word and believes in Him who sent Me has everlasting life, and shall not come into judgment, but has passed from death into life." We listen to this last greeting not with a feeling of sorrow and suffering, but with an atmosphere of hope and resurrection, because we know that Lynette is in the hands of our Lord.

May her memory be eternal!

+*Anastasios*
Archbishop of Tirana and All Albania

Introduction

"**N**OW WE HAVE TO LIVE WHATEVER WE HAVE EVER PREACHED TO others," Lynette Hoppe wrote in her diary. "I have been classified as having Stage 4 cancer (of 4 stages), and my prospects are rather grim. Nonetheless, I remain cheerful and hopeful and want to spend what years God grants me in joy and thanksgiving, serving as and wherever I can."

Lynette wrote this entry shortly after discovering the severity of her cancer, when she began an incredible journey of faith with her husband Nathan, through which she touched the lives of countless people. St. Francis of Assisi said, "Preach the gospel at all times; and if necessary use words." While Lynette and Nathan often preached the gospel with words over their eight years as long-term missionaries in Albania, it was with the unexpected news of her cancer that God called them to offer a new, unique, and unforgettable type of witness that used few words, yet influenced far more people.

My wife Faith and I had the privilege to be with Lynette Hoppe during her final week of life. She and Nathan amazed us with their way of facing illness, suffering, and death. On our plane ride to Albania on August 20, a week before Lynette would die, Faith and I reread all the journal entries Lynette had written throughout her twenty months of illness for the website www.prayforlynette.org. As moved and blessed as we had been the first time we read these entries, once again we felt the same inspiration and blessing. I even said to my wife, "This journal needs to be published so that others can be encouraged and enriched as we have been!"

Of course, we experienced Lynette's beautiful Christ-centered witness from the beginning of her missionary service. We welcomed the Hoppes to Albania when they arrived as new missionaries for the Orthodox

Autocephalous Church of Albania in 1998. We served together as co-missionaries for more than seven years. We experienced the Kosovo War and other trying periods together, and always respected and admired their Christian faith and witness during such times of crisis. We saw and tasted their love and hospitality.

From the time Lynette discovered her cancer, in December 2004, until her death on August 27, 2006, we kept in constant contact through weekly phone conversations and various visits—the Hoppe family came to our home in New England, and I visited them in Minnesota. We consider Lynette and Nathan as some of our dearest friends.

Although we regarded their faith highly during our years of service together, it was during her journey with cancer and her final months of life that we witnessed her genuineness of faith, more precious than gold, tested by fire (1 Peter 1:7) and purified to the level radiated by the saints throughout church history. Lynette and Nathan have truly set an unforgettable example for countless people of how to live and how to die in the Lord with faith, joy, peace, and love.

A Beautiful Death

Our visit during Lynette's final week of life will always remain one of our most memorable and divine experiences. Although Faith and I went to Albania to say a last goodbye to a dear friend and to offer whatever love and encouragement we could to her and her family, I must admit that the entire experience truly blessed us in a way totally unforeseen. I can describe Lynette's final days on earth as one of those sacred moments when eternity touches the present, when God blesses us with a glimpse of paradise. Truly, these last days were unimaginably beautiful.

This may sound like a strange way to describe the experience of someone in her final pangs of death. Yet instead of horror and tragedy, Lynette's last days reflected a piece of heaven. Love surrounded her. Love filled her. She awaited with joyous anticipation her greatest love—her Lord Jesus Christ. Thus, she exuded joy. An indescribable peace emanated from her room— a taste of the "peace of God that passes all understanding." A deep-rooted contentment and a steadfast faith filled her throughout the moments that she lay awake. Truly, a divine and heavenly atmosphere permeated her entire space.

Since death is a travesty of the divine image in which God created all of us, it has always intrigued me to hear someone describe the dying process as beautiful. How can the greatest enemy and fear of life—death itself—act as an impetus for beauty? Now, having been present during Lynette's final week of life, I can say that I have witnessed such an incredibly beautiful death event myself. The last several evenings we spent with her typify this beauty.

Lynette sat in her recliner, mostly with her eyes closed, her breathing slowly leaving her. At moments she would open her eyes, and one of us would talk with her. Someone was always holding her hand, caressing her feet, and reminding her how much love surrounded her. Her dearly beloved filled the bedroom—her sweetheart and husband of fourteen years, Nathan; her precious children, Tristan and Katherine; her three brothers, John, Brian, and Joel, and her sister, Sherry, together with their father, Lynn, who had come from different parts of America and Africa; her best friend, Gaye; her parish priest from Chicago, Fr. Patrick Reardon, along with Faith and me.

We sat around her bed until late each evening, filling her room with hymns and songs. Her family sang plenty of old, traditional Protestant songs—"Amazing Grace," "How Great Thou Art," "The Old Rugged Cross," "It Is Well with My Soul," and others—while Fr. Patrick and I offered Orthodox hymns of supplication and resurrection. In between songs, each of us would take turns sharing different memories of Lynette. Sometimes Lynette would smile as we talked. Once in a while she would whisper a word or two. Most of the time she just sat with her eyes closed, slowly fading into another world. The deep peace and presence of our Lord was thoroughly palpable.

By this time at night, only a few visitors came by. One evening, a dear Albanian friend and co-worker, Sonila, came to say her final farewell. Initially, Sonila hesitated to enter the bedroom, sensing the sacredness of the space. The experience also brought up strong emotions within her as she recalled the death of her own father when she was but a young teenager. Unsure about what she would face, she felt uncertain about entering.

Yet as she walked into the room, the experience of something special and divine overwhelmed her. She heard the singing, listened to a few stories, tasted the peace and love that enveloped Lynette, and clearly sensed God's deep and abiding presence. After watching for a while, she kissed Lynette farewell and walked out of the house. As I accompanied her to the gate and hugged her goodbye, she looked at me with eyes full of tears and quietly expressed that she had never in her life experienced something so beautiful. "It was like I tasted eternity."

She went on to contrast this death experience with the reaction surrounding her father's passing away when she was a young girl. Her family followed typical Albanian tradition by keeping her and any children far away from the dead body of her father. She never had an opportunity to say goodbye. Family members whisked her from one place to another, keeping her as far from death as possible. This reaction to terminal illness, death, and tragedy is common in contemporary Albanian society.

Lynette's openness with her illness, suffering, and ultimate death, however, stood in stark contrast to the mentality of so many. The fact that Lynette and Nathan had decided to return to their adopted homeland of Albania three months before, even though they knew she was dying, spoke much.

Just ten days before she actually died, Lynette was active in ministry at the Orthodox Church's summer camp, even speaking to the campers on the theme of death and dying. (Her final talk is included in Chapter 7.) She shared her twenty-month journey of cancer, suffering, pain, and saying goodbye, and left the girls spellbound. Never before had they heard someone talk so openly about having cancer and facing the possibility of death. Lynette's witness showed them how an authentic Christian who truly believes in the resurrection and lives in the community of the Church with faith can face the greatest challenges of life unafraid—even with peace and joy.

Throughout the last days of Lynette's life, her co-missionaries and dear Albanian friends took care of the countless visitors who stopped by to ask how she was doing. One precious friend, Kristina, a paralyzed Gypsy who was too often despised by Albanian society yet beloved by Lynette and the community of faith, came each day to ask how Lynette was doing. Kristina felt bonded with Lynette not only through their friendship and love over the years, but more so during the final months with their co-suffering of cancer. Shortly after Lynette was diagnosed, Kristina herself had discovered an incurable form of cancer in her throat. This unique bond inspired Kristina to have her husband push her in a wheelchair one hour each way through the crowded streets of Tirana, just so she could express her love for her dear American friend. This tender concern acted as a poignant symbol of the concern and love of countless others.

The Life of the Cross

Throughout Lynette's illness, many people asked me such questions as, "Why would God take away a dynamic, fruitful missionary in the prime of her life?" "Why would God take away a young mother with two dependent children?" "Why doesn't God hear the prayers of thousands around the world who are praying for her healing?" And ultimately, "Why do bad things happen to such good people?"

Too many of us, including lifelong, mature Christians, have allowed a superficial and erroneous understanding of faith, often preached by numerous televangelists, to distort or corrupt the true Faith that has been handed down in the Church throughout the centuries. From listening to these seductive voices, we think that God promises His followers health, wealth, success, and prosperity if only they pray and believe in the "abundant life" Jesus promises.

This so-called prosperity gospel, though, stands in total contradiction to the life of our Lord Jesus Christ Himself. Although Jesus was God Incarnate, He was born in poverty in a dark cave. He tasted life as a desperate refugee early on, growing up in a simple village family. Throughout His adult ministry, those He loved often misunderstood and rejected Him. He served people with love, doing only good, yet received ridicule, hatred, and persecution in return. Ultimately, whenever we look on Jesus on the Cross, we must remember the path to which He has called His disciples—a path on which we deny ourselves, take up our cross, and follow Him.

The Christian way is not a guarantee of comfort, good health, and long life. We only have to look at the two-thousand-year history of the Church and study the lives of the saints to see this. The vast majority of saints did not live long lives of comfort or health. Look at the greatest missionary of all, St. Paul. He depicts his apostolic life in his letter to the Corinthians in a shocking way—five times whipped with thirty-nine lashes; three times beaten with rods; once stoned almost to death; three times shipwrecked, even drifting out at sea for a night and day; numerous times imprisoned; threatened continuously by robbers, by his fellow countrymen, and by the Roman authorities; often traveling in hunger, sleeping in the wilderness; and possibly the greatest suffering of all, being rejected by the people he so greatly loved.

St. Paul understood suffering and could relate to the worst of turmoil, even though God called him to become a chosen apostle. And in addition to all this exterior pain, he says that "a thorn in the flesh was given to me, a messenger of Satan to buffet me, lest I be exalted above measure" (2 Corinthians 12:7–9). Some other inner cross tormented the apostle Paul to such a degree that he begged God to remove this burden. "Concerning this thing I pleaded with the Lord three times that it might depart from me. And He said to me, 'My grace is sufficient for you, for My strength is made perfect in weakness.'"

Here we see one of the greatest saints of our Church pleading with God to take away his suffering, and yet the Lord does not remove his cross. Instead, Christ teaches St. Paul an invaluable lesson: "My grace is sufficient for you, for My strength is made perfect in your weakness."

Our Lord calls us to follow the way of the Cross, which implies a life of sacrifice, possible suffering, and some form of death. Jesus prayed in His high priestly prayer on the night before He faced His Passion, "Father, the hour has come. Glorify Your Son, that Your Son also may glorify You" (John 17:1). Christ glorified God by obeying His Father's will and fulfilling His mission on earth through voluntarily accepting death, even the most humiliating, horrifying death on the Cross.

Crosses are a part of life, as Lynette so clearly came to understand. The crosses we bear in life are often mysteries we cannot understand. It may seem that we don't necessarily deserve them, especially when we compare our crosses to those that others carry, but this is part of the mystery of life.

God allows His precious saints, like the apostle Paul, to experience suffering and abandonment so they won't think too highly of themselves. It is precisely when we become too comfortable with ourselves, when we think too highly of our own accomplishments, when we feel proud of who we are, that we are at risk of trusting in ourselves and not in God. Lynette understood this wisdom of the saints throughout history. Her life was a true martyrdom, in the sense that the Greek word for "martyr" literally means "witness." She offered a powerful and memorable witness through her life and especially through her suffering and death.

Lynette's journal poetically and clearly describes her own understanding of carrying her cross while glorifying God. As she would often say to me, "So many people are praying for my healing, and I don't want them to think that God hasn't answered their prayers. He has! My healing, however, is taking a form that I never would have imagined at the beginning of this journey."

The Suffering Witness of Lynette

Although Lynette strived to live her life in Christ as a faithful Christian, missionary, mother, wife, daughter, teacher, mentor, and friend to so many, she probably never realized that her greatest witness to the Lord would come from a twenty-month journey with cancer, suffering, and death. She witnessed to her life in Christ throughout this saga by a deep faith, an inner peace, a radiant joy, a courageous love, and an undying hope.

Many people often wonder why a loving God allows any type of illness, suffering, and death to attack people, especially those who are in the prime of their lives and in the midst of a fruitful ministry. Lynette even had two young children, Tristan (age 8) and Katherine (age 6), who face their future without a mother. Yet it is precisely in the witness of God's faithful children during such times of tragedy, difficulty, and darkness that His light shines most brightly.

In the Old Testament we read:

But though a righteous man may die before his time,
He shall be at rest.
For old age is not honored for its length of existence,
Nor measured by its number of years;
But discernment is gray hair for mankind,
And a spotless life is the maturity of old age.
There was once a man pleasing to God and loved by Him,
And while living among sinners he was taken up.
He was caught up lest evil change his understanding
Or deceit deceive his soul. . . .
He was made perfect,
For in a short time he fulfilled long years,
For his soul was pleasing to the Lord;
Therefore, He took him early from the midst of evil.
(Wisdom of Solomon 4:7–14)

These words aptly describe Lynette's full life of forty-six years.

Lynette exemplified how such a path of illness and even death, when experienced with faith, can lead one into a fuller union with her Lord and even offer a witness more powerful and memorable than many lifetimes on earth. She became a contemporary witness of what saints throughout all ages have given to the world—a genuine, Christ-centered life of divine love and invincible faith in the prime of her life.

The saintly Bishop Gerasimos of Abydos of blessed memory once said, "Life is not a problem to be solved, but a mystery to be lived." Lynette embraced this divine, yet harsh mystery of life, and allowed it to hone her faith, deepen her love, and increase her compassion. She experienced the presence of God as never before through this inexplicable mystery.

Praising God for His Love

First, Lynette embraced an authentic Christian perspective on life, a view which never lost sight of God's presence and control in her life. "I do accept what God has given to me and do not view it as something 'bad' that has happened to me," she wrote. "Already I see the beauty of suffering and how it can give birth to humility, thankfulness, compassion, a clear vision of what is important, and a deeper love for Christ."

Her Christian worldview also gave her the ability to radiate joy and gratitude throughout her illness. St. Paul advises us to "Rejoice always . . . in everything give thanks" (1 Thessalonians 5:16, 18). I am not exaggerating when I say that at each stage of Lynette's illness, and especially when the medical news went from bad to worse, her first words to me would always be, "Well, although the news isn't good, still I thank God . . ."

She possessed the rare, divine ability to see God's hand at work in the midst of any and every situation. She held a deep-rooted attitude of gratitude, incarnating St. Paul's words, "Neither death nor life . . . nor things present nor things to come, nor height nor depth, nor any other created thing, shall be able to separate us from the love of God which is in Christ Jesus our Lord" (Romans 8:38, 39). I heard Lynette thank God shortly after she discovered her cancer. She thanked God after her cancer had metastasized. She thanked God after the cancer entered her bones. And even in the last days of life, when she informed me that the cancer had entered her liver and the doctors gave her only a few weeks to live, she still thanked God for His abundant grace and the love she felt from so many.

Lynette thanked God that her illness helped her learn to live in the present. She also thanked God for other lessons of life—lessons about God's love, about herself, about her relationships with her husband and others, and about so many other things. She even thanked God that He gave her the strength and grace to return to Albania, her adopted homeland, during her final three months of life, where she actively ministered in the youth camps up to her final days. To be honest with you, if I had not talked with Lynette so frequently and witnessed the authenticity of her gratitude, I'm not sure I could have believed it was so sincere.

Feeling the concrete presence of God and living with this spirit of gratitude gave root to one of the most visible signs of a true, living relationship with our Lord—a deep, spiritual joy and peace. In the midst of illness, suffering, and dying, with the temptation of fear and doubt ever lurking nearby, Lynette never lost that sense of deep, inner joy. Mother Teresa often said, "Never let anything make you forget the joy of our Risen Lord." Lynette lived by this principle, which she often expressed.

Overcoming Despair

Of course, Lynette's journey also included moments of discouragement, darkness, depression, and even despair. She described how traveling through the "valley of the shadow of death" often humbled her. In following the path of the saints, though, she learned that the closer she drew to her Lord, the more clearly she would see her own fears, faults, weaknesses, and sins. And through these moments of darkness, as well as through her physical suffering, she learned invaluable lessons: that faith is not a feeling but an act of will; that we are totally dependent on God, whether we realize it or not; that God's love and goodness never fail us.

Throughout this journey, Lynette and Nathan understood the priceless value of the Church—the Body of Christ that encouraged and nourished them along the way. Through her journal and the website www.prayforlynette.org, both Nathan and Lynette invited others to join them in her final journey. They reflected a genuine understanding of Christian community by inviting others to share their experience and walk with them— both by inspiring others through their example and lessons learned, and by unhesitatingly asking others to pray, visit, and help them in their moments of darkness. Lynette constantly gave credit to this cloud of witnesses who pounded the gates of heaven with their intercessions and prayers.

Death Is Not the End

A final sacred attitude that Lynette held was her paschal perspective on death. St. Paul said, "For me, to live *is* Christ, and to die *is* gain" (Philippians 1:21). Throughout her sickness, Lynette repeated this phrase. Shortly before she died, she shared with me, "Although I cry at the thought of leaving my dear husband and precious children, I simultaneously realize that our heavenly homeland awaits me, and I look forward to dwelling in the continual presence of our loving Lord."

This life is but a brief sojourn on planet Earth. God created us for eternity, and Lynette understood that eternal perspective so well. She had a passionate love for Christ, which filled her with the joy of going home. She mourned that she would not be physically present with her husband and children for many future events, nor be able to continue her ministry among her beloved Albanian co-workers and friends, but she truly believed that she was going home to that heavenly dwelling place which is in the loving presence of our Lord.

Lynette did pass away and join our Lord on August 27, 2006, but her funeral was more of a celebration of life and faith than a funeral of death. Many Albanian friends told me that they have never witnessed a death and funeral like Lynette's. For two days following her death, Lynette's body lay in repose in her home. Her Albanian students and friends, along with the missionary community, kept vigil day and night around her coffin. Psalms were read. Hymns were continuously sung. And crowds came to visit, seeing her beautiful body in front of a large resurrectional icon of our Lord.

At the funeral, Archbishop Anastasios eulogized Lynette by calling her a modern-day martyr of cancer. One reason the early Church grew so rapidly in the first centuries was precisely the authentic witness of the first martyrs. The willingness of the saints to die with hope, in the peace of God, offered a stark contrast to the deaths of their contemporaries. In fact, the manner and spirit in which the saints died not only influenced, but even converted many of their bystanders. This was the impact that Lynette's death had on those who witnessed it.

When her body was finally laid in the ground, following a moving ceremony led by Archbishop Anastasios along with Metropolitans John of Korca and Ignati of Berat, a host of clergy, and hundreds of friends, Nathan greeted everyone who came to console him with the words, "Rejoice! Christ is Risen!" People told me it seemed Nathan was comforting others, instead of the other way around.

Although Nathan, Tristan, and Katherine will sorely miss their wife and mother during the days and years ahead, as will all her dear friends and family, still we all can find great comfort in the incredible witness she offered to so many throughout her life and death. She is not gone and dead. She is just physically absent. She now dwells with our Lord, watching over us and interceding for us with her motherly love.

Lynette may truly repeat the apostle Paul's final words, "I have fought the good fight, I have finished the race, I have kept the faith. Finally, there is laid up for me the crown of righteousness, which the Lord, the righteous Judge, will give to me on that Day, and not to me only but also to all who have loved His appearing" (2 Timothy 4:8).

THIS BOOK YOU HOLD IN YOUR HANDS OFFERS A GLIMPSE OF THIS incredible woman of faith. Through the reflections of others, but mostly through her own writings during her final months of life, you will be nourished and inspired by Lynette's faith and wisdom, cultivated and forged through the fires of suffering and sacrifice. From her cross come gems of spirituality that I know will challenge and bless all her readers.

Please note that as you read this book, parts are taken from Lynette's personal journal. She would never have imagined that certain things she wrote would become public reading. We include these passages and thoughts, though, to help give a fuller picture of who she was and with what she struggled. In order to protect the privacy of individuals mentioned in the journal, some names have been changed.

Much of her writing, of course, comes from her postings on the website www.prayforlynette.org, which one of our co-missionaries, George Russell, created and constantly updated. George created a vehicle by which countless people came in contact with Lynette, and for that we are all grateful.

I know that one of Lynette's greatest hopes throughout her struggle was that God would use her final witness and "martyrdom" to raise up a new generation of Christians who would courageously walk the path of the Cross and follow our Lord by acting as witnesses of His love to the entire world—whether in America, Albania, or to the ends of the earth. May Lynette's hope see fruition!

Fr. Luke A. Veronis
Feast of the Dormition of the Virgin Mary
August 15, 2007

CHAPTER 1

The Foundation

L YNETTE HOPPE WELL UNDERSTOOD A LIFE OF CHRISTIAN WITNESS and missionary outreach from a young age. Although she was born in Indiana, her parents, Lynn and Marce Holm, took their four children, Sherry (age 8), Lynette (age 3), John (age 2), and Joel (age 1), and entered the missionary field of Uganda in 1963 under the auspices of the Conservative Baptist Foreign Mission Society (CBFMS).

For the next ten years, they lived in the capital city, Kampala, where Lynette's childhood memories recalled an idyllic existence in post-colonial East Africa. She and her siblings attended a British public school. She loved living in the tropics, playing outdoors year round. She enjoyed the expatriate missionary community, along with her Ugandan friends. She even began honing her artistic talents from a young age, when her parents arranged for a British parishioner in Kampala who had studied at the Royal School of Art in London to tutor her.

As a child living in the "Pearl of Africa," she wasn't aware of the revolutionary storm arising with Idi Amin, even though he was a neighbor of theirs. When Idi Amin finally attained absolute power in Uganda, he began his reign of terror, killing his compatriots, threatening foreigners, and forcing many missionaries to leave.

The Holm family left Uganda in 1973 and settled in Windom, Minnesota. The missionary spirit, though, was thoroughly ingrained in the family. Years later as adults, four of the five Holm children would serve with zeal in Christian ministry: Lynette as a missionary in Albania, Joel in Congo for the organization Food for the Hungry, Brian in administration for Wycliff Bible Translators, and Jon as a church planter outside of Denver.

Her father Lynn recalls Lynette's devout faith and zeal from a young age. When talking about Lynette, he often recalls an incident that took place after he received a position as a pastor in a local church in Windom. "The church offered me a minimal salary, but after a few years they decided they wanted to increase my salary. Lynette was old enough to be in the general assembly meeting. When the time came to vote, we excused ourselves and the church voted to increase my salary. When we came home after the meeting, however, Lynette met me at our front door. 'I don't like it that they voted to increase your salary,' she curtly informed me. 'Now we can't live by faith anymore!'"

Following uneventful years of high school, Lynette entered a three-year certificate program at Moody Bible Institute. Although she had a passion for missions, Moody opened her eyes to the world in a new way. She began thinking on her own, hearing other theological ideas that challenged her own beliefs. This theological atmosphere forced her to come to faith conclusions not simply inherited from her parents, but ones she truly believed in herself. The Moody experience, with its excellent music program, also helped fine-tune her musical talent. Lynette often performed in school concerts, even singing solo parts in Handel's *Messiah* and other classical compositions.

As a part of the missions major at MBI, the school required all students to take part in a summer mission experience. Lynette finished her coursework and went to Kenya, where she taught Religious Education and Christian Faith in the public schools for nine months. This fantastic experience only solidified her passion to serve the Lord as a missionary.

Since Moody Bible Institute did not offer an undergraduate degree, Lynette continued her studies at Northwestern College, majoring in the Visual Arts. Her decision to enter this field of studies represented a great transition for her, since she was expanding her vision beyond a strict study of the Bible. She understood the talents that God had given her and wanted to enhance them for His glory. She went to school for two years and completed her Bachelor of Arts in 1983. The following year she filled in for a professor on sabbatical, offering classes in art at Northwestern.

In the fall of 1985, Lynette began graduate work in Intercultural Studies (the former missions degree program) at Wheaton College. This same

year a young man named Nathan Hoppe began his undergraduate studies at Wheaton as well. Although Lynette had entered a two-year program,
she had no money for school and had to simultaneously work full-time.
She extended her two-year program into five years. Her future husband,
though, would say that this delay occurred through the providence of God,
because it allowed Nathan, who was almost eight years her junior, to grow
up and catch Lynette's eye.

Lynette finally met Nathan in the fall of 1988. As they took some classes
together, their friendship grew. Lynette would often read books for Nathan
and help him with his problem of dyslexia. They began attending the same
church—Christ Covenant Church. They had the common bond of being
missionary kids.

Nathan had grown up in the jungles of Colombia, South America. His
parents, Bob and Dottie Hoppe, have worked since 1964 with Wycliff Bible
Translators and other frontier mission organizations translating the Bible
into a tribal language. Nathan was born in the capital city of Bogotá and
spent much of the first thirteen years of his life among the Malayo Indians,
in a mud hut with a thatched roof. From a young age, both Lynette and
Nathan felt the call to dedicate their lives to serving their Lord as lifelong
missionaries, and this calling attracted them to one another.

As they spent more time together and got to know one another, Lynette
finally approached Nathan and expressed her deep interest in him, even
though there was quite an age difference. Hesitant at first, Nathan realized
the unique qualities of this beautiful woman and didn't want to carelessly
throw away such an opportunity. Thus, a month later he told her he wanted
to pursue a relationship.

Lynette graduated from Wheaton in December 1989 and soon thereafter began working for the college, developing her skills in graphic design.
Although their relationship grew over the following year, Lynette felt
Nathan wasn't serious enough, and she ended their relationship in January
1991. Nathan had just received his Master's in Theology from Wheaton and
promptly left for seven months to travel around the world. The two kept in
touch, though, and a year later, Nathan surprised Lynette by showing up
at her doorstep. The following month, he proposed. They were married on
June 28, 1992.

Before Lynette and Nathan married, they obviously had talked much
about their vision and calling to serve God as cross-cultural missionaries.

Nathan specifically wanted to involve himself in "church planting," but what church would they plant?

Since 1989, both Lynette and Nathan had attended the nondenominational Christ Covenant Church. This church community had committed itself years earlier to voraciously reading the church fathers while trying to discover the "apostolic Church." In their search, the community heard about Fr. Peter Gillquist and the movement of two thousand evangelical Christians who had entered the Orthodox Church after a similar journey. Fr. Gillquist and other former-evangelicals-turned-Orthodox came to speak at Christ Covenant.

Nathan and Lynette participated with Christ Covenant Church in their journey. The more the church community read the church fathers and studied church history, the closer the entire community grew to the Orthodox Church. "We felt good about Orthodoxy, and believed that it was truly the apostolic Church, but we couldn't find out anything about what the Orthodox Church was doing in cross-cultural missions," stated Nathan. "And we began to worry about this. We felt we couldn't enter a church in which we couldn't fulfill our calling as missionaries."

In 1993, Fr. Patrick Reardon and several other priests of the Antiochian Orthodox Archdiocese chrismated the entire congregation of Christ Covenant Church and brought them into the canonical Orthodox Church. Christ Covenant Church became All Saints Orthodox Church. The Hoppes, however, chose not to participate in the chrismations. They still had not figured out how to reconcile their dilemma of Orthodoxy or missions. As another year passed, though, both Nathan and Lynette came to the conviction that Orthodoxy represented the fullness of the Christian faith. They also came to the conclusion that if God really wanted them to be Orthodox and to serve as cross-cultural missionaries, He would open the door for both. They accepted chrismation into the Church on Palm Sunday, 1994.

Several months later, someone introduced them to the Orthodox Christian Mission Center (OCMC) in St. Augustine, Florida. This pan-Orthodox mission agency was the official sending body for all canonical Orthodox Christians in America. Their dreams came back to life. Shortly thereafter, Lynette met Fr. Dimitrios Couchell, the executive director for the OCMC, and the Hoppes expressed their interest in becoming long-term missionaries.

In May of 1995, Fr. Luke Veronis was acting as a liaison of both the

OCMC and Archbishop Anastasios of Albania, and he contacted the Hoppes. He invited them to think about coming to Albania and working under the auspices of the Orthodox Autocephalous Church of Albania. Nathan jumped at the opportunity and asked Lynette if she was ready to go. "Sure I'm ready!" she responded. "But where's Albania?"

Three months later the Hoppes had an opportunity to meet Archbishop Anastasios at the International Conference on Orthodox Missions held at Holy Cross Greek Orthodox School of Theology in Brookline, Massachusetts. As they discussed the needs and possibilities of missionary service in Albania, all parties agreed that Nathan should first attend Holy Cross to better familiarize himself with Orthodoxy. Thus, several weeks later Lynette and Nathan packed up their belongings in Chicago, and with no money and no scholarships but lots of faith, they traveled cross-country to Boston. Their All Saints Church Community gave them five hundred dollars to help them with their new beginning.

Nathan quickly became a full-time student and found a full-time job. Shortly thereafter, Lynette obtained a job in the Alumni Office of Boston University doing graphic design. Her two years of work in that office proved quite providential and invaluable, as she would refer back to this experience often in her graphic design work for the Orthodox Church of Albania.

Before an exhausting and overwhelming two years came to a conclusion, the Hoppes began planning their departure for the mission field immediately after Nathan's graduation with a Masters of Theological Studies in May 1997. Unexpected factors, however, delayed their plans. Three months before graduation, the entire country of Albania fell into anarchy and chaos following the collapse of a number of "pyramid" economic schemes that robbed eighty percent of Albanians of their life savings. All foreign embassies evacuated almost all expatriates, including most of the OCMC and other foreign missionaries.

At around the same time, Lynette discovered that she was pregnant with their first child. So Nathan and Lynette postponed their departure for Albania until after the birth of their son Tristan, which took place on December 9, 1997. The fulfillment of their lifelong dream would have to wait until after the New Year.

A family picture from Uganda in 1966. Lynette grew up as a "missionary kid" while her parents served in Uganda for ten years.

Lynette in Uganda, 1965

*Lynette with her
brothers and sister
straddling the equator*

*Lynette's senior picture
from high school*

Above: Nathan, Lynette, and Tristan at Holy Cross Theological School in 1997

Below: Archbishop Anastasios meets his newest missionary, Tristan Hoppe, in 1998

Lynette and Nathan celebrate the baptism of Mihali Tahiri, the youngest son of the refugee family that stayed with them during the Kosovo war

Lynette with refugees

Lynette (center back) in a group shot of the Good Shepherd girls' summer camp in 1999

Above: Family portrait, 2000

Left: Lynette and her children visiting Elisabeta, one of the "holy women" from Korca

Lynette and family in front of the statue of Albanian national hero George Skanderbeg

Family picture, April 2006

Lynette and her sister Sherry comforting her mother Marce, who was also dying of cancer

Lynette with her children, Tristan and Katherine, during her final weeks

Lynette & Nathan

Lynette at the official presentation of her book, Resurrection: The Orthodox Autocephalous Church of Albania 1991–2003

Lynette singing at an outdoor youth concert

Lynette directing an arts and crafts project at the summer camp

Lynette offering one of her talks on "Overcoming Evil with Good" at the girls' camp during her final weeks of life

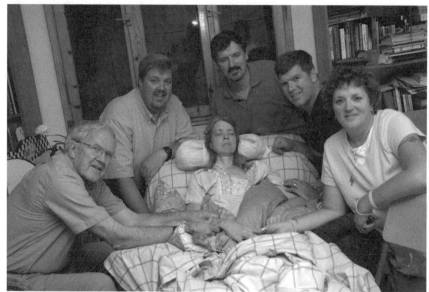

Lynette surrounded by her father, Lynn Holm, and her siblings Brian, Joel, Jon, and Sherry

Fr. Luke Veronis comforting Lynette during her final days

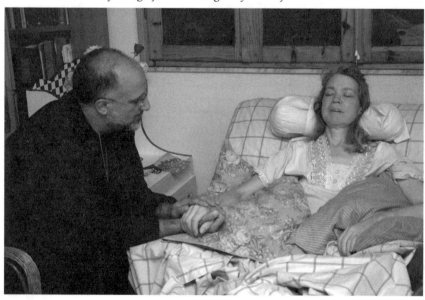

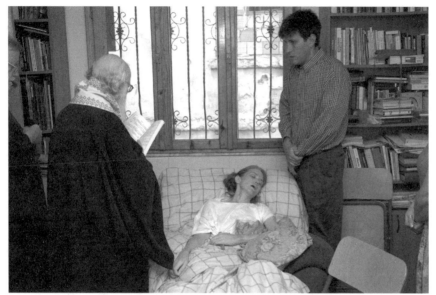

Archbishop Anastasios praying the Trisagion prayers for the departed

Lynette's body in her coffin

Metropolitan John of Korca, along with Papa Jani Trebica and Fr. Andon Merdani, offering the Trisagion prayers

Albanian women gather around Lynette's coffin, reading psalms and singing hymns as they keep a 48-hour vigil from the time of her death until her burial

Archbishop Anastasios, Metropolitan John of Korca, Metropolitan Ignati of Berat, and clergy from Albania and the US at Lynette's funeral service

Funeral procession from the Monastery Church of St. Vlash to the burial site in the village of Shen Vlash-Durres

Archbishop Anastasios holding the hands of Tristan and Katherine as they process to the burial site. Fr. Martin Ritsi, OCMC executive director, walks alongside.

Below: One-year memorial service. Lynette's tombstone with mosaic icon of her patron, St. Katherine of Alexandria. Inset: Back of the tombstone with an icon of the Resurrection.

CHAPTER 2

A Dream Fulfilled ❧

AFTER YEARS OF DREAMING AND PREPARING FOR LONG-TERM MISSION-ary service, Nathan and Lynette, along with their three-month-old son Tristan, finally entered the mission field of Albania on March 22, 1998. This chapter contains parts of their official newsletters, which they would send out several times a year to all their spiritual and financial partners who made it possible for them to be in the mission field. These snippets taken from newsletters dated 1998 to 2003 reveal the spirit, work, and character with which the Hoppes carried on their missionary service.

March 1998 ❧ Newsletter

THANKS BE TO GOD! AFTER THREE YEARS OF PRAYING, WAITING, and studying, our dream of doing missionary work in Albania is becoming a reality. On March 21, we will depart for this little-known country, still wounded by unspeakable suffering under an oppressive Communist yoke. We feel deeply honored to be given the opportunity to serve our Lord with the Orthodox Church of Albania under the outstanding leadership of Archbishop Anastasios. We pray that we will be worthy of this honor. After we arrive and acclimate to a new culture, we will begin intensive, formal study of the Albanian language. Although we have received some instruction in this ancient tongue, we know that only by living the language will we be able to learn it well. We are convinced that prayer and the mastery of language are keys to effective missionary work.

I will care for our three-month-old son, Tristan, and will also assist with Church publications. The need for Christian literature in Albanian is so great, and I will put to use my experience in illustration and graphic design. I may also teach English classes at the Seminary. Since there are so few theological texts translated into Albanian, the students receive instruction in English so that they can have access to more theological books. As a homemaker, I will face many unusual challenges. Albania suffers from a poor infrastructure, making water and electricity supplies erratic, at best. No doubt our kitchen will be well-stocked with buckets for holding precious stores of water. Caring for an infant in a city with poor medical facilities is cause for concern. We thank God that Tristan has not had a day's illness since his birth, despite the fact that he has been exposed to every sort of flu and cold.

Nathan will begin teaching at the Resurrection of Christ Orthodox Seminary, an institution devoted to the training of clergy and laity. Under the Communist regime, all churches were either destroyed or closed; all clergy were executed or imprisoned; and all manifestations of faith were outlawed. Now that freedom of religion has returned to Albania, the task of rebuilding the Church is dependent upon prayer and the training of effective ordained and lay leadership. Since the Seminary's inception in 1991, more than 85 of its graduates have been ordained and assigned to pastor churches throughout Albania. Many churches, however, still lack priests. Hence, the Seminary continues to play a crucial role in the future of the Church of Albania. Nathan has been asked to prepare courses in Old Testament Introduction and Patrology. Although he will begin teaching through an interpreter, he hopes to learn the Albanian language well enough to teach in it eventually.

July 1998　　　　　　　　⊱　　　　　　*Newsletter*

ON JULY 7, TWO DAYS BEFORE HE TURNED SEVEN MONTHS, TRISTAN was baptized at the cathedral in Tirana. Archbishop Anastasios led the service, assisted by Archimandrite John Pelushi (now Metropolitan John of Korca) and Fr. Luke Veronis. A small group of friends gathered to witness the event and were joined by four priests (besides those serving) and a deacon. The service was solemnly joyful. Tristan was quiet but alert throughout the service, squawking briefly only when the water was poured over his head. (He couldn't be immersed in the font because he refused to bend his legs. Fr. John used an old tin cup to pour water over his head.)

John Thompson, who flew in from Chicago to be Tristan's sponsor, commented that the baptism was so moving it made his entire trip worthwhile, particularly those moments when we processed around the baptismal font singing, "As many as have been baptized into Christ have put on Christ."

For me, Tristan's mother, the service was beautiful and touching. I felt myself almost physically bursting with joy. What a privilege we have been given to know Christ, to serve his church, and to lead our son in the ways of the Lord. May we, in turn, be found faithful, humble, and gentle, serving our God with joy and without thought of recognition or reward.

Fr. John commissioned a special icon of St. Tristan for the baptism and inscribed on the back these words for Tristan: "May the Lord bless you with the gift of loving Him more than everything else. 'Life is burdensome without love for God.' Blessed are those who love the Lord." *Truly our son has been blessed. Thanks be to God!*

August 1998   ✥   *Newsletter*

WE WRITE TO YOU IN A MOMENT OF UNCERTAINTY ON THE EVE OF a possible crisis. Three days ago the American embassy in Tirana announced that it would be evacuating all non-emergency personnel immediately and urged all Americans in Albania to leave if their presence was not absolutely essential. The reason cited for this sudden exodus was a specific threat directed against the embassy by Muslim extremists—those related to the recent bombings in Kenya and Tanzania and the extradition from Albania of known terrorists.

We were stunned by this announcement and spent hours trying

to get more information. Unable to get news beyond the official statement, we had to judge the situation based on the actions of the embassy itself. Was the situation serious enough to warrant our leaving? Nathan decided that he should remain in Albania. With the seminary slated to open in eight weeks, he felt that he had to stay in order to prepare for the heavy teaching load that has fallen on his shoulders. The question remained, should Tristan and I leave and go to the States for a while? Although there doesn't appear to be any immediate danger, the actions of the embassy indicate a serious threat. Yesterday two large commercial airlines flew into Tirana to carry out the embassy and U.S. Aid personnel. By today about 600 Americans will have left Albania.

We are not afraid. It does not appear that there is a general crisis in Albania. This threat is directed specifically at Americans. Now with all known American targets out of the country, we are left somewhat vulnerable. Although we don't want to run from a phantom enemy, we want to be wise in the face of a very serious threat.

After much consideration and prayer, we decided that Tristan and I should fly to the States and stay with my parents in Minnesota. We will leave tomorrow and stay three weeks, reassessing the situation thereafter. We hope that whatever danger may be lurking now will pass by then. I do not want to be away from Nathan for more than three weeks unless it is essential, and I will not rest easy until we are reunited. Besides, Tristan is on the verge of walking, and his father doesn't want to miss his first steps. Furthermore, I am in the middle of designing some major pieces that need to be ready in October, so I don't want to be gone for long.

We are sorry that our first official newsletter is an announcement that I and the baby are coming home, but these are the realities of life in Albania, where anything can and anything *does* happen. When we registered with the embassy upon our arrival, we were given a travel warning for Albania which urged extreme caution at all times. We have not taken the warning very seriously, although we seldom go anywhere after dark. This current threat is a startling reminder to us that the situation in Albania remains unstable.

Our Adjustment in Albania

This week marks the fifth month since our arrival in Albania. During these past few months, we have focused our attention largely on studying the language and adjusting to the Albanian culture and climate. We have, however, also participated in a few activities with the youth and with university students. Of those who attend the services of the church, about half are young people, many of whom are quite outstanding. These are the future leaders of the church, those who will carry the gospel to their peers and to the succeeding generations.

Nathan continues to prepare for teaching in the fall. Again, there is a shortage of teachers for the fall semester, so we would appreciate your prayers for more faculty. I struggle with the ongoing difficulties of doing design work in Albania. One of the things I would like to do while I am home is to buy software and perhaps hardware to improve the process of designing and printing the church's publications.

Christmas 1998 · Newsletter

"For behold, I bring you good tidings of great joy which shall be for all people."

THIS AFTERNOON AS I SAT WATCHING SIX LITTLE ANGELS STRUGGLE to grasp their choreographed routine for the Christmas program, I was reminded of the truly wondrous message announced by the angels. God came to us, entering quietly into creation through a hidden cave in a tiny town, yet he made possible the transformation of the entire universe. He came as Joy Incarnate, touching grief and turning it into hope and gladness.

Albania knows little joy, and even less hope. Etched in the faces of many Albanians are lines of despair, discouragement, poverty, and suffering. Their hope lies in economic prosperity, which most of them will never experience. Suspecting as much, their hopelessness deepens. It's an endless cycle of raised and dashed hopes. Our message is that Jesus is our joy, our hope, but it is not a message to be posted on a bulletin board. It's a message that must be carried in person, enveloped in love, and at times accompanied by a warm winter jacket, new boots, or parcels of food.

Our last letter to you in August was fraught with uncertainties. At the time, you may recall, we had received word from the American embassy in Tirana that they had received specific threats from Islamic extremists and were evacuating all non-emergency personnel immediately. All American citizens were urged to depart Albania, as well, if their presence wasn't absolutely essential. After much prayer and thought, Tristan and I left for the States on August 18 not knowing when we would see Nathan again. Initially our plan was to remain in the States a month, then reassess the situation. Just days after I returned to the States, Nathan sent an e-mail message stating that one of our Orthodox Churches had been bombed. It was a terrible omen, though unrelated to the threat against the American embassy.

But, thanks be to God, after five long weeks of separation, Tristan and I returned to Albania and were reunited happily with Nathan.

Although security remains a problem in Albania, we have not experienced any change in lifestyle due to the threats directed against Americans last August. During the day, Tristan and I go about the city on foot as usual, and never think even for a moment about the security issue. At night, however, we are much more cautious.

Winter has brought on power shortages throughout Albania. Each day we can expect to be without power for about five hours. There is no schedule to the outages, so it is difficult to plan around them. We just continue with our activities until our printer stops running, or the stove goes off, or the house is plunged into darkness. (Half of this letter was composed by candlelight.)

Kosovo

The ongoing struggle in Kosovo has drastically altered the situation in northern Albania over the past few months. Tens of thousands of refugees have poured over the mountains into Albania, finding shelter wherever they can. Some have managed to make their way down to central Albania to the major cities of Tirana and Durres. Most are suffering terribly from a lack of food, clothing, and other necessities.

The Orthodox Church has been distributing winter clothing and boots to 6,000 refugee children in about 26 locations around Albania. Many families find their way to the gates of our Archdiocese in Tirana, and the Church offers food, clothing and other necessities to those that it is able to help. Those with special needs are referred to other charities that are better able to assist them.

Unfortunately, much of northern Albania has fallen into anarchy, with four major families controlling the area. All of the relief agencies have withdrawn their personnel because the dangerous situation has made it impossible for them to continue their humanitarian efforts. This is tragic for the destitute Kosovo families who cannot be reached with aid. With the coming of winter, the mountains of the north are snowy and cold, creating conditions which serve only to increase the suffering of these refugees. The police have either abandoned the region to the bandits, or have chosen to cooperate with them.

May 1999   ❧   *Newsletter*

The Kosovo War

MULLET CAMP IS ACTUALLY AN OLD ARMY BARRACKS LOCATED IN a valley along the Erzenit River in Albania. The site is quite lovely, with a beautiful view of the nearby hills. The barracks themselves, which now house about 800 refugees, are in a dreadful state of disrepair. On either side of the barracks buildings, two separate tent camps have been erected, one housing about 1,200 refugees, and the other holding several hundred people.

When we first walked into the barracks, we were terribly dismayed to see how people live. On either side of the building two long wooden bunks had been constructed and were topped with mattresses and blankets. One hundred seventeen people shared this bunk space. There was no place to store anything except under the bunk, and the only place to sit was on the end of the bunk. The weather was still very cold and rainy. There was no privacy, no warm place to bathe, and no good health care in the camp.

Presbytera Faith Veronis, another OCMC missionary serving in Albania, had learned about the plight of pregnant Kosovar women giving birth soon after arriving in Tirana. One day, Faith asked if I could help deliver packages to five women and their babies at the Maternity Hospital. I agreed, and that day I met Violtsa Tahiri, white-faced, silent, and very sad.

Violtsa, aged 26, had actually given birth to her baby in Kosovo, but had been forced out of her home two days after giving birth. She and her family walked for a day-and-a-half through the forest in the rain without food or water, which meant she had been unable to produce much milk for her baby. After making their way across the Albanian border to the town of Kukes, they boarded a bus for Tirana. Upon arriving in the capital, Violtsa and her baby were admitted to the hospital, where they stayed for five days. On the day that I met her, she had asked to be discharged because she wanted to be reunited with her husband, Zef, and four-year-old son, Emmanuel, who supposedly were staying at the Sports Palace, a clearing house for refugees. I offered to drive her there, and she gladly accepted.

We didn't find her husband that day, nor that evening. As the day dragged on, Violtsa began to suspect that her husband was no longer in Tirana, and had perhaps been moved to a camp. I offered her a place in our home until we could find her husband. She stayed with us that night, and the next morning she asked if we could take her back to the hospital. Perhaps her husband would look for her there. She remained in the hospital most of that day. At 3 P.M., she called to say that her husband and sister-in-law had arrived from a camp about 20 minutes' drive out of town. We offered them a ride back to the camp, and soon found ourselves making the first of many trips out to the Mullet camp.

Nathan and I offered to keep her and her immediate family for a few days until they had more fully recovered from their ordeal, but Violtsa's husband insisted that the extended family should stay together.

We made several visits to the camp, supplying needs for clothing, shoes, new underwear, filtered water, dishes, a small gas burner and coffee pot, coffee (an essential to the Albanian diet), and other items. I also made up seventeen bags of clothing for babies and delivered

these around the camp. On Saturdays we fell into the habit of bringing the whole family in for hot showers, a real meal, and a chance to
escape camp life. We also washed their dirty clothes. Faith Veronis
kindly opened her home so that half the family could bathe there,
and she washed half their clothes. (Water shortages are a major problem in Albania.)

One day, upon visiting the camp, we found that Violtsa and baby
Mihail were not there, and we learned to our consternation that they
were back in the hospital. Mihail had come down with an upper
respiratory infection. Camp life had been too cold for the baby.
Violtsa and Mihail remained in the hospital for one week, and then
Violtsa announced that she was coming to stay with us. That was
three weeks ago, and we are still hosting this family.

The Tahiri family is Catholic. Until I met them, I didn't even know
there were any Catholics in Kosovo (there are about 100,000 Kosovar
Catholics living among the majority Muslim Albanians in Kosovo).
This has given us a common ground of faith. They join us for evening
family prayers and go to church with us. Last Saturday, we witnessed
the baptism of baby Mihail in the Catholic Church in Tirana.

It has been both rewarding and challenging to enter into such a
close relationship with a suffering family. We feel that we really have
been able to relieve a small part of their difficulties, and yet their
needs are overwhelming at times. Today, as Violtsa's sister-in-law,
Mira, was riding with me in the car, she couldn't stop crying. When
I asked her what was troubling her, she told me that she was worried about her brother, who supposedly is still in Kosovo. No one
has heard anything from him, including Mira's two sisters, who live
in Switzerland. We can only pray that Mira's brother is still alive
somewhere.

Violtsa and her husband are hoping to get to Holland, where
Violtsa's sister lives. Mira and her family are staking their hopes on
France and have made connections with a Catholic priest there, who
may help them realize their hopes.

We are highly skeptical that any of them will be able to get into
other European countries—it's just too difficult and many other
Kosovars have higher claims. One thing is certain for all of them.
They don't want to stay in Albania.

Nathan, along with keeping up with his teaching load, has taken upon himself the tremendous task of buying and delivering mattresses, blankets, pillows, sheets, food, and other necessities to Kosovar families who are being hosted by Albanian families in Tirana. There are some who have managed to collect enough money to rent an apartment but can't afford bedding, food, or clothing.

Thank you so much for your prayers, your concerns, and your love. Many of you have asked how you can help in this situation. The first and most important thing you can do is pray for a just and peaceful solution to the crisis, and for wisdom and endurance as we attempt to help those who come into our sphere of help. In addition to your prayers, we could very much use your financial support for these refugees. All sorts of items from baby clothes, to beans, to new underwear, to soap, etc., are needed for these people, who have come with only the clothes on their backs. All of these things can be purchased here more reasonably than in the States, but the needs are overwhelming. Meeting the needs of so many people requires large sums of money.

June 23, 1999 ✿ *Newsletter*

Returning to Kosovo

YESTERDAY, UNDER THE DARK COVER OF EARLY MORNING, NATHAN boarded a heavily-loaded minibus and departed for Kosovo. The laden vehicle was heading for a small village somewhere outside of Gjakova. Nathan was accompanying one of our Kosovo families— Mira and Ndue Tahiri, and their four children—back home. If all went well, they should have reached home by mid-afternoon yesterday. Because the phones in Kosovo are not yet back in service, I will not know what has happened until Nathan returns—hopefully, sometime tomorrow. This morning I was told that refugees were being turned back at the border—Kosovo isn't ready to receive its masses of citizens yet and wants to delay their return until next week. Since Nathan didn't return home last night, I assume he and his minibus crossed the border (or, perhaps, they're camped out nearby).

Violtsa and Zef Tahiri (the brother of the above-mentioned Ndue), and their two children (our house guests for two months) also left yesterday, having arranged for transportation with their uncle's family. I miss already Violtsa's sweet nature and kindness. Two weeks ago, after we settled her into her own little apartment, she took to baking us bread every day. I enjoyed visiting her, drinking freshly-brewed Turkish coffee, and bouncing three-month-old Mihail on my knee. Violtsa's pride in her plump little son was a pleasure to see. Mihail had never really had a home other than ours, having made his first long journey two days after his birth in Kosovo. He had been carried in his mother's arms through the mountains in the rain, unable to nurse because his mother had no milk to give him. She herself had had nothing to eat or drink during her hospital stay and for several days after Mihail's birth. She had been unable to produce any milk. Needless to say, when the family finally reached the Albanian border after their long ordeal, Violtsa and Mihail were rushed to the hospital. Mihail was thin and sickly, and Violtsa herself was in a serious state of exhaustion. (She walks with a limp because of an injury incurred during her own birth 27 years ago, and her walk through the mountains so soon after giving birth and her own disability, as she describes it, almost cost her her life.)

Now, Violtsa returns to face a difficult situation in Kosovo. Although the looting and burning of houses by Serb forces and the bombardment by NATO have brought on so much destruction in Kosovo, Violtsa's life as a village woman before the war began was not easy. Previously, her daily duties had included milking the cow (from which she made yogurt and cheese), baking bread on a wood stove, washing clothes for five people by hand, and cleaning the house. Her mother-in-law with whom she lives was disabled and could not assist her. Now Violtsa returns with an infant to care for along with her extremely active four-year-old. At our last meeting, she gave me a wan smile. I don't think she was ready to go home. Her life here had been infinitely easier. (Nathan will be giving careful attention to their circumstances and those of Ndue's family and will try to provide the things that they need in order to have a manageable life. That is one of his primary reasons for taking this trip to Kosovo. He loaded them down with enough food to sustain them for some time.)

Fortunately for the families of Ndue and Zef, their homes were not burned. Last week a representative from the Tahiri family was dispatched to Kosovo to discover what had become of their parents and what condition their homes were in. These families are among the few lucky ones. Not only did they find their parents alive, they still have a roof and four walls to shelter them. Their parents had refused to leave Kosovo and had survived on bread made from a large stock of flour stored before the war began, and yogurt and cheese made from the milk produced by their cow. Several times the Serb military had come, asking after their sons and looting their home, but they had left the aged couple unmolested and the cow undisturbed.

Nathan and I were completely unprepared for the mass exodus of the Kosovo refugees. We thought most would be cautious about returning home to possible burnt-out, mine-infested, looted homes and properties. But such has not been the case. The refugee camps are quickly emptying out, and the returnees are now numbering in the hundreds of thousands. I am worried about what they will eat, where they will find shelter if their homes were burned, and what will happen if they encounter mines and other explosive devices. No doubt the aid agencies will help, but it takes time to organize these things, and no one thought the war would end so suddenly. Understandably, the Kosovars would prefer to be home, suffering from want in their own back yards, rather than cramped in close quarters in a camp or apartment a day's journey from home. We can't blame them.

Although many of the refugees are leaving, many will still remain here for a few weeks or months. Some don't have the resources to return home. (All available modes of transportation are commanding exorbitant fares—$350 and up to hire a minibus). Besides continuing to provide food and other necessities for those refugees whom we know here, we will also be turning our attention toward helping refugees return home, and we will try to provide what we can for them to start life over in Kosovo.

But first, Nathan needs to return. If all goes well on this trip, he may decide to accompany more of "his families" home. Thank you for your prayers and gifts to help these refugees. You have helped to ease the pain and distress of an immensely difficult period in their lives. God bless you.

TWO NIGHTS AGO, NATHAN RETURNED SAFELY FROM HIS EXCURSION to Kosovo. The properties of the Tahiri family, three households in all, were largely intact, having suffered little loss from looting. Nathan was struck by how immediately life fell back into its normal routine. That first day home, Mira Tahiri milked the cow morning and evening just as before; the children wandered out into the garden to play; various neighbors, whom the family hadn't seen for months, came to drink coffee and gossip about local affairs. Violtsa was reunited with her two brothers and their families, none of whom she had heard from since before the war. (On several occasions, I had seen Violtsa weeping over the unknown plight of her brothers.)

The shopping district of Gjakova, the largest city nearby, was completely destroyed by Serb forces. Nathan saw blocks and blocks of rubble and scorched construction debris. Elsewhere in the city, about 10% of the houses were burned. Two of the most astounding sites of destruction were the police headquarters and the military base, both of which had been bombed by NATO. Though these locations were not leveled to the ground, they were rendered completely unsalvageable, with very little damage being done to any surrounding structures. Thankfully, Nathan neither observed nor heard of any incidents of retaliation by Kosovars against the Serb civilians in the area.

The road trip from Tirana to Gjakova took thirteen hours, seven of which were spent winding through the mountains on a miserable road flanked by a sheer, frightening drop. According to Nathan, "guard rails were not included in the budget."

Needless to say, I am happy to have Nathan home. He has spent the past two days visiting his refugee families to find out what their plans are. Most with whom he has spoken are anxious to go home as soon as possible. Some have already left. Nathan is giving serious thought to accompanying four to five heads-of-household to Kosovo to survey their properties. All of these men suspect that their homes have been destroyed. Nathan wants to analyze their situations and determine whether he can help provide temporary housing for them while assisting them with rebuilding.

Please pray for peace and forgiveness between the two ethnic groups in Kosovo. In his conversations with Kosovars, Nathan
tries to do what he can to promote reconciliation, but he often feels
like he's talking to a massive, stone wall. Fortunately, God can tear
down walls.

November 1999 &a *Newsletter*

Reflections of a Missionary Mom

WHEN I DISEMBARKED FROM THE PLANE ONTO ALBANIAN SOIL THAT
day in March, 1998, I was unprepared for the touch of icy wind and
the lightly falling snow that greeted me. Clasped in a baby carrier
at my breast was my three-and-a-half-month-old baby, Tristan, who
was just recovering from an ear infection.

Expecting the first signs of emerging spring in Albania, I was not
prepared for wintry weather. Thus, I had no warm coat or cap for
Tristan, and had only a lightweight blanket at hand with which to
wrap him. As we crossed the landing strip and headed for the terminal, a solicitous fellow passenger wound a scarf around Tristan's
head.

That first night in Albania was miserable. The temperatures were
far below normal, and the dampness and chill in a room barely
improved by an electric space heater made for little sleep. Anxious
that Tristan not catch cold, I bundled him warmly, pulled a cap on
his head, and settled him in the bed between my husband, Nathan,
and myself. Tristan was fine that night, but I shed many tears.

As I recall those first, uneasy days in Albania, I have to laugh a bit.
My nervousness then stemmed from a combination of new motherhood, uncertainty about health care available for an infant, the
newness of Albania, and the miserable, never-ending rain and cold
weather. Nonetheless, despite my fears, I never questioned the right-
ness of our coming to Albania, nor the timing of our arrival. And
I have never regretted raising a child in Albania, not only because
Nathan, Tristan, and I are a missionary family, but also because I have
found that children are an invaluable asset in missionary work.

Albanians love children, especially babies, and they are very demonstrative with their affection. Tristan, who is almost two years old now, has barely passed a day in Albania in which he has not been kissed, had his cheeks pinched, his legs shaken, or his nose tweaked. Being almost two, he most adamantly dislikes the pinching and prodding, but this seems to serve as little deterrent to his admirers. Tristan has served as a bridge in so many relationships. Just by being a child, he invites a greeting and attracts attention. This has helped Nathan and me to meet so many more people than we might have otherwise, had we been childless. It has opened doors into our neighbors' homes and has eased some of our awkwardness with the language. During the Kosovo crisis this past spring, when Nathan was making frequent visits to refugee homes, he often took Tristan, who served as a wonderful focal point and eased the language barrier.

Although my primary responsibilities as a missionary relate to being a homemaker and a mom, I do spend about 15 hours each week working in the publications office of our Church. A graphic designer by profession, I have been able to assist in producing calendars, brochures, logos, newsletters, and other printed materials needed by the Church. I thoroughly enjoy this work, but it would be impossible for me to participate in it were it not for the help of a very fine Albanian woman, Shpresa, who has looked after Tristan since he was four months old.

Raising a child in another culture can be of great benefit to the child. Both Nathan and I are the children of missionaries, and our worldview and life experiences are much broader because of our time spent in other parts of the world—I in Uganda, East Africa, and Nathan in Colombia, South America. Although any new culture takes time to adjust to, Nathan and I have had few problems acclimating to life in Albania, despite the difficulties that pervade this poverty-stricken, chaotic country. By living in such a place as Albania, Tristan has the possibility to learn that most of the world lives in much poorer conditions than in the States. He will learn that it is not the norm to have anything and everything one wants.

Furthermore, Tristan has learned to understand Albanian and, in fact, speaks more Albanian words than English words. He rattles off in Albanian all the animal names and noises (Albanian dogs say, "hum, hum," not "woof, woof," or "bow, wow"). With no difficulties, Tristan will learn to speak Albanian fluently, unlike his parents, who are still struggling. His faculty in two languages will make it possible for him to learn a third or fourth language even more quickly, should he so desire later on in his life.

We have never hesitated to take Tristan with us anywhere, whether it be into people's homes for visits, or out of town on extended trips. For example, this past summer we made a trip into Kosovo to see how some of the families we helped in Albania were faring back home. Knowing that many thousands of refugees were returning to Kosovo with their small children, despite fears over mines and instability, little food, and poor living conditions, we assumed that if they were willing to take their children into Kosovo, we had no reason to hesitate either. And, as we suspected, the situation proved no hardship for us with a small child.

We have taken Tristan with us on trips into some of the smaller, mountain villages of Albania, as well, and these have proven to be wonderful learning experiences for him. Although he has learned from books about many farm animals and tractors, by traveling in the countryside he had the opportunity to see these things firsthand for himself. Hearing him call out the names of the animals as he spotted them (mostly in Albanian) gave us no end of entertainment. Although it is unlikely that Tristan will remember any of these experiences, he will grow up seeing pictures of himself in various parts of Albania.

This past July, Tristan and I also spent two weeks at a university girls' camp held in a lovely monastery about an hour's drive from Tirana. While I assisted the girls with their craft projects, Tristan spent his time running around in the grass, chasing the monastery's flock of sheep, eating ripe plums directly from the tree, and passing the hottest part of the afternoon cooling himself in a small tub of water with his buddy, Paul Veronis. The girls thoroughly enjoyed having him around, despite the fact that he was reluctant to spend much time with any of them, and Tristan was relieved of the monotony of being apartment-bound in a dusty city.

On his very first Sunday in Albania, we took Tristan to church. During our first service, Nathan held a sleeping Tristan throughout the liturgy, which scandalized the women, who expressed vehemently that the care of babies should be in the hands of the mothers. After observing Nathan's effective care over some months, however, the women ceased to disapprove. We want Tristan to grow up loving our Lord, participating in the services of the Church, and knowing that he is always welcome in church. Nevertheless, having him with us in the service is very challenging, and with each new stage of his life, we have had to make adjustments in how we handle him during this time. We persist, though, because we want to demonstrate to the Albanians that church is for the family.

Raising a child in a politically unstable country, such as Albania, does present its challenges. Last August, after receiving warnings from the American embassy in Tirana and learning that the entire embassy was being evacuated because of threats directed against it, Tristan and I returned to the States for about five weeks. Had we not had children, I probably would not have returned to the States. Although it appears that there have been no obvious ramifications from those threats, the possibility of a political crisis or some other threat hangs like a permanent dark cloud over Albania. Each year seems to usher in some new crisis. This year it was the enormous flood of refugees from Kosovo and a fear that the war would spill over onto Albanian soil.

Although we choose not to live in fear of the ongoing political chaos and rampant lawlessness, we still have to be careful, particularly at night. In the past year and a half, four of the church's vehicles have been stolen, three of them at gunpoint. We never travel out of town at night, and we avoid traveling in the more isolated regions of Albania. Fortunately, it does appear that the security situation in Tirana (other than for vehicles) is improving slowly. When we first arrived a year and a half ago, few people took the traditional evening walk, or went out after dark. Now in the evenings, the main boulevard is crowded with promenaders, and the dozens of coffee shops scattered throughout the city are buzzing with conversation and laughter.

Despite the security problems, I have observed, paradoxically, that the realm of the mother and child is almost sacred in Albania. In the Albanian Code of Lek, a centuries-old code of behavior which is still honored by most, the women and children are to be protected. Thus, in my walking about town with my child, I have that odd sense of being both the protector of my child and of being protected because I have a child. This has been something of a comfort to me in this troubled land, where anything can and everything does happen.

As a family, we are in the beginning stages of our life as missionaries. If God allows us and if the need exists, we hope to spend many years serving our Lord in foreign parts, whether in Albania or elsewhere. We have no qualms about taking our children with us anywhere that God may lead us. Having Tristan with us in Albania has been a joy and a great benefit, and we look forward to welcoming our second child next April.

Advent 1999　　　𝕰𝕬　　　*Newsletter*

ADVENT IS UPON US—THAT SEASON OF THE YEAR IN WHICH WE PRE-pare for the coming of Jesus the Messiah. Tomorrow I will discuss this very theme—"Preparing for Christmas"—at a retreat for our priests' wives. In studying for this talk, I have been enriched in my own understanding of what it means to await the coming of Jesus. Words from *The Year of Grace of the Lord* have been particularly meaningful:

"The central idea of Advent is that it is the 'coming' of the Lord Jesus. One might perhaps feel that this term 'coming' is purely symbolic, for in fact Christ comes to us at all times, and even lives in us. Nevertheless, this approach and this presence of Christ, both of which are eternal, take on a special character at Advent; they somehow acquire an 'intensity.' A special grace of the 'coming' of the Lord is offered us."

The months since we posted our last newsletter have been full and varied. Throughout the spring and early summer months, our attention was focused on the Kosovo refugees and their needs. When the war "ended" (and we realize that it has not truly ended), most of the refugees returned home almost immediately. Their mass exodus left us surprised—even stunned. After their departure, so complete was their absence that it was as though they had never been here at all. In order to assure himself that the needs of his Kosovo families were being met, Nathan made four trips to Kosovo in the succeeding months. On one of these trips, Tristan and I accompanied him and were pleased to attend the wedding of the sister of our houseguest, Violtsa, of whom we wrote in our last newsletter.

During this visit, we were able to spend some time at the Serbian Orthodox Monastery in Decani. The monks we met there were wonderful, and our sadness deepened at the reality that peace is still so remote. Only God can heal the hatreds that have dominated this region for centuries.

The situation in Kosovo continues to be difficult, both politically and economically, and Nathan hopes to make one last trip there before Christmas to follow up on his families, who, along with power, water, and other shortages, are now confronted with freezing winds, rain, and snow. Kosovo has vanished from the news, but we ask you to continue remembering in your prayers this region and other regions of the world where war and ethnic hatred prevail. Whether we are aware of it or not, what happens to our fellow man affects us. Indeed, none of us is an island.

Duties at the Printing Office

In addition to keeping our almost-two-year-old son Tristan from stuffing his toys and snacks down the kitchen floor drain and teaching him that "no" is not an appropriate response when he is called, I continue to assist the church with its publications needs. Late last spring, a rash of requests for logos and seals kept me occupied: each of the new diocesan centers needed its own seal; the Archbishop wanted a personal logo; the Metropolitan of Korca ordered new letterhead; the new clinic needed a logo. The requests were endless. Each of these projects underwent multiple changes. Thank God in the end, they all got done, and I even managed to keep my mind.

Along with designing logos, I helped produce several issues of our English-language newsletter, "News from Albania," edited by Fr. Luke Veronis.

My fall projects included the production of our Year 2000 calendar, which went through a series of frustrating delays, including five days of citywide power outages. Rather than print the calendar on our own one-color press as was done last year, we opted to run the job at a state-run press. Formerly a huge publishing arm of the Communist government, this printing house had almost entirely shut down operations. When I first toured the facility, I was led through a series of warehouses where row upon row of one-color presses stood silent, unused—ghosts from the past. Tucked away in a corner was a Roland four-color press, also silent because the press house had no work. The irony of it was striking. For decades, this enormous complex had spewed forth Communist propaganda—a powerful weapon against the Christian faith, against the West, against anything considered an enemy of the state. Now I, an American, came to offer work—twelve large pages of photos and text illustrating the work of the Orthodox Church—a weapon, if you will, for Christ.

My current project is a 170-page color photo book illustrating the work of the Orthodox Church of Albania over the past ten years. I completed a first draft in time to present a bound copy to Ecumenical Patriarch Bartholomew during his visit, but the book is still in its infancy. Now that a copy is available for perusal, various people have come forward, proffering photos and information of which I was unaware. Their offerings will be incorporated where possible. God willing, this project will be printed by next February. I have a fixed deadline this time. We are expecting our second child early next April—a wonderful blessing from the Lord—but after the baby's birth, time for publications will be limited for a season.

December 2000 ❧ *Newsletter*

HOW QUICKLY THIS YEAR 2000 HAS PASSED. WE THANK GOD FOR THE good and the bad that we have seen and known. The good prompts us to be thankful; the bad compels us to be humble.

Our most precious blessing this year was the birth of Katherine Elise, who arrived April 12 in Minnesota. I returned to the U.S. in March in anticipation of the birth because medical conditions in Albanian hospitals make it risky to give birth here—the risk of infection being particularly acute. My parents very kindly opened their home to us, and we enjoyed an extended stay with them. Katherine is now 7½ months old, has four teeth, and just began crawling. She enjoys following her brother, who has reverted to crawling. A sweet-tempered baby, she is affectionate, delightful, and curious.

Second Term in Albania

Returning to Albania on August 23, we wiped down the inches of dust that had collected on our stored belongings, unpacked dozens of boxes, and settled into a new residence—a small, two-story, two-bedroom home with an external stair connecting the floors. Squashed into a crowded, noisy neighborhood, the house shares a common wall with the neighbors on three sides. Each week brings new discoveries of leaks and smells, noises, and well-established local residents—particularly cats, who make themselves at home in our kitchen if we forget to shut the front door. We are pleased with our home, a mere two minutes' walk from the archdiocese, where Nathan catches the early morning van to the seminary, and just a stone's throw from our church bell tower.

Design Progress

On the publications front, I recently completed the design of our church's Year 2001 calendar, which took almost two months to prepare because of complications with gathering photos, getting the text translated from Greek into Albanian, and producing 30 pages of four-color film. When the project was finally ready for the press, my children and I accompanied it to the print house, where we spent hours in the reception room waiting for the first pages to roll off the press. I don't think my children appreciated the significance of the occasion, but I was thrilled to see the tangible fruits of my labors.

Several weeks ago, I designed a PowerPoint® presentation illustrating the work of the Orthodox Church of Albania over the past ten years. This was shown in conjunction with a paper Archbishop Anastasios presented at an international symposium, "2000 Years of Christian Art and Architecture in Albania," held at the National Historical Museum. I had only a few days to pull together a show, but thankfully was able to draw on dozens of scanned images I had stored on my computer to be used for a book I am compiling on the same subject.

Several months ago I began giving thought to training others in graphic design. I wanted to find candidates with some talent and a lot of commitment to the church. Without even having to look for pupils, two young women approached me: Katerina and Marijeta, one of our seminary graduates. I have already begun working with Katerina, who is showing great promise.

Hour of Power

At the present time, Albania is suffering from a serious, state-wide shortage of power, and the prospects for improvement are bleak. Drought is probably the most immediate cause of the shortage, since Albania depends on hydro-electric plants to produce its power, and lake and river levels have plummeted, but there are other factors. Now, when we normally would be complaining about rain, mildew, and mud, we are enjoying balmy weather—but at such a price. If we have 8 hours of power in 24, we consider ourselves fortunate, but the situation is deteriorating, and power cuts occur without warning. When we're without power, we're also without water because we have an electric pump. To run office equipment requires power; hence, getting any work done is exceedingly frustrating. Nathan's parents very generously shipped us a generator, which we are sharing with our neighbors, fellow-missionaries Charles and Maria Linderman. Power from the generator will enable us to carry out some tasks—write lectures, print design drafts, etc., as well as run some household appliances, but we cannot run a generator 16 hours a day. Fuel prices are steep. I never thought I would see the day when I would pray for rain to fall in winter here, but that day has come.

June 2001 $\wp$ *Newsletter*

"He told me all that I ever did." With these words, the Samaritan woman, who had encountered Jesus at a well, urged her neighbors to come to Jesus. Her simple testimony—a teaser, if you will—brought the people out in droves, all of whom knew all that she had ever done. The Scriptures record that many Samaritans believed because of her testimony. St. Fotini, as we now know this woman, led her curious neighbors to Jesus, but ultimately, they were transformed by meeting the Lord Jesus himself. This is what they said afterwards to her. "It is no longer because of your words that we believe, for we have heard for ourselves, and we know that this is indeed the Savior of the world."

Two weeks ago a short-term mission team, sent through the OCMC, arrived in Albania for a three-week evangelistic outreach program. Leading the team was Fr. Peter Gillquist, who spent the first week training our seminary students and others in how to share their faith. This past weekend the seminarians had the opportunity to implement their training by distributing thousands of fliers at the University of Tirana, inviting students to talks by Fr. Peter. Despite the fact that the university students are now in the midst of finals, a good crowd attended the meetings and responded well to Fr. Peter's presentations of the gospel.

During the second week, the OCMC team, plus a group of our students and several of our missionaries, including Nathan, left for the northern part of Albania, where they conducted other outreach programs in the cities of Shkodra and Lezhe. Once more the students and OCMC team members distributed thousands of fliers and spoke one-on-one with people. These evangelistic meetings received hours of coverage on four national TV stations. Additionally, Fr. Peter was interviewed on the radio.

Our publicity for the campaign posed the question: "Looking for hope in a world without hope?" Albania is a country almost paralyzed by a lack of hope. Many here cling to a thin thread of hope that they might find some way of emigrating to the U.S. or a Western European country, whether legally or illegally. (A legitimate U.S. visa can be bought illegitimately for $10,000.)

By the time you receive this newsletter, this outreach program will be over and the OCMC team will have returned to the States. Please pray that those who have heard the Gospel of Jesus Christ through these efforts will be able to grasp the profound truth that God loves them and has provided hope through Jesus' death and resurrection. Pray also that those who participated for the first time in an outreach effort of this sort—our seminary students and catechists—will develop a vision for evangelizing their own country.

Third Draft Issued

My book illustrating the resurrection of the Orthodox Church of Albania over the past ten years is now in the third-draft stage. This book, which I now refer to fondly as my life's work, may actually get printed this year if all goes well. For the past two months I have focused my attention almost exclusively on this book, adding several new chapters, including a chapter illustrating the history of Christianity in Albania, and updating information on all aspects of the church's work; this involved meeting with each department and acquiring photos of new work. This project, which began three years ago as a 16-page flier, has now evolved into a full color, 270-page, cloth-cover/dust-jacket volume to be printed outside Albania.

Up until two months ago, I had been working on this project as a duty, but in the process of working on my new chapter on the history of Christianity in Albania, during which time I sent our church photographer around the country to shoot photos of the best-known, ancient Christian sites, I suddenly found myself becoming rather passionate about the church here. Perhaps it was discovering what treasures exist (for example, the *Codex Purpureus Beratinus,* or Purple Codex of Berat, a sixth-century manuscript of 190 pages containing the Gospels of Mark and Matthew) that lit a fire in me. I am now thinking of other books I would like to produce that might help to bring to the fore this Christian heritage.

Housing Refugees

Once again, we had the opportunity to house a refugee family for several weeks. This time, however, it was not a Kosovo family but our co-workers Fr. Luke and Faith Veronis and their two children, who suffered a devastating house fire on March 8, in which they lost their entire library, computer equipment and office furniture, and all their children's clothes, books, and toys. Additionally, almost the entire house was blackened from smoke damage. The fire started and raged while everyone was away from the house, so its cause remains a mystery, although a faulty voltage regulator is suspected.

Neighbors, friends, and church members rose to the occasion, offering hours of help with clean up, debris removal, and repairs. Family and friends here and at home in the States have piled the

Veronises with clothing and gifts for the children. New computers and furniture have been purchased, and the library is slowly being rebuilt. Over the past three years of working together, we have come to love the Veronises. Our time together served to deepen our love for them and to increase our admiration for their courage and stamina in times of adversity.

July 2002   ✌   *Newsletter*

MOST OF MY ENERGIES DURING THE PAST SIX MONTHS HAVE BEEN dedicated to working on my book. In June, I submitted a new version for Archbishop Anastasios' review, and am awaiting his suggestions. I am very anxious to finish this project, but there is still so much work to be done to size and touch up the approximately 500 photos in the book. Also, the text will need to be translated into Greek and Albanian for parallel editions.

We have decided to homeschool Tristan for kindergarten this fall and are now researching programs to use with him. Because of this, I want to conclude my current projects and give more time and attention to the children.

Summer Camp

One of the most important programs organized for our youth each year is the summer camp program. This past summer, three girls' camps were held at a monastery in the foothills of Elbasan, an hour's drive from our home. The boys' two-week camps occurred at Zvernec, a small island in the Mediterranean Sea.

I assisted with two of the twelve-day girls' camps, organizing the craft project and giving talks. Nathan gave a talk and showed our seminary presentation at one of the boys' camps. Tristan and Katherine went to camp with me, and enjoyed themselves immensely. Tristan was mesmerized by the large black beetles found in abundance at the monastery, and Katherine enjoyed chasing the monastery's flock of sheep. I enjoyed watching my children enjoy the outdoors, something they aren't able to do much in Tirana, a city that is either very dusty or very muddy, depending on the season.

My role at camp is to organize and implement the craft project, which, although optional for the girls, usually becomes a significant part of what they do during their stay at camp. Each year I try to organize a project that requires quite a bit of effort on the part of the girls, which teaches them persistence and patience. Those who participate have always done exceedingly well, and this year was no exception.

For this year's project, I hired a craftsman to make 250 trays, and then purchased paints, brushes, and stencils with which to decorate them. I painted several models myself to provide the girls with ideas about what they could do. Some did reproduce the pear sample, but most ventured out on their own, using the stencils or other patterns provided to make some very lovely trays. This craft was completed successfully by about 115 girls. Three girls' camps are held each summer, and this same project will be offered to the university-age girls during the third camp.

Each time I participate in the camp program, I see more clearly what excellent opportunities our girls have for spiritual and personal growth—opportunities that they might not have elsewhere. I thank God for the blessing I receive from being part of this wonderful program.

December 2003   *Newsletter*

"Now when they had seen Him, they made widely known the saying which was told them concerning this child. And all those who heard it marveled at those things which were told them by the shepherds." (Luke 2:17)

THE FIRST MISSIONARIES WERE HUMBLE SHEPHERDS WHO WERE blessed to hear the Savior's birth heralded by a glorious host. These received the message with joy and rushed to Bethlehem to find the child whose coming warranted this celestial announcement. After encountering the Christ child, they were bursting with news of him, and spread abroad word of his coming. What is the work of a missionary, but to do just this? To see for ourselves this Child—this

Savior of the world—and then to speak joyfully of him to others, telling of our own personal encounter with this One who has come to dwell among us: Immanuel, "God with us."

At this season of Advent, we thank our Lord for his great love, which brought him to a humble stable one starry night in Bethlehem long ago. We are grateful that he has called us to be his own, and has given us the privilege of bringing the good news of his coming to those in Albania. We are thankful also to you for making our labors possible through your thoughtful prayers and generous financial contributions. This newsletter brings a report on some of what has occurred in the past five months.

Children's Camps in Kosovo

Following the success of last year's camp for 450 children from an entirely non-Orthodox village in the Malisheva area in Kosovo, Nathan directed a second camp for children from the same area this past August. Seventeen young people from our church organized a variety of activities, including sporting events, a craft, and a talent show for several hundred children. The children were delighted with the program, and our young people participated with excellent spirits and much zeal. In running these camps, Nathan encourages leadership development among our youth. Although he serves as overall director, the responsibility for organizing and running the camp is delegated to our youth. Although the camps have no religious content, our young people seek to radiate the light of Christ through their love, care, spirit of cooperation, and good will. All from the village know that the camps are a gift from the Orthodox Church of Albania. Our young people stay in homes of the villagers and each day chant prayers with the blessing of their hosts.

Traveling in the States

This past August, we returned to the U.S. to visit our families and boost our financial and prayer support, which as many of you know had fallen quite low during the past two years. Over a period of two months we drove 14,000 miles and presented our work and the ministries of the Orthodox Church of Albania to 25 churches and home groups. We thoroughly enjoyed our time on the road, despite the many miles. Our children managed the hours in the car with good humor and seemed to adjust rather well to a new set of people and a new bed almost every night. We were delighted to meet so many new people and to visit with old friends.

Although we had engagements almost every night, we tried to take as many short excursions with our children as time would allow. As most of our miles were in the southwestern and western parts of the United States, we were able to see such spectacular sights as the Petrified Forest, Grand Canyon, Redwood Forest, and Arches National Park. We visited California and Utah for the first time, and Tristan had the opportunity to try "boogie boarding" in the Pacific surf, which he took to like a native Californian. Because we rely ultimately on God for our financial support during our travels, we were able to relax and truly enjoy visiting with people while presenting Orthodox missions to them. We met many who are interested in missions and want to be involved either in our work, in other ministries of the Orthodox Christian Mission Center, or in outreach efforts of other organizations.

Changing Role

Although my primary role as a missionary over the past five years has been to assist with Church publications, I have felt for some time that I ought to be more involved with people. I wasn't sure what that meant or how it might develop, but a most interesting thing occurred to launch my involvement in this area. It's a rather long story, but the short version is that I was asked to give a brief introduction to a recording of the first liturgy sung in the Albanian language (Boston, 1908) at an event sponsored by the State Archives of Albania, which has in its collection an 18-minute segment from this liturgy.

Despite the fact that almost all present talked amongst themselves during the entirety of my presentation, which opened with the words, "The fullest expression of the spiritual life of man is found in his relationship to God and his worship of God," there was one young woman who approached me at the conclusion of the event and asked if she could hear more about what I had said. I met with her for the first time several weeks later, and thus began a friendship that has continued for eight months.

Several years before we met, this young woman, Albana, in the depths of despair had called out to God for help. In the two years that followed this spiritual crisis, she had been searching for someone to talk to about spiritual things. God, in his providence (and good humor, I might add) used my short presentation, to which it appeared that no one was paying any attention, to pique her interest, and so she approached me.

Albana is from a Muslim family and knows little of Jesus and the Bible. I thank God for this opportunity to introduce Albana to Jesus and his desire to have a relationship with her. After that first visit, Albana and I began to meet regularly to discuss spiritual things. Just before I left for the States in August, Albana called me and said she wanted to be baptized and had the full consent of her parents to do so. I was so moved by her wishes, and so grateful to God for paving an easy path for her. Albana is very close to her family, and although they do not practice their own religion, her parents still might have objected to her choosing to follow Christ. I'm not sure how she would have responded had they objected. Since returning to Albania in October, I have been meeting regularly with Albana to teach her about the faith. *I ask you to pray for Albana as she deepens her knowledge of Christ and his salvation and prepares for baptism.*

In addition to meeting regularly with Albana, I would like to meet regularly with the young women of our seminary. My plan is to spend one afternoon and evening each week at the seminary, offering a graphic design course to those who are interested, and hanging out for the evening with any that are inclined to talk. *Please pray for me, as I would like to do all I can to be available to these girls in whatever way they need.*

CHAPTER 3

Martyrdom Through Illness &

IN THIS CHAPTER, WE ENTER INTO THE SOBER YET POWERFUL WITNESS of Lynette as she discovers her body racked with cancer. The chapter begins with a few excerpts from her personal journal and missionary newsletter composed several months before she learned about her cancer. These writings help the reader understand how the Lord was preparing her even before her final test. Her personal journal, along with her public epistles via missionary newsletters and postings on her website, details her spiritual struggle and gradual growth as a saint-like witness or martyr through her physical pain, suffering, and ultimate death.

February 23, 2004 & Email to a Friend

IT'S PARTICULARLY DIFFICULT TO ACCEPT THE DEATH OF THOSE that are young. We feel somehow that they're being cheated, especially if they have young children. The reality of our own frailty and the certainty of our own death are painful to face, too, but we're forced to look at them squarely when we see another suffer. I have asked God to spare me until my children are past the critical teenage years, but perhaps his will dictates otherwise. It would be very hard to have to leave the children while they're young and vulnerable, and Nathan, too, but I know he can take care of himself.

NATHAN IS AWAY IN KOSOVO, CONDUCTING CHILDREN'S CAMPS. He'll be back next week, but only briefly as he'll be heading to Pakistan shortly thereafter for three weeks. I've decided to focus my efforts during his absence on some much-needed "self-limitation." I also want to develop more of my inner self through reading, thinking, playing piano, and perhaps through a bit of writing. I'm going to have to be very disciplined about this as I will surely succumb to the urgent if I don't.

I feel that my whole orientation and mind set are rapidly changing. The driving force is the realization that Christ is by far and away our greatest treasure in life, and anything that stands in the way of gaining Him must be sacrificed. I do not know what this might mean for me, but I want to move forward to grasp at those things that will propel me forward.

Lately, I have been overwhelmingly convinced that in order to see Christ we must embrace suffering—if not our own, then the sufferings of others—and must curtail our desire for material things. Practicing this will be a big test for me, especially when we return to the States. I do not like what I become there in my mad frenzy to get as much as I can. If I can focus on serving rather than on getting, I will save myself from the immense burden of things.

I'm reading a biography on the life of Alexander Solzhenitsyn by James Pearce, and am being profoundly moved by it. I've liked the Russian authors Tolstoy and Dostoyevsky, and Solzhenitsyn is definitely in the same league with them. It is just the right thing to be reading now. He has exactly confirmed my thoughts about suffering and self-limitation, particularly with regard to material things. Suffering is essential to our spiritual growth. If we weren't suffering ourselves it was only because God was freeing us to take on the sufferings of others. At the same time I've thought that a desire for material things clouds our vision of Jesus, and that to clear ourselves from such a haze we must begin to detach ourselves from things. When I read the book on Solzhenitsyn I was amazed to read that he said exactly the same things—much more eloquently and convincingly of course, as they grew out of his experience in the Gulag Archipelago [Soviet penal system]. Now I'm trying to see what it means for me to voluntarily embrace self-limitation. I'm not sure how it should look on me, as it were, but I am asking God to help me tear away little by little those material things that I feel are so important.

June 2004   &   *Newsletter*

"Behold, the tabernacle of God is with men, and He will dwell with them, and they shall be His people. God Himself will be with them and be their God. And God will wipe away every tear from their eyes; there shall be no more death, nor sorrow, nor crying. There shall be no more pain, for the former things have passed away." Rev. 2:13

WHEN I LEARNED OF THE APPALLING MISTREATMENT OF IRAQI PRIS-oners by our own soldiers, I was appalled and grieved. For days I felt the terrible weight of evil and pain that torments our world and seems to crush anything good. In the midst of my heaviness, the plight of those nearby came vividly to mind—neighbors who are mourning the loss of a loved one, or are struggling to support sick relatives; the poor who come to our door almost daily seeking relief from their poverty, or begging for medicines to ease their pain; young people who are looking for hope in the face of disillusionment and despair.

What do we do? What can we do? I asked myself, agitated. Yet I knew the answer: We must spend our lives doing as much good as we can for others, helping them "one person at a time," as Mother Teresa used to say, and look beyond the "shadowland" to our eternal hope, which is to dwell forever with God, who will wipe away all tears.

Touching the Neighborhood

In previous newsletters, we've tended to focus on the programs or projects we're involved in. This time, we'd like to tell something about a few of our relationships.

Four years ago we moved to our present house, a simple structure just a two-minute walk from the cathedral and a three-minute walk from the church offices—an ideal location for us. After we moved in, I noticed that there were many young men who hung about in the alley not far from our door, or blared rap music from a car parked outside our gate. Neighbors in the house next door screamed at each other continuously, while their ferocious German shepherd raged at every passerby. Three elementary school boys hurled insults at us and whacked our stroller with sticks. Another group of children gleefully rang our doorbell and then ran away and hid just before we answered the door. Shortly thereafter, a drunken neighbor threatened to kill Nathan.

That was the final stroke for me. "We cannot live in a neighborhood with such people," I said. "They're too volatile." Nathan assured me that Albanians often dealt with conflict by shouting at each other and threatening all sorts of evil things, but usually dropped their quarrel afterwards. We would have to learn to look beyond the surface.

We didn't move from that house. Instead we made every effort to bring peace to the conflicts that erupted so easily around us. For example, several years ago, when we were losing our power for eight hours a day, we were given a generator and began to use it daily, sometimes up to four hours a day. The noise level of the generator (which was considerable, I must say) caused terrible conflicts with our closest neighbor—a single woman in her fifties, whose apartment window faces out onto our courtyard. This neighbor, Lumi, wouldn't confront us directly, but resorted instead to throwing things into our courtyard from her window, or setting her radio in the window and blasting out static noise. To our eyes, her behavior looked like that of a two-year-old. Our landlord said she was *"cmendur,"* or crazy, when we asked him about her.

At the height of our conflict, I decided to go and visit her to see if we could resolve the issue. When Lumi met me at her gate, she greeted me kindly and invited me in. Her eagerness to entertain me with what food and drink she had in the house was touching. For more than an hour I listened to her tell about her background and family history, her loneliness, and her ongoing battles in the law courts where she is struggling to regain her family's properties that were confiscated by the Communists. Her own cousins are opposing her bitterly in this conflict.

"I come home from fighting all day in the courts where there is no justice and want peace," she said. "But then I hear the noise of the generator, and it makes my head ache."

"It makes my head ache too," I said, and resolved to adjust our use of the generator. Lumi then went on to tell me that she was delighted to have us as neighbors because she felt safe with us. I went home bewildered by the complete turnabout in our relationship. Lumi joined us for Christmas dinner this past December and was delightful company.

Our other neighbors who fought all the time were actually twins, a brother and sister in their sixties, who were devoted to each other (we never could figure out the quarrelling aspect of their relationship). The brother, Kosma, died suddenly about six weeks ago, and his sister, Mara, who was crippled by polio years ago and cannot walk, has been wracked by grief. It has been so painful to see her suffer as she weeps for a brother who, she says, "has gone and left me all alone." We've tried to help bear her burden by having her in to express her grief over coffee. We've been to her home to hear it all over again. We've tried to give her our love, medicines to relieve her physical pain, and food to sustain her body. She also had flooding in her kitchen every time it rained, so we replaced her window and patched the wall. Mara's become a dear friend.

One of those wild elementary school boys, Renis, has turned out to be a polite and thoughtful boy (who would have guessed it?). He comes over to visit Tristan and is mesmerized by the American toys in our house. He and Tristan play well together, and Tristan's Albanian is good enough so that the two of them can communicate freely. We're glad to have him over.

And those young men that just hung about, well, they still hang around, but they always greet us politely, and somehow the music from their car stereo doesn't seem to occur as frequently or as loudly as before.

For the past few Christmases, we've baked cookies and distributed them to the families in our neighborhood. We've involved our children in the whole process of baking, decorating, and distributing the cookies, thus teaching them the importance of reaching out in kindness to those around us. The power of cookies to sweeten neighborhood relationships is incredible. This year I want to include even more families in the cookie giveaway.

We've opened a Friday night outdoor theater in our courtyard this summer so the neighborhood children can watch a film and eat popcorn with us. It's been a big hit with the kids, and even the adults and adolescents enjoy popping in. In August, we hope to host a week-long Bible school program for the same kids, offering Bible story, craft, games, and refreshments.

Perhaps through helping to heal the conflicts and hurts in our neighborhood, we will be able to introduce our neighbors to the Prince of Peace.

Theology of the Frog Prince

There are many people who come to our door each month asking for food, medicines, clothing, shoes, and cash. We don't know how they find us, but they do, and we see new faces at our door all the time. Many come from villages outside Tirana and travel by bus to our door. Over the years, we've adjusted our regular visitors to a system of coming once a month for a large bag of staple foods. Most are very happy with this program, but every once in a while someone shows up who has a different idea about what we ought to do for him.

Several months ago a short, worn and much weathered man came for food. I think he must have been going door-to-door seeking help and just happened upon our door. He said he was from a town some two-hours' drive from Tirana and had six children. We gave him a bag of food, and thereafter he began to knock on our door almost every day, sometimes several times a day. He came at 5:00 A.M. He came at 10:00 P.M. If I gave him a banana, I found the banana skin on my doorstep. If I gave him cheese, bread, and tomato, I found the discarded tomato core on the step. He began to rankle me, and I moaned to Nathan that this man wouldn't cooperate with my once-a-month food program. What could I do with him? Nathan suggested that I have simple foods available to give him should he happen to come by. The man was, in his own words, *"fukara,"* "a poor fool" and could not be reasoned into a "program." Furthermore, he was so hungry each time he came that he promptly consumed anything he was given (and dropped his garbage on our doorstep, I added).

As I puzzled over Nathan's suggestion, the tale of the Frog Prince popped into my mind. I have never liked that story because the heroine, a young princess, is not an exemplary character. She refuses to keep her word—not a good trait for a princess. She promises the frog that if he will help her recover her golden ball, which she had accidentally dropped into the pond, he can eat at her plate and sleep on her pillow. He recovers the ball, but later when he comes to claim her promise, she despises him, slamming the door on him, throwing him off the table and screaming when he hops onto her pillow.

After thinking about this tale, it occurred to me that Christ is like the Frog Prince. For some reason, he has chosen to visit us in a form that we find unlovely. ("That which you have done unto the least of these my brethren, you have done unto me.") If I want to find the Prince I must embrace the frog. To reject the frog (in whatever form he comes to me) is to lose the most precious and beloved of all princes, Christ.

As for this poor man who comes to my door, now he gets food each day he comes as well as a monthly bag of staples.

Such experiences give new meaning to the text in Gal. 6:9, "And let us not grow weary while doing good, for in due season we shall reap if we do not lose heart." In truth, doing good is very wearying, and it is tempting to try to escape it, but the reward gained by persisting, which is a greater capacity to love, is worth all the effort.

Employing Blerina

One day a young woman named Blerina came to our door. She had two children with her and was weeping. Her children were sick, she said, and her husband was violent and abusive when drunk. I gave her food and medicines.

After some weeks, she came again. This time she said she wanted work, not a handout. Did we have work? Nathan spoke with her and asked if she could record some Albanian books on tape for him. She said she could, and I asked if she could do embroidery. Thereafter, Blerina began to record books for Nathan and embroider napkins for me. For this work we paid her by the hour and by the piece. After numerous books had been recorded and 120 napkins had been embroidered (gifts for friends in the States during our travels), I said to Blerina that we couldn't keep up the employment, but I said I would ask God to provide her with work.

Amazingly, within a week, the director of a major relief agency with whom I had very little contact asked me if I knew of anyone that she could hire to do housework for her one day a week. I immediately thought of Blerina and asked her if she would like the job. She said yes, and shortly thereafter was hired by the director. Blerina was so reliable and so good at her work that she was recommended to others and within a short period had the equivalent of full-time work. Blerina's husband, who had been so violent, quit drinking and found occasional work.

Though there were many ups and downs and setbacks in this family's situation, gradually, there was a real change for the better. In time, Blerina, who is from a Muslim background, expressed an interest in having her children attend catechism classes at our church. She recognized that her children needed to have their spiritual needs as well as their physical needs met. Blerina herself also came to believe in Jesus and to thank Him for all that had been provided for her. She and her children are planning to be baptized soon.

As for Shpetim, Blerina's husband, he is at least open to the Christian faith. In time, we hope that he too will come to believe in Jesus Christ.

Blerina came by for a visit a few weeks ago and said that she would like to finish high school and train as a nurse. We applaud her ambitions and pray that somehow her husband will take responsibility for providing for the family, thus freeing Blerina to pursue her interest in health care.

The challenge of introducing Christ to needy families such as Blerina's to whom we have given much assistance is to ensure that they come to Him in true faith and don't act simply to please us, or to gain something from us. In Blerina's case, we know her faith is genuine.

Turning the Heart of Mr. Hoxha

I wrote last time of a young woman named Albana, whom I met under unusual circumstances in March 2003. For more than a year now, I have been meeting regularly with Albana, teaching her about Christ and the truths of the Bible. Over the months, our relationship has deepened into a meaningful friendship, which has been as much a blessing to me as it has been for her. Just a few weeks ago, Albana decided that she was ready to be baptized. She was exuberant in her anticipation of this important step in her spiritual journey.

Just four days before the baptism was to occur, however, Albana called me in great distress. Her father, she said, had absolutely forbidden her to be baptized. "We are Muslims," he said, "and should not abandon our traditional faith." Albana's father is a self-proclaimed atheist, so his attachment to a traditional faith has nothing to do with any real belief. It is simply a cultural issue for him. He told Albana that if she disobeyed him, he would refuse to speak to her again. Albana is not a child. She passed her twenty-third birthday a few weeks ago and is of an age to choose her own path. Nonetheless, we thought it best to postpone the baptism and wait a bit, committing ourselves to pray for a change of heart on the part of her father and also for the salvation of the whole family.

That all occurred last week, and we are now asking God for a miracle. Please pray for Albana and her family. She has resolved to go forward, but when exactly that will be, she does not know. To be baptized is a choice that could cost her dearly, and she must be spiritually and emotionally prepared for the consequences.

Developing the Curriculum

As I mentioned in our last newsletter, our seminary is now under the leadership of Bishop Ilia (Katre) from the United States, who has proved to be an excellent director, doing all he can to raise the academic level of the school.

Nathan has been working hard with the bishop and other teachers from the school to develop a curriculum that will better prepare the students for leadership in the Church. Please pray for this process. The caliber of our seminary students has risen in the past few years, but an improvement in the curriculum will attract even better students. For this fall, please pray that serious and devout young men and women will consider joining the ranks of our students.

Saying Goodbye to Good Friends

This July, Fr. Luke and Faith Veronis and their three children will be retiring after ten years of missionary service in Albania. We are grieved to lose them. They have been outstanding missionaries, and we have come to love and admire them deeply. Our friendship has grown close over the years, and our children are excellent playmates. We know that God will bless the Veronises as they return to the United States to serve the Church there, but we will miss them sorely.

The departure of the Veronises signals the beginning of some new responsibilities for Nathan and me. The university ministry and the work of the national children's office will fall into Nathan's lap, and I will take a leadership role in the girls' camp program.

At present youth leaders, who have been trained under the Veronises, are coordinating these ministries and have proved themselves to be capable, mature, and responsible. We would like to move these young people to a new level of leadership, giving them opportunities for greater maturity and independence. Our goal as missionaries is to replace ourselves with national leaders.

Team leadership of our OCMC missionary group also will fall to Nathan after Fr. Luke leaves. This role carries with it the need to support, guide, and advise the long-term missionaries in Albania.

Taking a Hike

For many years Fr. Luke and Nathan dreamed of making a serious pilgrimage/hike with Metropolitan John of Korca in the mountainous region of southern Albania. With Fr. Luke planning to leave in midsummer, the men decided that they either had to do it this spring, or it would never happen. Thus earlier this month Nathan, Fr. Luke and two other men from our team drove to Korca to begin this oft-discussed, but never attempted hike.

The Metropolitan himself planned the tour, which began just outside of Korca and ended in the village of Vithkuq. For two days, the company walked, sometimes in the rain, often in stiff winds, and passed through forests, scaled hills, and wandered amidst fields of flowers. The climb was not difficult but demanded endurance.

After it was over, the men spoke glowingly of the colorful wild-flowers, the glorious view of the mountains, the good conversations, and the exuberant feeling that they were like "hobbits on a quest." The hike, with its spiritual overtones, was so successful that the men are thinking they ought to make this trek with Metropolitan John an annual event.

Our Thanks

None of our work would be possible apart from our Lord Jesus Christ, who gives us strength in weakness, courage in distress, and love in the midst of suffering. To Him we give praise and thanksgiving.

And to you, dear friends, we also give thanks for the many ways in which you support us: through your prayers, your notes of encouragement, and your generous financial gifts. May God bless and refresh you and give you His joy and peace.

July 23, 2004   ✠   *Journal Entry*

LAST NIGHT AFTER A LATE MEETING WITH THE CAMP LEADERS, I went into the Church to pray and look at all the stars in the sky [the Church of St. John Vladimir was an old, destroyed monastery church with no roof]. The candles were lit over the icons and a lone lamp burned on the altar. It was so beautiful. As I looked at the vast night sky studded with a million lights, I felt that our problems were so minute when compared with the enormous universe. We will pass away, returning to dust, but it will remain. Others will come, but they will pass on too. God is great. God is good. He is with us and will help us. *O God our help and our home, come and abide in us and with us.*

October 31, 2004   ✠   *Journal Entry*

FALL SWEEPS THE COUNTRYSIDE, DROPPING CRISP COLORFUL LEAVES and blowing them in swift curls of current. The air is warm during the day but cool at night. This evening, I'm lying in bed in the girls' dormitory at St. Vlash. Varvara is abroad, and I'm the caretaker for a few days. I'm enjoying our stay. The children are free here and Tristan is loving all the bugs, frogs, cats and other creatures roaming, flying, buzzing or creeping around here.

Something within wishes to live here permanently, and something is contented in Tirana. Last year Nathan and I offered to be dorm parents for the girls, but the Archbishop said no. He said he prefers having an Albanian, but I can't believe that because for a long time there were Greek nuns staying here with the girls. It seems to me that it would be so good for us to live nearer the students, to invest in them, hear their stories and troubles, and be available to them. The girls get lost somehow, and after they graduate we lose them to Greece, non-Orthodox boys, or to indifference.

Nathan and I could model what a Christian family and marriage can be. I'm thinking I should write the Archbishop a long letter about this, but first I must ask Nathan what he thinks. He may feel that he is tied to Tirana because of overseeing the university and children's ministries.

The children are thoroughly enjoying being here at St. Vlash. Today Melania and Joana came to play, and the kids had so much fun being together. Tristan is in heaven with all the bugs and frogs and cats around. I've had such a strong feeling that we ought to move out here, not only for the sake of our children but also to be more a part of the seminary. It seems that we ought to invest deeply in a few people who can, in turn, invest in others. I in the girls and Nathan in the boys. We can still do things in Tirana—go bowling once a month, or go to the park. Go for dinner or to the movies. There's probably good shopping in Durres. Our kids can play with the Linderman kids, or the kids from the Children's Home of Hope. We'll see.

December 13, 2004:
Lynette discovers that she has cancer

BY THE GRACE OF GOD I FIND MYSELF AT A BLESSED MONASTERY ON the holy mountain of Greece, Mount Athos, called the *Pantokrator*. With the operation [on a child from the Children's Home of Hope in Albania] a success and the hospital in Athens absorbing the cost, I should be elated. Unfortunately, my heart and mind are as stormy and turbulent as the sea outside my window. I am looking at the miracle-working icon of the Theotokos called the 'Gerontissa' and wondering if she would work another miracle for our Lynette Hoppe.

On December 19, 2004, while reflecting, as I often do, on how painful it was to lose the Veronis family six months earlier, I received a call from Lynette. In her classic style she asks about everyone and before hanging up the phone she says, "Oh by the way, Charles, I have a painful mass under my left arm; is that something to be concerned about?" The feeling I had at that time I would not wish on the darkest of people, and to my horror that feeling was to greatly worsen.

In rapid succession, as if the Archbishop Anastasios built the Orthodox Clinic only to evaluate Lynette, she underwent mammography, X-ray, ultrasound, physical exam, and fine needle aspiration. Results: infiltrating carcinoma, with a lesion 5 cm in greatest diameter. I can now testify to why doctors should not treat family. I was now telling my best friends, Nathan and Lynette Hoppe, that she had breast cancer and much worse yet, it looked aggressive. As a surgeon, I have told more people than I want to remember they have this dreaded diagnosis and have found that this news tends to strip people of their facade and societal persona. Those that know Lynette will not be surprised to hear of her response. No one has ever responded like both Lynette and Nathan. First, she consoled me as if I had to engage this struggle instead of her. After a moment to consider what I had just said, she followed with this reflection of her heart: "Well, Charles, now I have the *blessing* of showing the Albanians that we are serious when we say that suffering is an important part of our spiritual growth." In fact during this entire process she has remained powerfully motivated to witness to her faith in God and her trust that His grace is sufficient.

The OCMC has done well by her missionaries by obtaining

insurance that allowed Lynette to be treated by some of the best in the world: the Mayo Clinic. I had hoped that my diagnosis was wrong, and that they would find that it was some benign process. Again in rapid succession Lynette underwent fine needle aspiration, mastectomy, bone scan, and CT. Results: Lobular Carcinoma, 18/20 lymph nodes positive, with metastasis to the thoracic spine. I was the 'update' person for our beleaguered mission team and the multitude of Albanians who dearly love Lynette and Nathan and continuously ask me about her. With each phone call from Nathan reporting on how Lynette was doing, I found it more and more difficult to pass such pessimistic news. I have been inspired by Nathan's strong faith and stability in dealing with his beloved wife's illness and prognosis. After an operation removing the tumor and complications with infection, Lynette and Nathan met the oncologist and discussed all the options. They resolved on the following treatment: focus beam radiation to arrest the growth of the thoracic metastasis and an oral medication to only slow the growth of the tumor.

At the time of writing of this update Nathan, Lynette, and their two children, Tristan and Katherine, are with Lynette's parents deciding on how they will spend the remainder of Lynette's blessed life. This brings me back to why I am on this holy mountain staring at a print of a beautiful miracle-working icon of the Theotokos. I ask you to lift up Lynette in prayer. We know that "all things work together for good for those who love God, to those who are the called according to His purpose" (Romans 8:28). *O blessed Theotokos, if it is within God's will, please do one more miracle of healing for Lynette. We could really use one right now.*

January 9, 2005 ❦ *Journal Entry*

IT HARDLY SEEMS POSSIBLE THAT ONLY TWO MONTHS HAVE PASSED since my last entry and yet life has changed so dramatically for us. I never expected to be where I am, and yet here I am sitting in a chair at mom and dad's house, recovering from surgery for breast cancer. I had feared cancer two years ago when I was having such pains in my hip area and wondered if I might have ovarian cancer or bone cancer. After having my female organs checked while in Greece, and finding out that there was no cancer there, I let the matter rest, even though I was still having such pains in my hip and pelvic area. When another doctor from Greece, who was visiting Albania, suggested that I might have a herniated disk in my back and recommended that I get an epidural, I agreed and received instant relief from the pain.

When the pain returned, I decided that I didn't want to spend my life getting injections to block pain, and so I started to work out to strengthen my back muscles. My program was working out well until the day I helped move furniture for Melanie and developed new back pain, this time not in my lower back, but higher up in the middle of my back. I asked Dr. Charles about that, and he said that back pain in that area was actually easier to overcome, so I let the matter rest and just took Tylenol for pain. That happened several days after my St. Nicholas Party on December 6.

Less than a week later, on the 13th to be exact, during a graphic design lesson I was giving to Alexia and Anjeza, I felt a sudden sharp pain under my arm. It was intense enough to draw my fingers to the area, and it was then that I felt the lump for the first time. Nathan called Charles about it that evening, and Charles asked if I had done a breast exam. I said "no," but later when I did one, I found a huge mass in my left breast. I was so shocked and wondered how I could have missed such a thing, for surely it would have taken time to grow.

The next day Vjollca and her four children came for a visit. We celebrated Christmas with them and then I drove them home. On the way back, I stopped at the clinic and had an ultrasound and mammogram done. Charles then did a breast exam. I had been assuming all along that I probably had an infection in the left breast, even as I had had nine years before, which cleared up with an antibiotic. After Charles examined me, though, I realized that wasn't the case. I did have something there that wasn't going to go away with a little medicine.

That evening I went with Christine to Julie's house to talk about home school stuff. The entire experience was surreal because I knew something immense was happening with me, but I wasn't sure and therefore, I couldn't say anything about it. I went on the whole evening as though life would continue to be the same indefinitely.

Wednesday afternoon, Nathan and I went to the clinic and had a fine needle biopsy done on the lump on my breast, and one under my arm. Usually the results take ten days, but these took one hour to come back. The diagnosis was medullary breast cancer—an invasive sort that had broken out of the initial tumor. I felt bad for Charles because he was so unhappy about telling us. He said it couldn't be treated in Albania, and that we would have to go to either Greece or the U.S. within the month.

The next few days were a blur as we tried to figure out when to go and what needed to be done. We decided to be open about my condition, and after Nathan told a few people, word quickly spread around the Church and among our friends and co-workers. People were very compassionate and caring. I was deeply touched.

One of the things I wanted to do before I left was to check the proofs on my book, so I flew to Greece on the 21st and was able to stay with [co-missionaries] Pete and Shannon [Sakalleriou] who had just had a baby the month before and were in recovery from a C-section. I was able to meet the Archbishop on Wednesday and had a wonderful visit with him. He had himself just undergone surgery for cancer of the thyroid and was awaiting further treatment, as the cancer had spread to other parts. Our shared illness served as a bond between us as nothing else could have done. . . .

The Archbishop checked the proofs on the book and gave his blessing to go ahead although he did want to add a map of Albania, which I did agree to. The Archbishop then gave me a magnificent icon of the Theotokos on which he had written such beautiful words of encouragement. . . .

I finished my business in Greece, and the following five days were a stressful blur. We tried to focus on saying goodbye to people, while packing and making arrangements for others to take over our responsibilities. Our departure was set for December 28 because we wanted to spend Christmas with our co-workers and friends. On the 23rd, I felt myself growing ill and realized that I was coming down with the flu. I loaded myself with drugs to be able to keep going, but also developed a sore throat and cough. This put a bit of a damper on the festivities, but I didn't want to miss out on anything. On the 24th, Shpresa baked and decorated many Christmas cookies, which the children and I distributed to our neighbors. I heard many say *"te shkuara"* ["get well"] and knew that Maro had effectively spread word of my illness among the neighbors, even as I had wanted her to. Katherine and I visited Lumi and took her cookies, and as was true so often before, I wished that I had done more with her, perhaps even taken her to the opera with me.

The neighborhood kids wanted to know when they would be coming over to decorate cookies. I apologized and explained that there would be no time before we left to do that project. I felt bad leaving these kids, as I felt that we were making good progress in our relationships.

On Christmas Eve, Albana and Georgia came for dinner, decorated cookies, and read together the Christmas story. We had a nice evening together. The children each got two gifts to open and they were very contented. I think Georgia must have been feeling very homesick that evening. She had, in fact, forgotten that we had invited her over for the evening. It seemed to me that when she arrived at our house, her eyes were red and she was very subdued. We had picked up a box for her from the post office and gave it to her. That seemed to cheer her up. I think she was genuinely homesick and distressed about being away from her family for Christmas.

Our evening went well with decorating cookies, eating dinner, and acting out the Christmas Story with the kids serving as Mary and Joseph, along with Katherine's horse as the donkey and her doll as baby Jesus. Georgia played the Angel Gabriel, Nathan the shepherd and King Herod, and Albana the wiseman. Then we shared gifts and the kids played for a while.

I was not feeling very well, despite all the drugs, and with the Divine Liturgy starting at 5:00 AM the next morning, we soon broke up our party. Albana slept at our house so that she could go to church with us the next morning.

The Christmas Liturgy was bright and warm. People were quiet throughout the service, which would have been unusual for any service, but was especially so because so many people were present in the Church. At the end of the service, Bishop Ilia [Katre], who was serving in the Archbishop's stead, said some very kind words about Nathan and me, and then told the congregation that we were leaving for health reasons. I had not known anything was going to be said so I wasn't prepared for it.

I got teary-eyed and had a hard time speaking with people after the service. Many came up and expressed their love and concern. I was very touched by it all. . . .

The remainder of our time in Albania went quickly. Sunday afternoon we had a Christmas lunch prepared by Ana Kruja at the Soup Kitchen. Lots of friends were there, including all our co-workers and the Van Cleaves. Bishop Ilia was also there, and at the conclusion of the meal he stood up and addressed the group, praising our labors and urging me, like an old Pentecostal preacher, to "put off the spirit of infirmity." I responded by saying very modestly that I accepted the will of God, but he said, "No, that's too passive. You must say, 'I reject this illness.'" I felt myself put on the spot a bit and was not comfortable with that kind of attention, but it passed. I did sing "Amazing Grace" with John Lena, and "O Holy Night" as a solo. It was good to sing.

Although we knew we needed to depart quickly for the States, we decided to spend Christmas in Albania with our missionary team and Albanian friends in order to encourage them and to celebrate with them this important feast of our Lord's birth, an occasion when missionaries often get homesick.

The love and prayers that were showered on us by those in Albania were deeply moving. I deemed the whole experience of being ill worth it just to see how people came together with such love and care for me. Loving sentiments were expressed by so many, and I was deeply touched by them all. I am beginning to realize that I am enjoying one of the rare experiences, a kind of "It's a Wonderful Life" experience, in which I have the opportunity to see what life is like, not as though I had never been born, but because I have lived.

Of course, not all of my interactions with others have always been so pleasant. One evening, I went to some friends' home for dinner. During the evening, I had an opportunity to sit alone with a doctor friend of ours. As I was telling him my thoughts about how I need to become more like a "Mary," who sits at the feet of Jesus and listens rather than being a "Martha," who frantically runs around doing good but not doing the "one thing necessary," my friend interrupted me as I developed this idea and said, "Lynette, I don't think you realize the seriousness of your situation. You need to prepare yourself for death." These words totally unnerved me. My encounter with this friend was my first experience of a "Job's friend," and it was terrible. Many others would come with their well-meaning, but hurtful and presumptuous comments or suggestions. But to offset these were many more wonderful people who expressed their love and concern so beautifully. These precious friends stepped up beside me, and now through their prayers and love, walk with me through this dark valley. Among these was Sister Argiro, who took my hand, squeezed it, and said, "I never knew how much I loved you." She gave us beautiful icons and holy oil as parting gifts.

There was Melanie Linderman, who came over to express her love, and said, "We need you. What an example you've been to all of us." Georgia Gillman's words were wonderful, "I've never met a better woman than you, and I haven't had enough time to become just like you." Many people have expressed such warmth through a look or a hug. Prokopi, whom Nathan told of my cancer, shared my situation with so many in the Evangelical Community. Many of these expressed love and concern.

The Russells offered to move into our house. That was a big blessing. The night before we left the girls' Winter Camp opened. Since I had originally planned to be at the camp and to give a talk on "peace," I decided to go for a couple hours to say goodbye to the girls and to say a few words about peace in the midst of difficulties. I did speak for a few minutes with Gabriela serving as my translator.

Charles Linderman, George Russell, and the three girls who work for Nathan—Ana Kercyku, Ana Baba, and Gabriela Bezhani—came to the airport to see us off. It was a sleepy farewell since it was so early in the morning and no one had gotten much sleep. Our trip was rather uneventful. Steve Keller picked us up at the airport in Chicago and took us to the Reardons' house.

That evening friends from All Saints Church gathered to see us. Fr. Pat anointed me with oil and did the prayers of healing. I was very moved by the love and concern shown by all, and by their generosity, which was considerable. It was also good to speak with Dennis and Constance about the possibility of them being appointed to serve in Albania. They might be able to make a very fine contribution to Albania.

February 2005   *Newsletter*

"We are hard pressed on every side, but not crushed; perplexed, but not in despair; persecuted, but not abandoned; struck down, but not destroyed. We always carry around in our body the death of Jesus, so that the life of Jesus may also be revealed in our body." 2 Cor. 4:8–10

LITTLE DID I KNOW, WHEN I WROTE IN OUR LAST NEWSLETTER, OF the amazing lessons I was learning from 2 Corinthians, that within two weeks of writing, I would find myself "pressed, perplexed, and struck down" in a new way.

Unexpected Diagnosis

On December 15, I was diagnosed with breast cancer by our co-worker in Albania, Dr. Charles Linderman, just two days after discovering a painful and swollen lymph node under my arm. Dr. Linderman urged us at that time to seek treatment in the States within a month. Thankfully, my parents live just 30 minutes' drive from the famed Mayo Clinic in Minnesota, so we opted to stay with them and seek treatment at that facility. This was a great blessing as we did not have to waste precious time trying to figure out where to go for medical care, nor did we have to worry about where to live during our six-months' stay in the States.

Did I have any clue that I was ill? No, I did not, although I had been suffering from some rather intense back pain, which has since been found to be a malignant tumor in my spine.

By the grace of God, Nathan and I were able to respond calmly to the news of my cancer. Of course, it was a surprise, but perhaps not a shock. It was as though we had been prepared for it through some rather challenging experiences in Albania over the past two years. For us this became the next stage of our journey—a "yea, though I walk through the valley of the shadow of death" part of the journey, perhaps, but not a sudden and terrible detour that would tear us away from what we considered to be our mission. Our mission now became walking by faith through cancer—a wonderful opportunity to experience the sufficiency of God's grace in a time of great difficulty. As Nathan and I said to each other at the time, "Now we have to live everything we've ever preached to others!"

Two Weeks to Pull Ourselves Together

The two weeks between diagnosis and departure for the States were very intense. [*See January 9, 2005, Journal Entry for a description of these weeks.*]

On December 28, we left for the States and moved into the newly finished basement in my parents' home. My father had just completed work on the space a few weeks earlier. It was almost as though he had been anticipating our coming. On December 30, I had the first of what would be many, many visits to Mayo Clinic.

Treatment and Prognosis

Six weeks have passed since then, and I have been poked, prodded, anesthetized, sliced, stitched, aspirated, drained, biopsied, weighed, hospitalized, radiated—and the list of [verbs] grows each week. I had a full mastectomy on the left side, and 22 lymph nodes were removed. Cancer was found in most of those lymph nodes, and a malignant lesion was discovered in my spine. This tumor was treated with two weeks of radiation therapy, which was completed the end of January. I have been suffering from some side effects of the radiation, most particularly extreme fatigue and indigestion. I have started the next stage of treatment, which is hormone therapy to block the production of estrogen in my body. (This form of cancer is estrogen fed.)

I have been classified as having Stage IV cancer (of four stages), and my prospects are rather grim. Nonetheless, I remain cheerful and hopeful and want to spend what years God grants me in joy and thanksgiving, serving as and wherever I can.

I will need to be scanned every three months to see if the cancer has spread to other organs. Since the cancer already has metastasized, humanly speaking, this is very likely. I am trying to do all I can to fight the cancer by boosting my immune system, radically changing my diet, and getting exercise and proper rest.

Bearing Up Emotionally

People always want to know how I am doing emotionally. In general I am very much at peace. Although I pray for healing, I do accept what God has given to me and do not view it as something "bad" that has happened to me. Already I see the beauty of suffering and how it can give birth to humility, thankfulness, compassion, a clearer vision of what is important, and a deeper love for Christ. These are blessings that I did not expect. I have had the joy of seeing how many people love and care for me. I have heard of so many that are praying for me and am touched by their love and concern. I have never received so many cards and flowers in my life, and I am delighted and encouraged by them.

Despite all this, I do have times of discouragement. In those moments, I try to remember all the blessings I have experienced—and there are many. I take comfort in so many beautiful words in the Psalms and other passages of Scripture. I remind myself often that "His strength is made perfect in my weakness," and I am seeing just how weak I am and how desperately I need God's strength.

I also find myself repeating throughout the day phrases from the morning prayers, such as, "Teach me to pray, to believe, to hope, to be patient, to forgive, and to love." I pour my heart into these prayers because they express what I truly need. Also, I pray for others. My own situation helps me to feel much more deeply the sufferings of others and drives me to pray more earnestly for them. If any of you has special prayer requests, I would feel blessed to be entrusted with them.

Family Support

Nathan has been amazing through all of this. He has supported me through every step of the treatment process. He's been my companion on every trip to the clinic and through two hospital stays. He has had to observe several rather gruesome procedures and has been assigned some rather nasty tasks in my care, but he's done it all with a very level head and much good humor. He also has managed to pick up some great skills in medical care. The most precious thing, though, is the fact that his love for me has grown through this experience, and he expresses it often. I feel myself to be the most blessed of wives and cannot imagine having to go through this without Nathan's love and strength to sustain me.

My family also has been wonderful. My parents welcomed us into their home and have been so supportive through their love and prayers. They've also played a major role in caring for our children during our many visits to the clinic. My brother's family and my sister, who live nearby, also have been immensely helpful, especially with child care and providing us with a cell phone.

Our family in Christ also has been wonderful. We have heard of people all over the U.S. and the world that are praying for us. I have been amazed by the vast network of caring Christians that rises to pray for an afflicted sister in Christ, and I am so grateful that they are "pounding the gates of heaven" (as one friend expressed it) for me.

Since most of the treatments that tie me to Mayo Clinic have been completed, we are now giving thought to traveling around the U.S. to visit friends, family, and many of you who have supported so generously our work in Albania. We look forward to seeing you and expressing in person our thanks for your encouragement, prayers, and financial support. This will also serve as our bi-annual speaking tour, which we had planned originally to do this fall. At the completion of our tour in July, if my three- and six-month scans show no new cancer growth, we plan to return to Albania to resume our work there.

We would ask you to pray for us—for healing, strength, wisdom, and grace. May God bless you for your love and concern.

April 8, 2005 ✥ *Journal Entry*

HOW HOPEFUL, ALMOST PRESUMPTUOUS I WAS OVER THE PAST month with a promising Detoxification and Nutrition Program I got involved with. I had made the mistake, however, of not consulting with Nathan before dropping the hormone therapy [recommended by the Mayo Clinic]. When we finally met after two weeks of being apart, we had some hard words about what I had done. Nathan was hurt that after two months of making decisions together, we were not working together at all. He did not agree with much of what I was doing and was almost hostile. I felt a terrible despair at his lack of support. I told him how much I needed him to support me and said I would die for sure if he didn't. For two days I was in such a state of despair that I could almost feel myself getting physically worse. I knew that if I did let everything go—if I just gave in to despair and stopped working to get well—I would die very quickly.

All I could do then was pray that God would let down a rope to pull me out of my despair. This image was from my recurring "day dream," where I would walk out on a narrow stone bridge that spans a chasm and suddenly find that the bridge has vanished. Although I don't fall, I'm left suspended with no support and no ability to move to safety. As I begin to panic, I hear a voice saying, "Look up." I look up and see a silvery rope coming down through the darkness. I grab on and am pulled to safety.

I prayed for a rope then and thought it would come through a letter, a phone call, or a visit. But it didn't. Instead, it came in the form of a thought which I had during one of my afternoon walks. The thought was very simple. "The joy of the Lord is my strength." This simple thought drove away my despair. The next day I received a card from Mel Bodger, who expressed the same thought to me. "I'm praying that the joy of the Lord will be your strength!"

The path is still not easy. I feel little support from Nathan for this nutritional program, but at least he's not openly hostile. I have confessed my wrong in making decisions without consulting with him first, and have said I would try to do better in the future about talking things over with him.

May 12, 2005   ✥   *Journal Entry*

YESTERDAY I WENT TO SEE DR. CALDWELL, AN ACUPUNCTURIST. I had been to see him about six weeks before, and in that session he dealt with the impact of emotions on the body. I had given him a full "emotional history," and he commented that because I had been emotionally distant from Dad, I had a hard time accepting that other people could love me. I have felt this very much from friendships— I've always wondered how anyone could like me, even with Nathan.

I couldn't quite accept that he loved me, and I couldn't quite accept that God loved me either.

Dr. Caldwell and I discussed the whole issue of guilt and how, in his experience, many Christians were uptight and bound by their sense of guilt. I think I've had a combined sense of self-righteousness and guilt, an odd mix.

After my first visit to Dr. Caldwell, the children and I flew to Boston to begin a six-week tour of the East Coast. Fr. Luke, Paul, and Theodora met us at the airport. We hadn't seen the Veronises in nine months, and had a wonderful reunion. Faith took such good care of my food needs, and made me organic salads and soups and such. In the morning she prepared a plate of kiwi and bananas, which I really came to enjoy.

[*See June 2005 Newsletter for a description of this visit.*]

June 3, 2005   ✌   *Journal Entry*

I'M SITTING IN AN OLD FOREST IN NORTHERN WISCONSIN. THE LATE afternoon sun is sending its golden rays slanting through the trees. It glints on the bright green leaves of young maple saplings and falls off the fern beds scattered here and there across the forest floor. The trees, oak and maple and fir, are tall and stately, their upper branches interlocking high above to form a sort of canopy. A light breeze rustles through the maple leaves and sways the fir boughs. A soft blanket of fallen leaves and dry pine needles covers the forest floor. Here and there great tree roots have broken through the floor and resemble serpents. Birds twitter in the branches and call cheerfully to each other. The surface of the lake shimmers through the trees. Wind rushes through as though bearing tidings from afar.

We've been staying at the vacation cottage of Chris and Nancy Lemons. It's been a wonderful ten days for us as a family, and we've really enjoyed one another. Nathan and I have been restored to each other so beautifully. He keeps saying, "Thanks for letting me back into your life." I realize that in many ways I have been exceedingly willful, doing my own thing without including him in the picture. I have been doing this for years, and it's a hard habit to break, especially when I really want something. I must learn not to cherish any thing above him, or above God for that matter.

Nathan's family is accustomed to discuss everything before deciding collectively. My mom, on the other hand, tends to do whatever she wants regardless of what anyone else says. At the same time, she is exceedingly concerned about what everyone thinks, especially her family. I myself have almost been crippled at times by this same fear of what others think. Oh, to be delivered from it. I see how necessary humility is for true freedom, but humility is so hard to attain.

The other thing I must remember is not to judge others, but to remember always that I would have been worse or done worse given the same circumstances. When I judge the speck in my brother's eye, it is a sure sign that I have a plank in mine. If I tend to my own plank, I probably won't see the specks in the eyes of others.

June 2005   ☙   *Newsletter*

THROUGHOUT MY ILLNESS, I HAVEN'T THOUGHT ENOUGH ABOUT spiritual healing. Being a missionary, I suppose, made me feel that I ought to be a pillar of spiritual strength. My awareness for the need of spiritual healing began as I started praying the Akathist to St. Nectarios of Aegina. Someone had very kindly sent me this Akathist Prayer for healing, along with some holy oil from the tomb of St. Nectarios. As I prayed this service day after day, asking St. Nectarios to intercede with Christ on my behalf, I began to realize that the prayers were just as much about the healing of the soul as they were about the healing of the body. Here's an excerpt:

> *To the faithful that turn to thee*
> *And extol and bless thee, O Saint Nectarios,*
> *Do thou grant unto them strength and health*
> *Of both soul and body, O most blest of God.*

There are many prayers like this throughout the Akathist, and as I prayed them day after day, they began to sink in. I began to think about Jesus' healing ministry and how often he said to those who sought physical healing, "Your sins are forgiven." The sick sought physical healing, but Jesus gave them the healing they really needed—spiritual healing. Their bodies would die eventually anyway, but their souls, which would live on, needed to be healed of spiritual infirmities. Jesus gave the sick what they asked for, but he also gave them what they truly needed.

I started to pray for spiritual healing, though I didn't really know what I was looking for. I believe my prayers were heard, though the process began through a nearly debilitating emotional/spiritual crisis.

We had begun our travels around the United States by this time and were in Massachusetts staying at the home of our dear friends, Fr. Luke and Faith Veronis, with whom we worked for seven years in Albania. I was beginning to experience a lot of pain in my neck and lower back, and the pain was radiating down my legs to my feet. When one has metastatic cancer, it is tempting to think that every ache and pain is the unchecked spreading of the disease throughout the body. I was sure that my days were *really* numbered. In my mind, I began to see God as judge, and I have to confess that I was terrified. "I haven't done enough, I haven't done enough," I repeated to myself over and over again, and though I could quote all sorts of Scripture passages to myself about my works not being sufficient for my salvation, or about the fact that we are saved by God's grace, etc., I could not console myself. Then I thought of all the sins I had ever done, and I started wailing another mantra, "I'm not good enough, I'm not good enough," and on I went deeper and deeper into despair.

This was a blessed state, though, for suddenly a simple but profound truth that I had learned as a child finally hit home to me: "For God so loved the world that he gave his only begotten Son that whosoever believeth in Him should not perish, but have everlasting life." Until that moment, I don't think I had ever really understood that God *loved* me, but it hit me hard then and my soul was flooded by that love. Fear and despair left me, and they have not returned. Though I knew it in theory, I had never experienced it in truth: My salvation was not about me. It was based entirely in God, who is Love.

I don't think I had ever really understood the idea of repentance either. I was rather self-righteous, and my self-righteousness had made me blind to my spiritual need. To be able to feel truly and deeply, to the point of despair, that I truly was the chief of sinners became the first step in my spiritual healing. Until that moment I hadn't seen or felt how desperate was my need for God.

At about this time, visitors in the home of Fr. Luke brought me a book, *Come Away My Beloved,* written by Francis Roberts. The author had sent the book specifically for me, and it was the perfect thing for me to read at that time. The book was designed to be read as a daily devotional, so each day I read a section, and each day I wept, for I was reminded over and over again of how much God loves me and has called me to a higher life. Each day I was filled with joy. Then I read a passage from the Scriptures, and this too came home in a new way. Since the season was Lent, I was reading in Isaiah, and I read, "Though your sins be as scarlet, they shall be white as snow; though they be as blood, they shall be as wool." How many reminders I was finding of how much I am loved and how much I am forgiven. I was very grateful to be in the Veronises' home at that time, for Fr. Luke was a tremendous help to me in working through these critical issues, and when we left this home to move on to our next destination, I was deeply at peace.

This has begun the journey of spiritual healing. There are many more wonderful things I am experiencing and reading, but it would make this update too long. I will just say that I recently finished reading *The Mountain of Silence* by Kyriacos Markides, and found it to be another one of those amazing things that was given to me as a gift for my spiritual journey. It has brought home to me the need for serious spiritual *askesis*, especially in the area of disciplined and unceasing prayer, and the absolute necessity for humility before any real spiritual progress can occur. These are great challenges for me, but I want the end result so badly—a profound experience of the Grace of the Holy Spirit and oneness with Christ—that the struggle is immeasurably worthwhile.

Thank you for your concern and prayers. I have begun to realize these past few months, as I have heard about all the people that are praying for me, that this outpouring of love and prayers is not because of who I am. It is a consequence of who these praying people are. They are people filled with divine love. This has been a great inspiration to me, and I hope I am learning myself what it is to reach out to others in love.

These prayers have put me on a path to healing of soul and body, and I bless you for your part in it. I pray that God will supply all your needs—both those you see and those he sees.

On June 9, Nathan will be leaving for Albania to attend the graduation ceremony of his students at our theological academy. He will also be going to Kosovo to oversee two children's camps reaching about 800 children from two villages. Please pray for safety and for the success of these camps. Nathan will be away for about three weeks. I, and the children, will be staying with my parents in Minnesota during that time.

This week and part of last week, we have been staying at a cottage in northern Wisconsin. Someone very kindly offered our family a getaway at their second home. This has been a wonderful time for us. Our children have enjoyed hiking in the woods, chasing after frogs, dragonflies, and every other kind of creepy crawly, and fishing for anything that will bite. We have loved the beauty and silence of the Northwoods, and are so grateful for the chance to retreat for a while before Nathan heads to Albania.

My scan is scheduled for June 7. This should give me some indication of what the cancer is doing. On the night before, from 11 P.M. to 2 A.M., I would like to be in prayer. I want to pray for myself even as Jesus prayed for himself on the night of his betrayal, "If it be Your will, let this cup pass from me. Nevertheless, not my will, but Your will be done." I also want to pray specifically for others who are struggling with serious health issues, so if you know of anyone, please e-mail their names to me.

CHAPTER 4

The Shadow Encroaches

CANCER CONTINUED TO METASTASIZE THROUGHOUT LYNETTE'S BODY. In addition to her own suffering, Lynette faced the added cross of discovering that her mother was diagnosed with cancer in her liver. Now in the same house lived two women with terminal cancer. At times, the burden of witnessing her mother's agony seemed greater than Lynette's own struggles. Yet, in the midst of an advancing shadow, Lynette remained positive and hopeful. She lived in the present and was able to create beautiful memories with her family. One surprise in the midst of her sorrows was a desire to return to Albania. During this visit, her Albanian family overwhelmed her with love, and she even had the privilege of participating in a book signing for her newly published work on the resurrection of the Church of Albania.

June 21, 2005 ✿ *Journal Entry*

I HAD A BONE SCAN ON JUNE 7. THE RESULTS WERE NOT GOOD. THE cancer has spread into my ribs and pelvic area. I guess I shouldn't have been too surprised. For several weeks I have been experiencing a lot of pain in my pelvis and upper back. The cancer explained the pain. My disappointment that my nutritional approach had not served to stay the cancer was great. I had been such a proponent of natural healing that I think I had taken up a cause. If my efforts had succeeded, I would have said, "I did this," or "My program did this."

Nathan commented that I would have preached the virtues of good nutrition with missionary zeal. I saw at once all my arrogance and willfulness in insisting on my own way and not listening to others.

June 26, 2005 &a *Journal Entry*

I MUST WRITE SOMETHING HERE THAT, AT LEAST AT THIS TIME, I cannot share with others. Two days ago I felt strongly the urge to read the passage from John's Gospel about the raising of Lazarus. It moved me in ways I never have been moved before. "This sickness is not unto death; it is for the glory of God, so that the Son of God may be glorified by means of it." I have felt for some time now that my illness was for the purpose that God might be glorified in me and through me.

Not long after I read this passage, Fr. John Chakos, an OCMC Board Member and the spiritual father of Fr. Luke, called me. That morning before he called me, he too had been reading this passage and meditating upon it. I tried to express to Fr. John that I wanted to know how to walk in the grace of the Holy Spirit each day, if I get well and no longer have the reality of death driving me. How could I do this? I asked him to ask Elder Efraim [of St. Anthony's Monastery in Arizona] that question. I think I already know the answer. I must go into the desert and learn a serious spiritual askesis. It is the gaining of deep habits of prayer and meditation that will build up one's spiritual resources. This daily habit will be the daily habit of asking for the grace of the Holy Spirit to live each day. I'm a little intimidated by the desert for I know there are many terrible temptations there. Also, I have no spiritual guide, so it is easy to be deceived. I must not rely on my own resources, or I will become confused.

Yesterday I read again the story of Lazarus. This time I was struck by Jesus' words to Martha, "Did I not say to you that if you would believe you would see the glory of God?" I was overwhelmed by these words and kept repeating them over and over again to myself, especially during my walk last evening. I began to feel that perhaps my healing would be a dramatic one, so that the power of God would be seen so obviously. I began to anticipate it, and even pictured different healing scenarios. This, I think is the confusion of the desert. I do anticipate with joy that I will see the glory of God because I do believe, but I cannot anticipate how.

Today as I read the passage again, I was struck by another of Jesus' statements. When Jesus tells Martha that her brother will rise again, she says, "I know that he will rise again in the resurrection on the last day."

Jesus answers, "I am the resurrection and the life; he who believes in me, though he dies, yet shall he live."

I thrilled to hear these words this morning. It is the Master of the Universe who stands before us and in His hands is the power over life and death. The resurrection isn't some vague theology relegated to the end of time. Jesus is the resurrection. I have been filled with these thoughts this morning and am delighting in them.

July 11, 2005 ✌ *Journal Entry*

I'M IN DESPAIR TODAY. A TERRIBLE TEMPTATION HAS COME TO ME. I knew some weeks ago that God was calling me to go into the desert—that place of really learning to walk by faith and not by sight, a place to learn serious spiritual askesis, a place to leave off all encumbrances. I knew there would be serious temptations, for how can faith be purified except it be tried by fire? I was afraid that I would not even recognize the temptations, and perhaps there may come many that I won't recognize, but this one I do see and it is terrible. I cannot even speak of it to anyone because it could cause such hurt.

It came to my mind today that Shpresa [an older Albanian woman who had helped care for their children and take care of their house] had been brought into our lives so that she would be there to take care of the children after I was gone. It almost seemed to me Shpresa was a sure sign that I would die. I mentioned this to Nathan, and he said that I should be thankful that Shpresa would be there for the children should I die. He is right and I do see things that way in my mind, but my heart is bleeding.

My emotions are telling me that things are already in motion for me to be replaced. Thus, my death soon is certain.

Stories like mine always have tragic endings, for who learns anything from a happy ending. So many people say they have been inspired by my life and responses. I have to say that all that is the work of the Holy Spirit, for I know how feeble my efforts have been and how any positive responses I may have are entirely by God's hand. Therefore he is simply multiplying His own efforts.

I have taken this temptation to God and have given it to Him. I cannot overcome it on my own because I don't have the resources within to fight it. My consolation in all of this is that if I die I will be united with my true bridegroom, Jesus, for whom I have such a longing now. I won't know pain or sadness or sorrow in heaven, but only joy and gladness.

If I give in to my temptation, I will pull away from Nathan and the children, as though I had lost them already, rather than enjoy each day still given to us. My husband and children do not belong to me. They belong to God and are merely loaned to me for a season to be a blessing to me and a means of my salvation. I am with them to love and serve. I cannot hold on to them, but must release them. I must thank God for the wonderful years we have had together and not mourn the loss of those that might be given to someone else.

Nathan is a great source of joy to me these days. He is acting so sweet and attentive to my needs and is enjoying each day with me. I forget so often that this is a time of suffering for him as well, and that if I die it will be a great source of grief for him.

The day after my last bone scan, when we realized that I was getting worse, not better, we took a walk through the nearby cemetery, and I very haltingly brought up the fact that we needed to think about where I was to be buried. I said, "Perhaps I could be buried here. Then you could bring the children to see my grave when they come to see their grandparents."

Nathan's response was so beautiful. "You are my love, my treasure. We'll choose some place to be buried together."

I wept at his words and was so moved by them, for they spoke such love. Nathan suggested that we find a monastery where we can be buried, perhaps Holy Dormition in Rives Junction. Fr. Pat and Denise are coming for a visit next week to talk about these things with us.

Last week Nathan and I were able to get away for a night to celebrate our anniversary. I wanted to surprise Nathan and made a reservation for us at Mansion Hill Inn in Madison, where we had spent one night of our honeymoon 13 years ago. Nathan very thoughtfully rented a Cadillac so that I could ride in comfort. On the trip over we reminisced about different experiences we had in the 17 years since first meeting. We have many wonderful memories together!

Our time at Mansion Hill was wonderful. Nathan told me afterwards that it was the best experience of his life, and I was so touched by this, knowing how many amazing experiences he has had in his life. Everything about our time together was wonderful—our walk, our fabulous dinner, our times of rich intimacy, our talks, our breakfast, our time at the health food store, and our picnic. These are precious memories for us, ones that we can recall, should God grant me life. We've decided that we will go again every two years—to the same Inn and room.

In the past month, I have come to see that Nathan and I have the opportunity to have an extraordinary marriage!

August 2005   *Newsletter*

"I will bless the Lord at all times; his praise shall continually be in my mouth. My soul makes its boast in the Lord; let the afflicted hear and be glad." (Psalm 34:1, 2)

I HAD A BONE SCAN AT MAYO CLINIC ON JUNE 7. THE NIGHT BEFORE the appointment, I spent a few hours in prayer, preparing myself for the outcome of the scan. Among the prayers I read was the Akathist to the Mother of God, "Healer of Cancer." Included in the booklet containing the Akathist was a short sermon on healing by Metropolitan Anthony of Sourozh, which I read around 2:00 A.M. The sermon was profound and I knew it, but my brain was rather fuzzy at that hour and nothing would stick in my head, so I said to myself, "I had better read this again tomorrow when I'm more alert."

I did not have a chance to read the sermon again the next morning before my bone scan because the procedure was scheduled for an early hour. By 10:30 A.M. the scan had been completed, and with typical Mayo Clinic efficiency, I had my results by noon. The picture was discouraging. . . .

At such times as these, I do not tend to express my emotions very openly, even with my husband. I like to process things privately and talk afterwards. Hence, on the ride home from the clinic I was very quiet. It was a hot day and all I could think of was bathing my disappointment in a tub of scented water. Unfortunately, my efforts to soothe myself that way were a colossal failure. First of all, I could not get the tub stopper to hold the water, so all my fragrant water drained away. After I gave up on that, I grabbed the sprayer with the thought of showering away my discouragement, but for some reason, the showerhead became detached, leaving the hose writhing about like a snake and shooting water all around the bathroom. I started laughing and crying simultaneously, then grabbed the hose and shut off the water. After a few minutes, I collected myself, mopped the floor, and went and crawled in bed for a nap. I knew that prayer was the best means of coping with such disappointment, and I ought to have poured out my heart to God first.

I went through the usual fears at that point. What had I done wrong? Hadn't I prayed the right prayers or been fervent enough? Why hadn't my nutritional program worked? It had done wonders for others.

I did not dwell on these questions for long, though, because I realized that I was approaching things very immaturely. God was not out there waiting for me to get just the right combination of words and sincerity. He was merciful and compassionate and infinitely above any sort of pettiness. He also was good, and everything he ordered on my behalf was for my good.

I read Metropolitan Anthony's sermon on healing again and spent many hours thinking about it. Here are some excerpts from the text:

Time after time we hear accounts in the Gospels about people who were healed from illnesses and in the Gospels this appears so simple and clear: there is a need, and God responds to it. So the question arises: Why then does this not happen with all of us? Each of us needs physical healing, or healing of the soul; but only a few are healed. Why is this?

When we read the Gospels, we lose sight of the fact that Christ did not heal each and every person. One person in a crowd would be healed; but many others, also ailing in body or soul, were not healed. And this happens because—in order to receive the action of the grace of God unto healing of body or soul, or of both—we must open our-selves to God. Not to healing, but to God. . . .

What then do we do? We must ask ourselves some serious ques-tions; and when we come to God, asking Him to heal us, we must pre-pare ourselves beforehand for healing. To be healed does not mean to become whole only in order to go back to the same kind of life that we lived before; it means to be whole in order to begin a new life, as if we realized that we died in the healing action of God; that the illness was of the old man in us. . . . This old man must die in order for the new man to live. We must be ready to become this new man through the death of the old in order to begin to live anew. . . .

Are we capable of receiving healing? Do we agree to take upon our-selves the responsibility of a new wholeness, in order to enter again, and yet again, into the world in which we live, with knowledge of our renewal; to be light, to be salt, to be joy, to be hope, to be love, to be giv-ing back to God and man?

I understood that I had not been ready to be healed. Had my nutri-tional program succeeded, I would have given credit for my healing either to my program or to myself, and I would have been insuffer-ably proud of it. As Nathan commented to me later, "You would have preached the virtues of nutrition with a missionary zeal."

Until my bone scan, I hadn't been able to see how willful, arro-gant, selfish, and independent I had become since starting on the nutritional route, but as soon as I recognized these spiritual dis-eases in myself, I immediately repented of them as well as of all the pain I had caused Nathan, who had felt shut out for months. I was completely humbled and silenced by this experience and knew that my worsening condition had been a necessary step in my journey. I thanked God then for the disappointing results, which had brought my proud head so low.

I do not believe that preparing to be healed implies that if I make "enough spiritual progress" God will find me worthy of being healed. God acts according to what he deems best for me, and that may mean not healing me. Preparing for healing means that I pray for and seek healing of soul, so that, should God heal my body, I can rise from my bed of illness ready to live a transformed life, becoming light and salt and joy and hope and love in the world.

Nathan and I had just one day together between my bone scan and his scheduled departure for Albania. (He was planning to be gone for three weeks.) It was a precious day for us as Nathan and I sought each other's forgiveness and faced together the reality of my failing health. . . . We have grown more deeply in our love and commitment to each other in the weeks since my bone scan.

We have not yet answered the question of where to be buried, but we are pursuing this and all the other practical questions that accompany the closing of life. We are not assuming that death is inevitable by any means, but we are preparing for it. My faith in the power of God to heal has grown considerably since hearing the results of my scan. I have spent hours poring over the amazing story of Jesus' raising Lazarus from the dead, and have been thrilled at Jesus' words to Martha, "I am the Resurrection and the Life. He who believes in me, though he dies, yet shall he live." The Lord of Life is not dismayed by my worsening condition, even as he was not disheartened by Lazarus' death. This makes his compassion and grief over the suffering of Mary and Martha all the more poignant. He knew that Lazarus would live, yet he wept at the depth of human suffering that was poured out before him. Though I may now be beyond hope of healing by medicine or nutrition, I cannot get beyond the power of God to heal or raise me, if He chooses to restore me to health.

I find myself very grateful for each stage of this new part of the journey. Getting worse rather than better has been exceedingly humbling, and I have so needed to have my pride exposed and ripped away. I see now that my nutritional program was not really a failure. Though it did not achieve the results I had hoped for, it did achieve the results I needed—strict discipline of the body. This has led me to realize how much I need just as much discipline in the area of my heart and soul and mind—a detachment from all those material things I had thought so essential to life and comfort. I feel so much freer now knowing that I can walk away without regret from all the material things I used to cling to with such devotion. Jesus' words, "He who would come after me let him deny himself, take up his cross daily and follow me," have taken on new significance as I see in myself the importance of stripping away all those encumbrances that keep me from truly seeking after God with my whole heart.

The cancer that seems to be running free in me has begun to make its presence known in acute and continuous pain. This has brought on a completely different dimension to my journey. Pain is a great leveler. It strips one of all pretenses and brings one down to bare realities. Although I have experienced the grace of God at every stage, I realize now how much I have relied heavily upon my own resources of a generally cheerful disposition and a rather stoic nature. Pain has knocked these out of me without any apology. In my immense discomfort, I have not complained, but I have wanted to find a dark corner in the basement, curl up, and give free rein to my misery. I have discovered also how much I was trying to put up a brave face before God. I wanted him to applaud my efforts. It seems ludicrous, now that I think about it. How can He possibly help me if I try to manage on my own and spurn the help he so freely offers?

The Psalms are filled with expressions of pain and fear and suffering. I'm allowing them to tutor me.

O Lord, rebuke me not in thy anger, nor chasten me in thy wrath.
Be gracious to me, O Lord, for I am languishing;
Lord, heal me, for my bones are troubled.
My soul also is sorely troubled.
But thou, O Lord—how long?
Turn, O Lord, save my life;
Deliver me for the sake of thy steadfast love.
For in death there is no remembrance of thee;
In Sheol who can give thee praise?
(Psalm 6)

This is the right place to be, for as I empty myself of pretension, I now have the possibility to be filled by God.

Nathan and I are in contact with a very gracious Christian doctor, Dr. Tom Miller, who is working in hospice care. This doctor is helping us to work through pain management and is also helping us to understand those last stages that might be ahead. It is hard not to be alarmed by them and to agonize over the road that may lie before me, but now I express all my fears to God, pouring out my soul to him. I'm no longer ashamed of these feelings. Afterwards, I can then let go of them and say, "Thy will be done." I know this will be a continuous prayer for me through all the days ahead.

I am so grateful for the opportunity to fellowship in the sufferings of Christ. I don't think I could have understood what that expression meant before experiencing pain myself. Now, I try to picture myself in the garden with Jesus, sharing in his agony as he asks to be released from the cross. I weep with him, then bow my head with him as he humbly submits himself to the will of God. Jesus could have gotten out of his sufferings at any moment simply by calling upon his Father to send forth the armies of heaven. But by his strength of will he chose to endure the cross for us, and I love him for this.

Several weeks ago, I purchased a book called, *The Royal Way of the Cross*, by François Fenelon. As with the other books I have read during this period, it has been just the right thing to feed my mind and soul. The first chapter, "Seeing Our True Spiritual State Before God," was a necessary beginning for me, for Fenelon opens by saying, "In order to make your prayer more profitable, it would be well from the beginning to picture yourself as a poor, naked, miserable wretch, perishing of hunger, who knows but one man of whom he can ask or hope for help; or as a sick person, covered with sores and ready to die unless some pitiful physician will take him in hand and heal him. These are true pictures of our condition before God. Your soul is more bare of heavenly treasure than that poor beggar is of earthly possessions. You need them more urgently, and there is none but God of whom you can ask or expect help. Again, your soul is infinitely more sin-sick than that sore stricken patient, and God alone can heal you."

As I sat contemplating this passage, I realized that I couldn't in myself create this tremendous sense of unworthiness, and so I asked God to help me. Amazingly, my prayer was answered almost immediately as God brought to mind Qemal, my "Frog Prince," a poor Albanian man about whom I had written in our newsletter from Albania last fall. Qemal is the most wretched, miserable, pitiful, inarticulate, and desperate person I have ever encountered, and I had come to see him as an image of how Jesus comes to me—as my prince, still in the form of a frog, whom I fail to recognize. Now, as I thought about Qemal, I suddenly saw myself as that same sort of wretched, impoverished, pitiful person before God, and I was humbled. The image was so vivid, so fitting.

Qemal was far ahead of me, though, for he was fully aware of his own wretchedness, calling himself a fool, and relentlessly begging that his needs be met. He had no pretenses before people, and knew he was pitiful. I, on the other hand, had tried so hard to be respectable before God and thus was missing out on the depth of his mercy and compassion.

I was deeply struck by this image and asked God to fix it in my mind so that I would approach him with a sense of unworthiness, of desperation for my need for Him.

I am thankful that God brought Qemal to my mind. By who he is, this poor man has modeled for me some profound theological truths. I see him not only as an example of how Jesus comes to me, but also of how I ought to go to Jesus.

My prayers are simple now. I pray that God, through my sufferings, will grant me a pure heart that I might see him. I ask that He help me to love Him with all my heart, and I thank him for his abundant and continuous blessings.

As a family, we are living one day at a time. We make few plans, for we do not know what tomorrow holds for us, and now we have a new cross to bear on top of my own cancer. My mother recently was diagnosed with liver cancer, which may already be metastatic. She has lost about 60 pounds and is very weak. She will be meeting an oncologist at Mayo Clinic this week to see if there are any treatment options. With the advent of her illness, I am experiencing a whole new range of emotions that I did not feel for myself—anxiety, helplessness, hopelessness—and this is demanding a new level of faith from me. I am now feeling for her what she has felt for me since learning of my cancer. I am so grateful that I am here with her. Neither of us has much strength, but we are being cared for in the most amazing ways. Besides the care we are receiving from Nathan and my father, other family members have graciously stepped up to help. My sister was here for a week-and-a-half, and then my brother and his family came for two weeks and took charge of meals, laundry, child care, and cleanup. Nathan's parents are here now to help us for two weeks and we are so grateful for all they are doing. When they leave, my mom's sister will be coming for two weeks. I know that God will continue to provide the care we need, and He will grant us the grace to walk each step on the road ahead.

We thank you for your prayers, for your letters and phone calls. I do not know how we would have made it thus far without them. Your love and compassion have been a blessing and an inspiration to us. We feel ourselves to be surrounded by an army of caring people around the world.

We also want to thank you for your prayers for Nathan during his trip to Albania and Kosovo in June. His time there was very productive as he was able to meet with many different people, listening to their joys and struggles and giving them guidance and encouragement. The children's camps in Kosovo also went very well. Twenty-four young people from our church in Albania organized and implemented activities for about 900 children. Nathan and his team members were very encouraged by the openness and enthusiasm they encountered. Please pray for the ongoing ministries of our National Children's Office and the University Ministry.

On another note, I forgot to mention in my update in June that my book, *Resurrection: The Orthodox Autocephalous Church of Albania, 1991–2003*, is now in print. I received the first two copies—one hardcover and one soft cover—in February and was delighted to have in my hands the fruits of almost seven years of effort. Pages from the book can be viewed on the "www.prayforlynette.org" web site, for those that want to have a look. . . . All proceeds from the sale of the books will be used for ministry in Albania.

September 2005 ❧ *Newsletter*

"Come to me, all who labor and are heavy laden, and I will give you rest. Take my yoke upon you, and learn from me; for I am gentle and

lowly in heart, and you will find rest for your souls. For my yoke is easy, and my burden is light." (Matthew 11:28–30)

THESE ARE SOBER DAYS—DAYS OF ANXIOUS WAITING AND SOME SADness—but they are not without joy and hope.

My mother's condition continues to deteriorate. It is difficult to watch her grow more feeble with each day that passes and feel such helplessness in the face of her failing health. I feel like I ought to be able to help her get well, despite the fact that just five weeks ago her doctors at Mayo Clinic said there was nothing that conventional medicine could offer her and that she probably did not have long to live. Each day I ask myself, "Is there something I can do to help mom turn around her condition?"

I have found that it is much more difficult to watch someone I love suffer than it is to suffer myself. Someone else's suffering brings home the hard truths of our mortality and the inevitability of death. It forces us to face the uncertainties and fears that hang like a black shadow over that dark and lonely valley through which we must all pass. When I think about my own suffering, I am consoled deeply by the thought that I will not really be alone on that final journey. My Lord will be with me, but that consolation doesn't turn the valley into a bright, happy meadow.

Someone asked me recently if I ever felt excited about the thought of going to heaven. I had to say, "No." I have felt a tremendous sense of joy at the thought of being united with my Lord, who is the "true desire and the ineffable joy of those who love [Him]" in a place where "the voice of those who feast is unceasing, and the gladness of those who behold the goodness of [His] countenance is unending" (from the Prayers After Communion). I have been greatly comforted by the fact that Jesus has gone to prepare a place for me so that where he is, there I can be also (John 14:6). I feel that Jesus awaits me with gladness, that my death will be "precious" to him. My thoughts about heaven linger on the joy of being with Jesus, not on what the place will be like. It is enough for me to know that He will be there. I also thrill to the idea of being present in the company of some amazing people who have gone before me—apostles, prophets, martyrs, saints, my grandfather and C. S. Lewis. I hope not to be ashamed to be in their glorious company because of my pitiful efforts here on earth, but I am consoled by the fact that heaven will be a place full of mercy and grace.

Excitement, it seems to me, is something one feels when one is looking forward to an event and sees an untroubled path in front of him. Joy, on the other hand, is something one can hold onto in the face of suffering, knowing that the suffering will pass in time, but that the joy will remain because it is rooted in something deeper, not in the circumstances that surround it.

Although I do have a great sense of joy, I also feel a deep sadness at the immense tragedy of the human condition—the terrible burden of our separation from God, the presence of evil in this world, poverty, illness, selfishness, greed, unending hostilities between nations and peoples, the inability of many families to get along, and so many other horrors. Jesus wept over these things, and expressed his desire to console "as a mother hen gathers her young under her wings," but his people refused his offer. I never felt his grief until I began to experience suffering myself. Then I began to identify with his sorrow, as well as with the misery of so many who had come to my door in Albania seeking relief from pain or illness or hunger or cold. Although I had tried to meet their physical needs, I don't think I commiserated with them very deeply. For this reason and for many other reasons, I am so grateful for my own pain. Now I can have a much deeper sense of compassion for the sufferings of others.

I understand so much better, too, how much our Lord identifies with the sick and the suffering, the poor and the imprisoned. He is close to those who are in misery and wants us to be his face, his hands, his eyes, his feet—giving, loving, visiting, praying—for those in need. I have been reading some of the writings of Mother Teresa, and she is a wonderful example of "being Jesus" to the suffering.

Thinking about the sufferings of others—from that of my mother to that of those in other parts of the world—helps me to take my mind off myself. When I think of how blessed I am to be well fed and clothed, warm and comfortable, loved and cared for and tended with the best medical care, I am ashamed to call my experience suffering at all. Behind all these blessings is the mercy and grace of my Lord, who has made his love and presence so very real to me, and who calls me continually to follow him with my whole heart.

Apart from our sadness over my mother's condition, these are very happy days for Nathan and me and our children, perhaps the happiest we have ever known as a family. I have learned so much in the past few months about how to be "subject to my husband." I mentioned before that I had developed the unprofitable habit of making independent decisions about some things, and hadn't realized how difficult this had been for Nathan during the thirteen years of our marriage. Nathan isn't the sort of husband who gives orders and expects unquestioning obedience. He likes to make decisions based on discussion and agreement. We have had some amazing opportunities in the past few weeks to work on this area of our marriage.

The most dramatic in my mind was when we were considering the idea of my undergoing chemotherapy. The idea had been proposed to us by our primary caregiver, who urged that we consider it as it could produce some good results. Nathan was eager to pursue the idea, so we scheduled a visit with the oncologist. I had my reservations about such treatment. I didn't want to have to feel terribly sick in the hope of maybe feeling a little bit better later on. On the other hand, I didn't want to be stubborn and refuse treatment if it could help.

I admit to feeling a great amount of anxiety in the days that led up to our appointment with the oncologist. It seemed to me that Nathan and I were on opposite sides of the fence on this issue. How were we going to agree on a decision, and how were we going to choose the right decision? I fretted and fretted about this until I finally said to myself, "Look, the Lord knows your needs and he will give you the answer when you need it, not before. Ask the Lord for wisdom and ask him to give you and Nathan consensus in this decision." I did pray earnestly about it and I also stopped worrying about it. When the appointment came, we met the oncologist, and his perspective was that the chemotherapy might add some months to my life, but that it was not likely to add years. He did recommend that I undergo treatment.

When Nathan and I discussed the issue later, Nathan said that if I didn't want to do chemotherapy, he wouldn't push it because he understood that it wouldn't profit me much and probably would reduce radically my quality of life for the duration of it. I was so relieved by his words. In the end, the decision was very easy to make, and I was so grateful that I had learned to "cast my care on the Lord," knowing that he would grant us an answer when we needed it.

Nathan and I continue to delight in each other's company. Frequently as we say goodnight, Nathan says to me, "You're a joy to me. I'm so glad we had this day together." He is helping me to focus on the blessings of today and not on the uncertainties of tomorrow. Jesus' words in Matthew 6 have taken deep root in him. "Do not be anxious about tomorrow . . ." Nathan could wallow in his own fears about the future—How will he manage the children alone? Will he have to grow old alone, falling sick and having no one to take care of him? Being more melancholy by nature, it would be tempting for him to give into despair, but he is choosing to be grateful for the good that we are experiencing today, and not [focusing] on the difficulties that may or may not come tomorrow.

C. S. Lewis, in his book, *The Screwtape Letters,* which I am reading these days, has a great chapter on this idea of living in the present. Uncle Screwtape, the senior devil, advises his nephew, a junior devil new to the business of tempting, to get "his patient" living in the past, or better yet, in the future. "Humans," he writes, "live in time, but our Enemy (God) destines them to eternity. He therefore, I believe, wants them to attend chiefly to two things, to eternity itself, and to that point of time, which they call the Present. For the Present is the point at which time touches eternity. Of the present moment, and of it only, humans have an experience analogous to the experience, which our Enemy has of reality as a whole; in it alone freedom and actuality are offered them. He would therefore have them continually concerned either with eternity (which means being concerned with Him) or with the Present—either meditating on their eternal union with, or separation from, Himself, or else obeying the present voice of conscience, bearing the present cross, receiving the present grace, giving thanks for the present pleasure.

"Our business is to get them away from the eternal, and from the Present. . . . We want a man hag-ridden by the future—haunted by visions of an imminent heaven or hell upon earth—ready to break the Enemy's commands in the present if by so doing we make him think he can attain the one or avert the other—dependent for his faith on the success or failure of schemes whose end he will not live to see. We want a whole race perpetually in pursuit of the rainbow's end, never honest, nor kind, nor happy now, but always using as mere fuel wherewith to heap the altar of the future every real gift which is offered them in the present."

Living in the present is a moment-by-moment effort. I still find my mind wandering off into the future on occasion, but I try to pull it back. I want to live fully today, being patient with my children, helpful to my husband, attentive to my mother, and rejoicing in my Lord.

Several weeks ago, I was thinking about Jesus' words in Matthew 6 specifically with regard to eating. "Do not be anxious about . . . what you shall eat. . . . Is not life more than food?" In mulling over these verses, I realized that I had allowed myself to become obsessed by food—organic food, health food, raw food, whole grains, the right supplements—all under the guise of "healing." I thought myself excused from moderation because I was fighting a serious illness. When I realized how mistaken I was, I repented immediately and was ashamed that I had been so excessive.

I'm moderating myself now, but that doesn't mean I'm not careful about what I eat. I read a lot of books on diet and its effects on cancer and the immune system, but now rather than being so earnest about it, I try not to take any of it too seriously. Nathan teases me regularly about my latest diet guru (meaning the latest health book I'm reading). A few months ago, I couldn't have laughed at such jokes, but with my repentance has come the realization that my diet quest really ought to be laughed at, and I'm doing so myself now. The good thing is that, although he jokes about it, Nathan is willing to eat the stuff I'm making—the lentil dishes, the quinoa tabouli, the spinach salads with flax oil dressing, and other such things. (I haven't subjected him to the seaweed yet.)

One of the gifts God has given me recently is a spirit of deep contentment. I am contented with the cross I have been given, because I know that it is rooted in the goodness of God. Because God is good, all that he sends us is for our good. I love Hudson Taylor's comments about this. He says, "All God's dealings are full of blessing: He is good, and doeth good, good only, and continually. The believer who has taken the Lord as his Shepherd can assuredly say . . . 'Surely goodness and mercy shall follow me all the days of my life.' Hence we may be sure that the days of adversity, as well as days of prosperity, are full of blessings." (Hudson Taylor was an incredible missionary, who spent over 50 years serving in China during the 19th century.)

This means, then, that even if the thing given to us looks "bad," it is given so that we might learn to detach ourselves from this world and cling to God. To be given a cross, then, is an honor, for it is God's way of wooing us. We listen better when things are difficult because we suddenly become aware of our desperate need for God.

I have experienced such delight in the nearness of God these past few months, and this makes my illness so worthwhile, but I want to love God, not for his gifts and for the consolation he brings, but for himself. I have days when I feel spiritually dry, but these are precious, too, because at such times I choose to love God and to pray anyway. I know that my feelings will come and go, but my love must remain an act of the will. I enjoy those days when my spirits are riding high because I feel profoundly the presence of God and hear his voice in the wind as it passes through the trees, but I am more thoughtful and sober when I don't feel such things and simply choose to believe that God is near because he has said so. This, I think, is the beginning of faith.

In conclusion, I want to comment on all the prayers that are being offered up to God for my healing. I know it is tempting for people to think that their prayers are not being answered because I have not been healed of cancer. But the truth is that prayers are being answered in the most miraculous ways—perhaps not for healing of body, but certainly for healing of soul. Nathan and I can attest personally to the real transformation that continues to take place in our own lives and in our marriage. We've also seen people close to us undergo dramatic changes for the good. In my mind, healing of soul is the greater gift, for it has bearings on eternity, whereas healing of body is only temporary.

And who knows? It isn't over yet. Perhaps healing of body is still to come. I rest confident in the purposes of God. If he still wishes to use me for good in this life, he will spare me. If he has accomplished his purposes, he will take me. This truth helps me cope with the thought of leaving my children, for it encompasses the idea that God will accomplish his purposes for my children as well. If he takes their mother from them while they are young, he has his reasons for doing so, and because he is good, his reasons are good. He will provide for them. When I succumb to anxiety about the future, I still shed tears over the thought of leaving my children, but my struggle is emotional. It is not spiritual, for I rest contentedly in the will of God.

I want to thank those of you who have been praying for us. We feel ourselves sustained and transformed through your prayers. We had some very stressful months this summer with the diagnosis of my mother's illness and concern over who was going to care for my 95-year-old grandmother, who was living with us at the time. My mother had been caring for her for four years. When it became clear that she could no longer provide the care my grandmother needed because she herself was beginning to need care, we began praying for a solution to my grandmother's needs. In the end, my mother's sister, who is a nurse, took my grandmother to live with her in Montana. We had some anxiety about grandma adjusting to a new situation at her stage of life, but she is happy and doing very well. We are so grateful to God for providing for her.

We thank you for praying for our children's school needs. When it became apparent that I was not going to be able to homeschool the children, we looked at the public and Christian schools in Plainview. After some deliberation, we decided to go with the Lutheran Church school, which is a small, closely-knit community. The decision was a good one for the children are very happy there, and their teachers are willing to be flexible to accommodate our family's particular needs. It also provides a loving Christian environment for the children while they are away from home. We are very thankful that the children did not exhibit any fears or reluctance about going to school. On their first day, they went right into their classrooms without any tears or clinging or hesitation.

About a month ago, I felt a very strong desire to make a short trip to Albania. Up until that time, although my desire had been all along to return to Albania to serve, if God granted me health, I had not felt up to making a visit. I'm not sure what changed. Perhaps it was a strong desire to see people there, to encourage them, to bear their burdens. Also, I think I realized that my condition might worsen, making it impossible for me to go later. At any rate, we have scheduled a trip for September 23–October 6. My caregivers at Mayo Clinic have cleared me to go. My caregivers in Albania are more apprehensive, fearing that perhaps complications could arise during our time in Albania. At the time that we made our decision to go to Albania, I was feeling quite well, better than I had in months. This past week, however, the pain set in again and is much worse than it has ever been. We still feel that it is God's will for us to make this trip, and I would appreciate your prayers that I might feel well for our two weeks of traveling. It is hard to reach out to people when you are feeling awful yourself, and I do want to be able to minister to others.

We are so grateful to those of you who have continued to support us financially during this time. Knowing that we have such strong support behind us relieves us of financial worries, which often burden those dealing with serious illnesses.

A big "thank you" also to those who have written by e-mail or regular post. I love getting cards in the mail or messages on the computer and wish I could answer every one. You all say such wonderful, encouraging things that keep me going from day to day.

God bless you.

December 2005   ☙   *Newsletter*

AFTER RETURNING FROM A TRIP TO VISIT FRIENDS IN BOSTON IN June, I felt that I didn't ever want to travel again. Even going as far as Rochester, a town 30 miles away, seemed overwhelming. I was contented to stay at home, sitting beneath a canopy under the magnificent maple tree in my parents' back yard and watching the finches and chickadees quarrel at the bird feeder or the squirrels sport in the trees around the yard. I thought I'd never travel again.

I don't know what happened to change all that, but in early September an overwhelming desire to visit Albania came over me. Perhaps it was the feeling that if I didn't go now, I would never be able to go. I wasn't getting any better, so waiting would only make it less possible. I told Nathan that I wanted to go, but I thought he would tell me it wasn't a good idea. On the contrary, he was very supportive. If I wanted to go, he would do all he could to make it possible.

We began to make plans for our trip. Nathan consulted our doctor in Albania, but the doctor was very apprehensive about the idea. If I took a sudden turn for the worse, he said, it would be very difficult for him to get me out of Albania. Most airlines do not like to carry seriously ill passengers. Though we were a bit discouraged by the doctor's words, we decided to go ahead with our plans to travel. My desire to see our wonderful friends and co-workers in Albania was growing each day, and I felt that if this desire was from God, he would take care of me. One of our chief concerns was regarding my hemoglobin. I had been getting regular blood transfusions for several months because my hemoglobin had dropped very low and my body no longer seemed able to produce it. We made this a matter of prayer and fasting.

We booked our tickets, packed our bags and prepared to leave, but as our departure approached, I began to feel worse and worse. I started running a fever and was wracked with pain. I knew that I could not go in such a condition, but would I ever get to feeling well enough to travel? We postponed our trip for a week, knowing full well that I might not be feeling any better in a week. On the day that we originally were to have flown, I was sitting in a chair downstairs. It was evening and I was feverish and uncomfortable. I was feeling the worst I had ever felt. Suddenly the front door of the house opened, and my father walked in with the pastor from his church. My father had seen how miserable I was, and out of compassion had brought the pastor over to pray for me. After the two of them and Nathan laid hands on me and prayed, a remarkable thing happened. I felt a definite change in my body temperature, a cooling down. By the next morning, I was feeling much better and was certain that the change in my condition was a result of the prayers that had been said for me.

Over the next week, I had time to regulate some new slow-release pain medication that had been prescribed for me and also to manage its unpleasant side effects, which included terrible sleepiness that usually hit late morning each day. By the time we were to leave, I was feeling much better and was prepared to take on our adventure with enthusiasm. One thing, however, began to unnerve me that week as we waited to see how things would go with my health. On two occasions, as I was in that half-conscious state after waking up from an afternoon nap, I felt an overwhelming dread—the fear that I might get trapped in Albania. I told myself I was being silly and pushed it aside, but it lingered in the recesses of my mind and came back later much more forcefully.

Several days before we were to leave, my hemoglobin was checked again. I had hoped that after praying so hard, it would go up so that I wouldn't have to worry while we were away, but it had dropped again, though not at such a rapid rate. I was given two units of blood then and prayed that it would hold me for the ten days that we were to be away.

We departed as planned on October 3 from Minneapolis and flew to Albania via Washington D.C. and Vienna. At every step, whether it was check-in or security or boarding, things went unusually smoothly. Each time as we disembarked, I was met by either an escort with a wheelchair, or by a handicap vehicle, which meant I did not get exhausted by having to walk across the airports.

Because I needed to be able to stretch out and sleep during our trans-Atlantic flight, I flew business class, while Nathan and the children flew coach. Although I was not happy about being separated from my family, I was very grateful to be traveling in such comfort, which had been made possible by a very generous gift from a dear friend. However, my fear of being trapped in Albania did strike again just after I boarded the plane. As I heard the plane doors being shut and bolted, I panicked. I have never had a panic attack, but at that moment I was overwhelmed by fear. I said to myself, "I'm going to have a panic attack, and then they'll put me off the plane." Then I panicked about panicking. I wished over and over again that Nathan were with me, but he was in the back with the children, and I couldn't run back to him because we were preparing for take-off. All I could do was to begin praying slowly and rhythmically, "Lord, have mercy. Lord, have mercy. Lord, have mercy." I repeated that phrase over and over silently. In the back of my mind I also prayed, "Lord, you've promised your strength when we are weak, and now I am terribly weak." Gradually, my fears began to subside, and I took in my surroundings. "How many times in your life are you going to fly business class?" I asked myself. "You ought to enjoy this, because if you get well, you'll never fly like this again." I did enjoy myself on that flight. I was seated next to a very nice gentleman, who, upon learning why I was flying to Albania, was extremely kind and compassionate to me. His wife had had breast cancer, and, although she had been cancer-free for over six years, was still very fearful about the cancer returning. We had an interesting conversation during dinner, which helped to allay further my fears. I thanked God many times afterwards for his grace for that trip.

I thought that when I arrived in Albania, I would be overwhelmed by my emotions. I was sure that I was going to fall down and kiss the ground. I didn't. It was all too familiar—the sights and sounds of the airport—and the old habits and rhythms of living in that context came right back. It was as though we'd been gone just for a holiday. Even my facility in the Albanian language came back. In fact, I was even better in my use of it because I forgot to be self-conscious about my ability and just talked, whereas in the past, I had always been so concerned about speaking correctly that sometimes I wouldn't say anything at all. My ease in speaking the language stayed with me throughout the entire visit, and I was so thankful to God for granting me this gift of communication.

We spent ten very happy days in Albania. Grant and Carina Van Cleve, missionaries with YWAM and very good friends, had graciously offered to move out of their spacious apartment during our visit so that we could have their living quarters to ourselves. It was a perfect setting. We could receive guests there, but I could also get away as needed during the day to rest. Located on the ninth floor, the apartment offered a wonderful view of the city, but also provided a reprieve from the bustle of people and cars and relief from the busyness of our schedule.

Our time was filled with wonderful conversations with people. There was so much to hear and see. We had missed these dear friends. During our visit, we didn't think so much about work. That would always be there. We thought about how much we loved these precious people and what joy we had in being together with them again, sharing our hopes and concerns. We met people for lunch and dinner almost every day, including Archbishop Anastasios, who invited us for a private lunch at the Archdiocese and was extremely kind in his attentions to us. Sometimes we ate out; at other times friends came to us, bringing a meal with them. Sometimes it was traditional Albanian food, and I thoroughly enjoyed sampling the local cuisine again.

We rejoiced with those who were rejoicing and struggled together with those who were struggling. Nathan arranged many meetings with co-workers and friends and was able to do some work while we were there. We spent a day at the seminary, visiting with Bishop Ilia and the students, who prepared a lovely program for us and afterwards gave me flowers. As we sat at lunch, I noticed that our table was spread with a white cloth and strewn with flowers. I learned afterwards that the girls had done that especially for me—something they had learned at camp the previous year when we decorated for our garden tea party. I was so pleased. They were so good at taking a few simple ideas and making them their own. This is what our work was all about—equipping others so that they could continue on their own.

Our children took to Albania and their friends as though they had never been gone. I marveled at how true it was that they were most at home in Albania. Until this year they had known little of the States. Tristan remembered much of his Albanian, and seemed comfortable speaking it. Katherine didn't remember words, but did understand quite a bit.

If I have to choose a highlight of our stay, I would say it was the event promoting my book, *Resurrection,* to the public. A number of pictures from this event have been posted to this website, so you can see them, if you're interested. The event, which was held at the Gallery of Arts, was organized by our co-workers George Russell and Ana Kruja, who went to great lengths to plan an incredible event. I had no idea such an event was being organized until after we arrived in Tirana, and at first I was quite daunted by the idea. Although I have done a lot of public speaking in my life, since becoming ill I have found myself reluctant to do anything public. I knew that for a book promotion, I would be expected to give a speech, and the idea seemed overwhelming. However, I was pleased at the thought that a public launching of my book would bring visibility to the tremendous work of the Orthodox Church that had been accomplished over the past fourteen years under the leadership of Archbishop Anastasios. Because of this, I set aside my own reluctance to participate and embraced the project with enthusiasm.

The event came off beautifully, though it began with some rather unexpected incidents. The first was that a parishioner who had been very active in the church from the first days of its reopening brought to me his list of complaints about the book. I had left out some important people, and had recognized some who were much less significant. This unsettled me a bit, but I tried to answer as kindly as I could and recommended that he write a book in which he could articulate details about events and people that had been active in the early 90s.

The second incident was an interview by the Albanian national television station that was present to film the event. I had not known a television crew was to be there, and when I arrived they asked for an interview to be done in Albanian. I have never been comfortable making speeches in Albanian without any preparation, and the thought of doing one that would be televised nationally terrified me. I asked if Nathan could help me, and they agreed to this. I called Nathan over and the cameras began to roll. There wasn't even time to think. Nathan gave a short speech and then the cameras turned to me. To this day I do not know what I said, but to my relief, the day after the event my former language teacher called me and was ecstatic about my appearance on TV. "You did wonderfully," she exclaimed. "I didn't hear any mistakes." I can only say that this was another manifestation of the tremendous grace of God that was present with us throughout our visit in Albania.

After the interview concluded, I felt much more relaxed. Nathan and I were seated at the front with Archbishop Anastasios and Bishop Ilia, who offered a few words of explanation about the nature and purpose of this book. Metropolitan John of Korca, with whom we have become very dear friends over the past ten years, delighted us with a surprise appearance and also said some words. I made my own presentation in English, and being out of practice in working with a translator, ran ahead of her at times and had to backtrack. As I was speaking and surveying the crowd, I had a strong sense that this book was something that we had all done together. I had interviewed or requested photos from so many of them. All had been eager to help me and had given me far more information than I ever could have incorporated into one volume. I said to them, "This book is not my work, but our work."

The greatest blessing for me in doing this book project was working so closely with Archbishop Anastasios. I have come to cherish this outstanding Archbishop as a man of God and one who loves deeply—both God and those under his pastoral care. He was so kind to me throughout the process of writing, editing, rewriting, and editing again. He was always patient, always thoughtful, and always full of good ideas and suggestions. The book is good because his hand was ever present in guiding and correcting me. I thank God that the project is done, and marvel over and over again at God's timing in bringing it to completion just before my cancer was discovered.

Our trip to Albania seemed to conclude so quickly. Toward the end of our visit, I got exceedingly tired. We had been running at a pace that I could not sustain. The last two days I had to lie down at every free moment. Sometimes when people came to see us at the apartment, I had to stretch out on the couch and converse reclined.

I had not had any blood work done during our stay in Albania, so I didn't know what was happening with my hemoglobin. I didn't feel any of the usual symptoms that come with low hemoglobin, though I assumed it was dropping because it had in the past. Thank God, I did not feel any anxiety about it; I just hoped it was not falling too rapidly. Overall, I had felt very good throughout our stay. I was so thankful that God gave me strength and "health" for the duration of our visit. Everything was a delight to me and so wonderfully familiar. I felt at home, and as a result forgot to be afraid of "getting trapped in Albania."

At the end of our visit as we stood at the airport saying goodbye to friends and co-workers, I could not help but let the tears come. I did not want to leave. My heart was breaking. If things were different, I wouldn't leave, and if things changed I would be back immediately.

Our return trip went smoothly until we got to Washington. There, we missed our connecting flight to Minneapolis. Since we had felt ourselves so sustained by people's prayers during our entire trip, we were puzzled by what was happening. We were able to get rerouted to Minneapolis via Chicago within a few hours, but we were exhausted after twenty hours of travel and didn't relish having to add another six hours to our trip. While waiting for the flight, the children, for whom it was now early morning in Albanian time, stretched out on the seats in the waiting area and went to sleep. When we finally arrived in Chicago some hours later, we found that our second flight had been canceled. We would have to stay in Chicago until the next day. This turned out to be a great blessing. As soon as we heard that we were stuck in Chicago, we said, "Let's stay for the weekend." We had an overwhelming sense that our circumstances had been altered to bring us to Chicago. Our home parish is in Chicago, and we have many friends there. With only an hour's notice, good friends from church took us in and housed us for the weekend. When we got to their home that night, we went straight to bed and were spared another flight and a long drive home.

We spent a wonderful weekend in Chicago, visiting with friends and catching up on our sleep. On Sunday we spoke to the parish about our trip to Albania and they responded with gratifying enthusiasm for the work there. When someone offered to drive us to Minneapolis the next Monday, we accepted with enthusiasm. We had had enough of planes and airports, and were delighted at the prospect of driving to Minnesota in a comfortable car with good company.

Since returning home, I have struggled a bit with being content. I had been experiencing so much contentment prior to leaving, and see now that sometimes these lessons have to be learned over and over, that I haven't learned them as deeply as I thought. My pride says, "I should be past this," but humility says, "I will be learning these things throughout my whole life."

My discontentment comes from something good. All my desire is to devote my life to the service of Christ in Albania. There is so much to be done and so few people to do the work. I am thankful for the dedicated people—both Albanian and foreign—who are giving themselves so wholeheartedly to the task, but I want to be there also. It's not that I feel I have some great contribution to make, but I love Albania and its people and want to be there, struggling under its burdens and rejoicing in its triumphs.

Nathan has been wonderful in this whole process. He could be chomping at the bit, impatient with this "detour" that has taken us away from the people and work that we love. But his mind from the beginning has been that this journey of cancer is the "work" that has been given to us for now. We are to be faithful to our Lord while walking this path. I am so thankful for his good spirit, despite the fact that he longs to be back teaching and directing programs in Albania.

I feel so strongly the need to learn patience in this process. I think patience is at the root of contentment. This is the great virtue of the saints, and it is my wish to emulate them. My mentor during much of the past six months has been François Fenelon, Archbishop of Cambrai, France, in the seventeenth century. His letters giving spiritual counsel to his many correspondents have been published and have touched me deeply. I am reading the third collection of his letters, *The Seeking Heart*, and continue to be transformed through them. He writes so much about bearing suffering well, and this has helped me bear mine more graciously. I want to quote a passage from the book I am reading at present.

I am sorry to hear of your troubles, but I am sure you realize that you must carry the cross with Christ in this life. Soon enough there will come a time when you will no longer suffer. You will reign with God and He will wipe away your tears with His own hand. In His presence, pain and sighing will forever flee away.

So while you have the opportunity to experience difficult trials, do not lose the slightest opportunity to embrace the cross. Learn to suffer in humility and in peace. Your deep self-love makes the cross too heavy to bear. Learn to suffer with simplicity and a heart full of love. If you do you will not only be happy in spite of the cross, but because of it. Love is pleased to suffer for the Well-Beloved. The cross which conforms you into His image is a consoling bond of love between you and Him.

Pray for strength and faith enough to trust yourself completely to God. Follow Him simply wherever He may lead you and you will not have to think up big plans to bring about your perfection. Your new life will begin to grow naturally. I know you want to see the road ahead rather than trusting God. If you continue this way, the road will get longer and your spiritual progress will slow down. Give yourself as completely as you can to God. Do so until your final breath, and He will never desert you.

These are great words of encouragement and consolation, and I am so thankful that I have found these writings and other wonderful texts that have been used by God to help me along this path.

I want to conclude this update by telling you about the results of my blood test. About a week after we returned from Albania, I went to the clinic to have my hemoglobin checked again. Miraculously, my hemoglobin level had not fallen at all. I was so amazed and thankful that God had sustained me physically as well as emotionally during our stay in Albania. My level has dropped since then, but at a much slower rate so that I haven't yet had to go back for a transfusion. I would appreciate your prayers for this blood issue. I will be going in next week to have the hemoglobin checked again.

January 2006 ♈ *Newsletter*

(Summarizing the Year 2005)

[This was a printed newsletter sent out to all of the Hoppe supporters via post. Although those who had access to the website already knew many details, the Hoppes wanted to keep all their supporters, including those without internet access, aware of what was happening. Some repetition with previous newsletters has been omitted.]

Philip found Nathanael and said to him, "We have found him of whom Moses in the law and also the prophets wrote, Jesus of Nazareth, the son of Joseph." Nathanael said to him, "Can anything good come out of Nazareth?" Philip said to him, "Come and see." (John 1:45, 46)

ABOUT FIVE YEARS AGO, I GAVE A TALK TO OUR ALBANIAN PRIESTS' wives on the theme of Journeying toward Christmas. In this presentation, I focused on the main feasts of the church during the Advent season, including the feasts of the apostles Andrew and Philip. In John 1, the Gospel account where each of these apostles is introduced to Jesus, the phrase "come and see" is used, and this call fits beautifully with our journey toward Christmas. We are called to "come and see," to draw near to Jesus. At Christmas time, we approach an infant, born as foretold by prophets and heralded by angels, who, on that first night, chant the wonderful news, "peace on earth, good will toward men." No ordinary infant, this child is announced as one who will "save His people from their sins," and we are led immediately to Pascha, to that bright sadness of his death for our life.

I have given this talk several times over the years, and it comes to my mind again this season, especially the call to "come and see," for we have been given a new way of coming and a new way of seeing through my cancer, which was diagnosed almost exactly a year ago. God has given us suffering so that we might see his love and goodness. It is his way of wooing us, and we are honored that he seeks us so unrelentingly. With joy now, we are walking along the path that takes us from that self-serving desire of wanting God for my healing to the place of loving God for himself alone.

Spring Tour

Many of you have followed the course of our lives over the past year through the website, www.prayforlynette.org. For those of you who do not have access to the website, I will summarize the months since our last newsletter in February.

I had just come off of radiation therapy when we last mailed a newsletter to our readers. At that time, cancer had metastasized to my spinal column and had formed a tumor. Thankfully, the cancer had not invaded any other organs.

During the spring months, I was feeling fairly well, and we toured parts of the eastern United States, visiting friends and supporters and presenting our work in Albania. Our travels took us to Chicago by the first week of May, and we were able to celebrate Pascha in our home parish, which we had not done for nearly ten years. It was a blessed time for us. We were delighted to be among so many long-time, dear friends for this most joyous celebration, and we were moved by the services sung in English by our beloved priest,

Fr. Patrick Reardon, whose deep voice resonated the Paschal hymns with such jubilation.

After Pascha, our plan had been to head west for a tour of the opposite coast, but I had begun to feel overwhelmed by our travels. It was too hard to travel and try to attend to my health needs. We decided instead to return to my parents' home, and canceled the western leg of our journey.

[. . .]

Over the summer, pain came and went. When I felt it forcefully, I spent a lot of time in bed. When it subsided, I was able to enjoy a fairly active life. By mid-September, however, the pain set in in earnest and didn't subside as it had in the past. At that time, I had to begin taking pain medication 24 hours a day. MRI scans in September showed small tumors throughout my spine and neck, but no fracture points. Other tests were given to see if the cancer had spread to my brain, lungs, and liver. It had not and I was very thankful that those organs would, at least for a while, continue to function normally.

I have not had any scans since September. My assumption is that the cancer continues to spread as my pain increases. Periodically, I receive blood transfusions to boost my hemoglobin, which dropped to critically low levels in July. Each month I receive a bone strengthener to help keep my bones from disintegrating too rapidly. These boosters cannot bring about healing; they can only prop me up for a while. Consequently, I have many ups and downs. When the pain becomes unmanageable, I am much less active, but during my good weeks, I can lead a relatively normal life, and for this I am very thankful.

Second Cancer Diagnosis

In July my mother, with whom we have been living this past year (along with my father), was diagnosed with an advanced case of liver cancer. By the time her cancer was discovered, there was nothing that could be done for her. She has been trying some natural approaches to healing, which, although they have not cured her, may perhaps be giving her some additional months of life. She does not have any energy, but she still pulls herself out of bed each day and dresses herself. She receives visitors and keeps up with other friends by phone. It has been so difficult to watch her grow weaker each day, but we rejoice that her spirits have been good. All of my siblings and their families will be coming for Christmas this year, and we are all looking forward to a sweet time of remembering our wonderful years together and sharing our love for each other. This may be the last we will all be together this side of our heavenly home.

Nathan's Work

Nathan has been keeping up with the work in Albania as best he can at a distance. He makes numerous phone calls to Albania each week, following up on people and encouraging the young leaders who are still officially under his direction. He made trips to Albania in February and June this year and was able to be present to oversee the children's camps in Kosovo.

While here in the States, he is also doing what he can to promote missions among the Orthodox churches in the Minneapolis/St. Paul area. He has been encouraged by the interest he is encountering at several parishes that are considering supporting long-term missionaries as a part of their regular annual budget. He hopes to continue visiting parishes to discuss this need and to urge them to include missions as a part of their own community's "mission." Several times a month, Nathan has been preaching at the Greek Orthodox parish that we have been attending this year. We are grateful for Fr. Nick Kasemeotes and the parishioners who have taken us in as though we were family and showered us with love.

[. . .]

Watching and Waiting

What is happening now? We wait, we pray, we carry out our day-to-day activities with as much patience as we can. Nathan does so much to take care of us. He gets the children up in the morning, feeds them, gets them ready for school, and then takes them to school. After that he tends to my needs. Later he collects the children from school and prepares dinner for all of us. We do not know what lies ahead. Apart from divine intervention, there is no hope for my healing, but with God there is always every hope. We submit ourselves to the good and perfect will of God and await his good pleasure. It is our hope and prayer to return to Albania, but when that may happen, we do not know.

In the meantime, we are very happy in our setting, despite the many challenges of my, and my mother's, illness. . . .

The experience of having cancer has brought so much good into my life that I cannot help but be thankful for it. God in his mercy desired that I might "come and see" Him. He had been calling all along, but I hadn't been listening very well. I am so thankful that in his love he persisted. We have drawn near and found him full of love for us. He has been so good to provide all that we have needed over the past year, and we marvel at how many people are praying for us. Almost every day, we learn of new people that remember us to our Lord, and we thank God for the showering of love and support that we have seen. This is a foretaste of that great community of love we will know in heaven, and I thrill at the thought of it.

We want to thank all of you for your prayers and support. It is impossible for us to adequately express our thanks, but please know that it is deeply felt. Through your prayers we have been showered with the grace of God for each day. A special thanks to those who have continued to support us financially this year through designated gifts to the Orthodox Christian Mission Center. This support has allowed Nathan to continue working with his ministries in Albania and also to care for me at home.

In this newsletter, it is not possible to express all of our thoughts. I have written much for the website, www.prayforlynette.org. If you want to view pictures of our recent trip to Albania, or read some of my thoughts from this past year, you can access them via the Internet.

"Come and see" is the call of our Lord this Christmas. Let us, like the shepherds, run to where our Lord is, for he desires that we, like the Apostle Andrew, should come and see where he is—in a place of salvation, peace, love, and joy.

"Glory to God in the highest and on earth peace, goodwill towards men."

CHAPTER 5

Entering the Valley of Darkness ❧

Although Lynette had moments of sadness, doubt, and despair throughout the first year of her illness, for the most part she maintained an extremely optimistic and hopeful attitude. The joy, hope, and faith she radiated almost seemed unreal to many of her friends. I remember using her website journals as a part of my church's weekly Bible Study group. We spent five weeks reading through her journal and discussing the spiritual gems within.

As we read through the first year of journals, however, some of the group began to feel discouraged, because they thought Lynette's overall upbeat reaction to cancer appeared too unbelievable. They couldn't relate to her because she seemed too "saintly." I told them to wait, because Lynette's journey through her own "valley of the shadow of death" would come. And indeed it did. Her journal entries from the start of the new year take on a different tone as she enters into what the saints call the "dark night of the soul."

February 2006 ❧ Newsletter

A shadow fell on me. It drifted in with the New Year, following on the heels of departing family members, who had come to celebrate a last Christmas with mom. We had been a happy tangle of people—21 in all—and our joy at being together was tinged only slightly by sadness. We knew that, very likely, mom wouldn't be there for the next Christmas gathering.

As for the shadow, I thought perhaps it was the natural ebb of emotions that often follows elation, but it hung on for days, growing in magnitude and darkening all my heart. I grew afraid of it and felt that I wouldn't be able to escape it. An existential angst gripped me, something foreign to me, as I have never struggled with God's existence. God had always been real to me, and so to face the question of his existence now seemed to me a kind of failure, a sign that here, at the end, I would fall from faith.

It all seems so ridiculous now, but at the time I was terrified. All day, every day as a sort of desperate mantra, I would cry, "Lord have mercy, Lord have mercy." My prayers were those of the abandoned: "Lord, don't let me go. I cling to you. Where can I go if not to you? There is no other place." For several weeks I struggled under this black pall. I reminded myself of everything I knew to be true about God, but those things left me unmoved. I knew I simply had to hang on, but I was afraid I would never recover the joy that had marked most of my days since my diagnosis.

During this time, I started to feel that it wasn't right for me to pray for my own healing, but at the same time I so desperately wanted to be healed. I felt that all my prayers were motivated strictly by the desire to gain favor in the sight of God so that he would heal me. My sincerity in prayer sputtered like a wet candlewick.

In the end I decided to take a day to fast. As a rule, being sick, I don't fast, although my diet is such that I eat little meat and dairy, so I don't have to remove much to fast. The day I did fast, I had to lie in bed most of the day, as I had no energy. Nonetheless, despite my weakness, my mind was extremely clear. As I prayed, the thought came to me that my faith was being tested, something that had not occurred to me during the entire period of my illness. I had seen this bit of suffering as a way of purifying my character, or a means of drawing nearer to Christ, but as an all-out testing of my faith, no. It also occurred to me that perhaps I was being attacked by the Evil One, whose wily arrows had managed to strike at a profoundly vulnerable spot, wounding me in spirit.

As I considered this idea of the testing of faith, the confusion in my brain that had clouded my thinking began to dissipate. I was relieved, almost happy at the thought that this was a trial from without, not a failure from within. Arming myself, then, was the next thing to do, with Truth being the chief weapon. I looked at the passages on faith, especially in the writings of St. Peter. "In this you rejoice, though now for a little while you may have to suffer various trails, so that the genuineness of your faith, more precious than gold which though perishable is tested by fire, may redound to praise and glory and honor at the revelation of Jesus Christ." And later in the chapter, "Therefore gird up your minds, be sober, set your hope fully upon the grace that is coming to you at the revelation of Jesus Christ." I knew I needed to learn fortitude and perseverance. I was so easily dismayed and discouraged by difficulties. Here was an opportunity to learn to persist in my faith, even when things looked so dark. I needn't fear the shadow, for Christ was there, even as he had been for Peter, who, after climbing out of the boat in faith to walk fearlessly to meet his Lord, had been overwhelmed by the cacophony of the storm and had faltered.

As in the case of Peter, I had begun to focus on the storm raging around me—on my illness and bleak prospects for healing, on departing prematurely from my husband, children, and ministry—and I had despaired and started to sink.

But probably the most profound idea about this dark period came from a dear friend of ours, Fr. Luke Veronis, who calls almost every week to inquire after my physical and spiritual well-being. As I was telling Fr. Luke about the shadow and my sense of utter spiritual desolation, he said simply, "That is what being poor in spirit is all about." It had never occurred to me to think this way, so his words struck me deeply.

I spent considerable time meditating on the first Beatitude, something I hadn't done before because the idea of poverty of spirit seemed too much in conflict with everything I thought ought to be true about my spirit. I had always dismissed from my mind the idea of "poor in spirit," thinking it must just be some kind of expression that I didn't comprehend. The idea that it really did mean *poor,* that is, "destitute," or "poverty-stricken," hadn't ever occurred to me, but now I saw it does mean just that, *poor.* I had seen the wasteland of my own spirit and had been utterly dismayed by it.

My experience under the shadow, rather than being some kind of spiritual failure, was actually a gift to me—the gift of seeing my spirit as it really is, as poor and utterly desolate—not as I had tried to dress it up so that God would be pleased with me—but as truly in rags. Now, seeing myself thus, rather than being dismayed, I ran and threw myself joyfully and with complete abandon into the arms of Christ—He who is Love, who is the Bridegroom. He took me as I was—poor and wretched—and adorned me with lovely bridal clothes and offered to me the Kingdom of Heaven. "Blessed are the poor in spirit, for theirs is the Kingdom of heaven."

In the shadow lay a blessing. I saw that now, but the testing of my faith was also there, and will always be, I think, for in this life the Enemy of our souls is never far and he seeks our destruction. Christ is much greater, of course, but we must be vigilant over our own souls as well, "alert and roused to action," as we state in the morning prayers. I have seen so often in the daily prayers the request that we be protected from the attacks of the Evil One, and I see that these aspects of our prayers are to be taken very seriously. Those who wrote the prayers down for our good and our use spoke out of long and deep experience of these things.

As to fortitude and perseverance in times of difficulty, I am grateful to have seen so vividly my own failure in that area so that I may, with God's help, begin to build upon my character. I have said to my children many times when they get to crying over small things, "You need to be tougher." I say that to myself as well, "Be a little tougher. Show a little fortitude."

After I finally emerged from under the shadow, I decided that we needed a whole lot more humor around our house. I said to my mom one day, "We are too glum, too serious. We need to lighten up and look for the irony in things." There are many humorous aspects to this business of being sick. It just depends on how we choose to look at them. We can cultivate a merry heart, which, according to Proverbs, "doeth good like medicine." It is our choice. Even though our situation is so serious, it is possible to be much lighter at heart in the face of death because we have such great prospects beyond the grave. What joy will be ours, what freedom from that which limits us here—our weak bodies and minds, our small understanding and narrow vision. No more pain, no more fears, no more pills and shots, no more potions and lotions.

One final lesson I learned from being under the shadow for a time was that I will be at peace during these days only if I am fully reconciled to dying. I would like to live, but I must accept that I may be dying and be at peace with it. This peace comes from knowing that there is a far better place to which I am going and that Jesus will be there. If I refuse to accept death, then I will be fearful, agitated, and restless, and will struggle with trusting in the goodness of God.

Psalm 141 says, "Precious in the sight of the Lord is the death of his saints." At a first glance, this statement can be startling. How can death be precious to God? At a second read, we realize that what is precious is actually our homecoming, our being united with Christ, who awaits our coming with joy. Death is only the means of bringing about this union. To see death from God's perspective is a great gift, then, because it can help to ease the pain and fear of our passage through the dark valley. What abandonment we can have to the fathomless love of God, and what anticipation of the joy we will have when we are in heaven with a community of people bonded by love.

I just finished reading a book by Joseph Pearce called *Literary Converts*, which tells of the conversion experiences of many famous English writers of the last century, including G. K. Chesterton, Evelyn Waugh, Malcolm Muggeridge, and many others. I was so delighted with this book, and was particularly struck by those passages that spoke about how these great writers died. They inspired me deeply as they approached the end of their lives with their longing to be free of this flawed life and to be joined with their beloved Christ.

When I was in college, I wanted more than anything to be an intellectual—not one of the dry, stuffy sort, but one endowed with good humor and a quick turn of phrase—witty and wise, you might say. Well, that never happened, and now that I am married to an intellectual, I see how much work it is to be bright—one has to read a lot of heavy stuff and then try to keep all that knowledge filed in one's mind so that it can be called up on a moment's notice. I see what I've been spared. I also see what everyone else has been spared, as I certainly would have been the dry sort that had everything to prove and no sense of humor at all.

Anyway, all that to say, as I read *Literary Converts,* all my longing for intellectual prowess came back, but I realized that I could enjoy the genius of others without coveting it. And that, it seemed to me, would be what heaven was all about. We would be bound together in a community of love, purged of all our weaknesses and pettiness so that we could truly enjoy one another, laugh together, be quick-witted or very dull, with no one to care, as it wouldn't matter. And all this made me long for heaven and that marvelous community. I could join in a conversation with G. K. Chesterton, Hillaire Belloc, and Ronald Knox, said to be "the wittiest man in Europe" in his day, and I would not be out of place. No one would scorn me for my feeble wit.

Thoughts of Heaven

Heaven. How much it occupies my thoughts these days. I long for it—that city "whose builder and maker is God" (Heb. 11). I stretch my brain trying to contemplate how wonderful it will be, that anything we've ever thought was beautiful or magnificent here is a mere shadow of what will be there. The wonders of nature—the high and fearful mountains and rich forests, splendid waterfalls and glorious vales of wildflowers, the planets and distant, mind-boggling galaxies—these are but a small sampling of God's creative genius. The manmade wonders of ancient days, from the pyramids of Giza to the hanging gardens of Babylon, and all the modern wonders—fruits of man's genius, the gift of God—these are but trifles compared to the magnificence of what will be in that city.

"I go to prepare a place for you . . ." (John 14). There is a place for me in that last and great city. I won't show up at the gates of heaven and be escorted to a bureau that will find some "accommodations" for me. I am expected, and my place is in order. In this regard I cannot speculate, and I don't even try. I only know that whatever "place" may mean, it will be beautiful, light-filled, magnificent, and joyous because Jesus will be there, and He is my Joy, my Light, my Hope—everything, really.

I see so much healing occurring in my soul—things that are too private to write about. Areas in my life that I didn't even suspect needed healing have been touched at a depth that makes me gasp with wonder. I had no idea of my own need, nor of the gift of healing that lay before my very eyes, just waiting to be grasped. Whatever may lie ahead, I embrace it with thankfulness, for I have been so deeply blessed and touched.

A friend wrote to me recently and said, "Your words come from an experience few are granted, and fewer still record, and you've given yourself and your Lord and your family in ways which will transform all of your readers. Maybe you can grant or convey to us the grace of that luminal space, the borderland you occupy, have so graciously occupied for a year and more now." I loved her use of the word, "borderland," for it struck me that even if, by the miraculous touch of God's hand, I were to get well, I would want to live all of my life in that borderland—that place where one has sight of the great City of God and yet remains with a foot on earth. I do not doubt that a vision of the heavenly city would transform what I did on earth; it would color all my actions with love, and drive me to set aside that which encumbers and distracts from the Good. I would want this vision of heaven to grow more vivid each day and fill all my mind. How it would lessen the fear of death and uncertainty, detach me from the desire to accumulate possessions, and give me compassion for those who suffer and struggle with fear. It would remind me that I am an exile and pilgrim here. My true home is in that Great City with God, and I must spend my life journeying to that city, doing all the good that I can along the way, helping the poor, the sick, the suffering; bringing comfort to those who are lonely and timid; and sharing Christ with all.

You may ask, how is our life going? I have my ups and downs. When I am up, I can function fairly normally, though I tire easily and have to rest often. When I am down, the pain sets in and drives me to my bed. At these times, I try to remain cheerful and remember that life is short and our sufferings are but for a little while. I also try to be thankful that I still do have good days and am not yet bedridden.

One thing that I am enjoying immensely is doing crafts after school with my daughter Katherine, who loves artsy things. I am teaching her to sew, and we have made several little projects together. She also loves painting and will paint alongside me as I work on an icon of the Theotokos. I've taken to making clothes for her doll and love doing that. Tristan has an engineering mind and loves building with Legos. He also loves displaying his structural achievements for all our visitors. The children are enjoying school, although Tristan less so as he thinks school interferes with play time, and he dislikes homework. Both children are involved in the AWANA program at my parents' church. Each week they do a fair amount of Bible memory work and do so with great enthusiasm, delighting in the rewards that come with memorizing verses well.

Nathan has been stalwart and patient. He attends to the needs of the children and my needs as well. He prepares all of our meals and shares kitchen clean-up with my father, who spends most of his time looking after my mother. Nathan also spends many hours on the phone to Albania, following up with people there and encouraging them in their struggles. He is thinking of making another trip to Albania, perhaps in March. We would appreciate your prayers for this. It is hard for me to have him away, but I feel that it is very important for him to visit at this time.

We have enjoyed visits from many friends, including a recent visit from our beloved Metropolitan John, bishop of Korca in Albania, who, during a recent trip to the States, came to see us. We were so pleased and honored by his visit.

We continue to be so grateful for your prayers, your letters of encouragement, and your love. These are sustaining us through this difficult period of our lives. We are also very thankful for all the people who are bringing us meals. This gives Nathan time off from kitchen duty and allows him to focus on other things. We are so happy to be part of that great community of love, and it has been our joy to sample some of that sweet fellowship that we will enjoy in the City of God throughout eternity.

May 2006 — Newsletter

Christ is risen! Truly He is risen!

As Bright Week draws to a close, my mind is drawn back to the journey of Holy Week, a time of walking with Christ through his last week on earth, remembering soberly all the events leading to his crucifixion and burial, and rejoicing at his glorious resurrection.

God showered me with grace this year, enabling me to feel well enough to attend almost all of the services of Holy Week, beginning with the Bridegroom Matins and ending with Agape Vespers. The services were quiet, meaningful, blessed, and marked all week by anticipation of that great moment when Fr. Nick Kasemeotes would announce, "Christ is risen."

When the vigil of Pascha came we were ready, for we had been building our expectations all week. Christ arose, breaking the chains of death, and our joy was immense for we knew that the work of our redemption had been completed. At last, we were free from the stranglehold of sin and misery.

Several things struck me this year. First, the extravagant love of the woman who anointed the feet of Jesus with precious ointment, then wiped it off with her hair. This woman had experienced Jesus' love and goodness firsthand and wanted to reciprocate in the only way she knew how—by giving without reservation that which she treasured most. She was not trying to gain something from Jesus. She poured out her treasure because she wanted to show him how deeply she loved him. The ointment was worth more than a year's wages and probably couldn't be replaced. There were some present for this demonstration who were horrified by what they perceived to be wastefulness. These rebuked the woman, but Jesus corrected them and called the anointing "a beautiful thing." This is what I so long for in myself: to love Jesus because he is good, not because I want him to be pleased with me, not so that he'll provide what I think I need, not out of a sense of duty. I want to love him for himself alone and to give unstintingly that which I most treasure, whatever *that* may be.

In each Divine Liturgy, we are invited to come to the Eucharist "with the fear of God, with faith, and with love." It seems to me that this is how we should approach God at all times. The "fear of God" implies that we ought to tremble before him, for he is terribly Good, and no one can stand before him. We forget this and get casual and careless in our approach to him. We need to come in humility, remembering that it is only because of his grace and mercy that we can approach him at all. But "fear" is tempered by love, and this makes us bold because we know that he loves us excruciatingly and has given all so that we might come to him.

As I look back over the past year, I wish I could say that I have made leaps and bounds in the area of loving God more deeply. I don't even know how one measures such things, but I do know that loving God demands a detachment from things. So does service to him. There is a profound prayer that the priest prays in the liturgy during the cherubic hymn that most of us never hear because it is said silently, but I have seen it written in a service book and have been struck by it often. It reads, "No one bound by worldly desires and pleasures is worthy to approach, draw near or minister to You, the King of glory. To serve You is great and awesome even for the heavenly powers." Though this applies specifically to priests serving the liturgy, I think it can apply more broadly to anyone in the service of Christ. I have thought of it often with regard to missionary service. We cannot be bound by worldly desires and pleasures and expect to be able to give love and devotion to our Lord. The world will always win. This fits also with loving God moment by moment. I cannot be caught up in the love of things and expect to love God at the same time.

You'd think with my illness that a detachment from this life would have come automatically, but this has not been the case. I have had to struggle with this and to be intentional about it. Let me give an example. Last year, I began to feel strongly that I ought not to put too much attention on my appearance, especially on my hair. I'm ashamed to admit it, but I used to go to the hairdresser almost every week in Albania. It was inexpensive, and the results were wonderful. I wanted to look good, and so I put a lot of emphasis on my hair. I think that is why, in my quest last year for healing of soul as well as body, God convicted me about this emphasis. It wasn't that I began to think it was wrong to go to the hairdresser or to color my hair. These are neutral things. The problem was with my focus. For me, then, healing of soul meant that I needed to be free from excessive concern about my appearance.

As a result, I stopped coloring my hair and let the natural color grow out—a rather long process with a lot of unattractive steps in between. My hair came in quite gray and really didn't look very good. In those first six months, I was tempted many times to go back to coloring my hair. I resisted, however, because of my desire to keep battling my vanity. Fortunately, I have gotten to the point where it doesn't matter any more. My body is perishing—not just because I am dying, but because life is brief—and it seems ridiculous to me now to put too much emphasis on it. I have to say that there is a great deal of liberty in being detached from one's appearance.

I've tried to detach myself from other things, as well—material possessions and such—that I have wanted to hold close. It's a long process of letting go, but by the grace of God, it is possible.

I was struck by something else during Holy Week this year, and that was the contrast drawn between Peter's repentance and Judas's regret. Both were guilty of terrible sins against Jesus, but whereas Peter wept and repented, coming back to Jesus and seeking his forgiveness, Judas regretted bitterly his betrayal but did not repent. He chose instead to take his own life. Regret is unproductive unless it turns into repentance. One of the things I have done as I face death is to reflect on my life, and I have spent many hours regretting certain things that I have done, and certain things that I have not done. This has not always been a positive exercise, as I have tended to dwell on regret and a sense of failure. I have had to learn to turn my regret into repentance, seeking God's forgiveness for my failures and sins, but then moving on from that to embrace God's love. To harbor regret and never repent and accept forgiveness is to deny the efficacy of Jesus' work on the cross. I can be forgiven of my sins because Jesus died for them. If I live in regret, unable to accept forgiveness, I make God out to be a liar, saying, in effect, that God does not love me and did not give his son for me.

I take great comfort in the tale of the prodigal son, who comes to his senses after a terribly wasteful life and runs home to his father, seeking his forgiveness. The father, who has been waiting anxiously for his son's return, embraces him with love. Without a doubt, that prodigal son loved his father much more than the older son who had never led a dissipated life, for the younger knew how much he had been forgiven. I often visualize myself as that prodigal running home to the father, begging for his forgiveness and basking in his overwhelming love.

It has been wonderfully liberating to recognize that I don't need to "succeed" spiritually in order to find favor with God. I come to him, not on the basis of what I have done, but on the basis of what he has done. If I were feeling spiritually successful right now, I might be in danger of believing that I didn't need to repent anymore. To be certain, I will never get to the point where I have attained a level of spiritual maturity that puts me beyond the reach of temptation and sin. In fact, the more I approach God with the proper fear, the more vividly I will see my own sinfulness and desperate need of his saving help.

These past three months have been very challenging for me. I went through a dreadful period in February and March, probably the worst time I have had in all the months of my illness. Part of it was triggered by medication, part by the progression of my disease and perhaps by other things as well. I began to have terrible anxiety attacks and bouts of deep depression. These were completely different from the down period I experienced after Christmas. They were overwhelming and dark and frightened me immensely. When a wave of anxiety would wash over me, I would sometimes go running into my mom's room and beg her to pray for me. She would do so with great love and compassion, asking God to protect me from evil, if the source were the Evil One.

At that time, I went to see a doctor who advised us that perhaps my medication for nausea was causing the anxiety attacks. I stopped taking that medication and the anxiety went away. The depression, however, continued, and I was prescribed an antidepressant, which, over time, seemed to help diminish the emotional lows and dark thoughts that had been troubling me.

I still do not know what caused the depression, but several very good things have come out of it. One is that I learned that I must press on regardless of how I feel. Depression is terrible, for it makes everything seem so pointless. There is this heaviness, a loss of appetite or desire or interest in anything. There were many times when I did not feel like praying, or going to church, or reading the Bible or other spiritual texts, but I chose to do them anyway and tried not to feel discouraged by my lack of earnestness or devotion. I chose to be obedient and "to cling to my God and place in Him the hope of my salvation." I often had that sense of simply hanging on, as though I were in a boat on a stormy sea and could do nothing but cling to the mast and hope I wouldn't be washed overboard.

I did notice during those miserable days that I had been in the habit of judging my spiritual state by how I was feeling. If I felt joyful or loving, then I was doing well. If I felt empty or despondent, then I wasn't doing well. I have since come to realize that faith is not about how I feel, it is an act of the will. I *believe* because I *know* something is true, not because I *feel* good about something. This realization will help me in the days ahead. I do not know what chemical imbalances the cancer may cause in the days to come, nor what may happen with my emotions, but I do know that I must simply hang on to what I know in my mind to be true. I have to admit, though, it is a great consolation to feel a love for God and the joy of the Lord!

The other thing that came out of my depression was a great sense of humiliation. This was a very good thing for my soul because I might otherwise have been tempted to think I was doing really well spiritually—a model of spiritual prowess. Well, that idea got shot down with this latest round of struggles. One doesn't get puffed up about depression. I would have said all along that it was only by the grace of God and through the prayers of people that I was managing to plod along, but I might have been giving myself a great deal of credit at the same time. Now I can say without a doubt that it truly is the grace of God that holds me and sustains me because I've been there on the edge, wondering if I were going to fall into some abyss. Thankfully, God was there in the darkness. Even though I had a hard time seeing him, I knew he was present because he said he would be. "I will never leave you, nor forsake you." This was a great comfort, and I clung to it tenaciously. It is very humbling to recognize how truly great is our need for God. He gives us these terrible moments to find that out, and so we must be thankful for them, but we must also live every day with that sense of total dependence on him, whether or not we are aware of our need.

Physically, I have been feeling quite well for the past few months. I haven't had to increase the dosage of my pain medication since the middle of February. For this I am very thankful. My hemoglobin had been falling much more slowly, and this past week it even went up a fair bit, which was a real surprise—a miracle. I hadn't had a blood transfusion since the end of January, but received one yesterday to prepare me for the months ahead. Because of this, and because of a sense of God's leading us to do so, we are planning to return to Albania for a few months. We are delighted with the prospect of being back "home" and being able to continue our work there. I will try to help out and participate as God gives me strength and energy. Nathan will still need to help me out a fair amount, but I do have my housekeeper, Shpresa, who can take over some of the things Nathan has been doing, especially meal preparation.

Our date of departure is May 17 and we would appreciate your earnest prayers for ease of travel for all of us, as well as grace for living and serving once more in Albania. There is little medical care available for me in Albania, but our co-worker Charles Linderman, the surgeon who diagnosed my cancer in the first place, will be checking me regularly. Please pray that my hemoglobin will hold steady. This will take a miracle, but we believe in miracles.

It is difficult for me to leave my mother at this time as well. Although my dad is her primary caretaker, there are still some things that I do for her, plus, she enjoys having a daughter nearby. It may be that my sister, who works from home and is fairly flexible with her schedule, will be able to come and stay for some extended visits with my parents. Please pray for my mom and for my dad and my sister. There will be some difficult adjustments ahead for them.

We will be pulling our children out of school about eight days before the conclusion of the school year. Both of the children's teachers are very understanding about this and have been extremely congenial all year with regard to our family's needs. Our children are enrolled in a Lutheran church school, and over the past six months members of the church have dropped by with meals for us and have offered help in so many other ways as well.

We thank God for his mercy and grace to us and for his provision for our every need. I also thank my good husband, Nathan, who has taken such good care of us over the past year-and-a-half. He has blessed us with a joyful and willing spirit and has not balked at any of the things I have asked him to help me with. I have had many ups and downs emotionally and spiritually, and he has been such a steadying force for me.

The costs of our tickets and other expenses for returning to the field are quite high, and we would appreciate any financial contributions that any of you might like to make to allay these costs.

We continue to be extremely grateful for your prayers for us. We are also thankful for those of you who have continued to support us so generously during our time in the States. You have eased our financial burden tremendously.

Thank you and God bless you.

CHAPTER 6

Memories for Nathan

IN HER FINAL YEAR OF LIFE, LYNETTE DESIRED TO LEAVE CERTAIN MEMO-ries for Nathan and her children. I remember mentioning to her on sev-eral occasions that she should set up a video camera and just talk into it. Even videotapes of such things as playing games with the children, sitting around with the family, or joking around with one another would become priceless treasures for her family in the future.

In one of the many letters Lynette received from people around the world, a woman described how her mother had died at a young age back in the early 1970s, but before dying she had recorded her own voice on a cassette player. This woman went on to share how that scratchy, unprofes-sional tape had become an heirloom for the surviving family.

I reminded Lynette about this several times, and even tried to press the issue with her once or twice. She understood the value of such things, of course, but walked that fine line between doing things for her family's future without her, and trying to live in the present with hope for a miracle of recovery. Thus, she hesitated to videotape herself or record anything too soon. Another factor was simply that she was too busy living in the present, making the most of each moment, and thus didn't find the time to write or do all that she wanted to.

In this chapter, however, we do see Lynette's attempt to begin writing a personal memory journal specifically for her dear husband. She recalls their history together, remembering their first encounter, Nathan's initial reaction, their courtship, their break-up, their marriage and honeymoon, and the love that grew over the years and blossomed fully during their final months together. She often repeated to me, "This illness is helping us go from having a good marriage to having an extraordinary marriage. Even if we were to have been married for another thirty years, our love might never have reached the stage that it has reached now through this journey and illness!"

As the dates of the entries reveal, Lynette began this journal six months before her death, and after several months of putting it aside, tried to finish it during her final days on earth. She had many plans of other things she wanted to leave both Nathan and her children, but she kept putting them off. Thus, she only began writing notes to her children weeks before she actually died, and it was then that her physical abilities started to fail. She did have the strength, though, to sing some of her favorite songs for her children on a CD during her final days.

I'm sure that another factor that led Lynette to hesitate to write the memories and notes she wanted to write was her perfectionism. As my wife Faith reminded me, "Lynette didn't want to just write her children a note. She wanted to write them a children's novel." In fact, long before her illness, Lynette talked about actually trying to write a children's novel. She loved the fantasy writings of C. S. Lewis and J.R.R. Tolkien and dreamed of creating a novel through which her children could learn the virtues and values of life. Such desire for perfection surely played a role in her delayed attempts to finish memory books and the like.

March 11, 2006   ❦   *Lynette's Memories*

I WRITE THESE OPENING WORDS IN A HAPPY STATE OF MIND. THIS is really saying something, as I have been so troubled lately, and feelings of joy have been rare. My heart is full of love and gratitude to you for the tremendous love and patience you have shown during this period of my life. I feel cherished and even nourished by your love, and know that together we will be able to get through it . . . "and all will be well . . . and all manner of thing shall be well."

I remember well our first meeting. It was at the "Wild West House" and you were chief cook. Most of the food being served had been gleaned from one of the several grocery stores in the area. We had been invited to lunch after the Sunday morning service at Oak-dale Community Church by your roommate Wayne, with whom I worked at the College's physical plant.

I had never seen you before, which is rather surprising as your appearance was rather striking: you were tall, dark from a summer tan, and had long dark, dark hair that flowed down your back, and a long beard that framed your handsome face. You were unsmiling most of that first day we met, and I found you a bit formidable. We sat next to each other at a large table. The most memorable thing about the meal was the fantastic sweet rolls that you had made and served as dessert. It was during this meal that you learned I was the parking coordinator for Wheaton College. I was sure from that moment on that you despised me, as you had had several run-ins with the former parking coordinator during the previous year and had not formed a good opinion about him.

I determined then that I would try to win you over to a better opinion. So that evening, I came back to your house under cover of night and put five tickets on your car, which was legally parked. The offenses ranged from such things as "hating the parking coordina-tor," to "just in case you park illegally and we miss ticketing you" and other absurdities.

And that was our first encounter!

. . . I don't remember when my feelings toward you first began to change. Perhaps it was when you hugged me goodbye that summer's beginning. I felt close to you somehow. It was after a party at our house that fall of 1989 that I really began to admit to having feelings for you. You came to the party dressed in a suit and your hair had been cut short. You looked very good. These feelings grew in me and one day I just had to say something to you about them. I knew that you regularly studied in the STUPE, so I went and found you there and asked if I could talk to you. You agreed and we went outside to a stone bench to talk. I said that I hadn't meant to develop feelings and didn't expect anything in return, but just had to tell you that I had developed strong feelings for you. You listened and then said very kindly that you were flattered, but I was much too old for you.

I left you then, determined to put my feelings behind. I started trying to avoid you. We had a class together with Dr. Scott, and I had been accustomed to sitting in the front row with you. Now I moved to the back row. You were determined to be kind and began sitting with me in the back.

I don't know the details of your change in feelings toward me, but I do remember noticing that you began to pay more attention to me. I didn't take it as anything but kindness toward me. It seemed too much to hope that you really cared.

Our first official date occurred the same day. We—that is you, me, and Gaye—went to visit All Saints, or Christ Covenant Church as we knew it then, for the first time. We drove downtown and walked about Chicago. You held my hand for the first time.

March 16, 2006 ❧ *Lynette's Memories*

CHRISTMAS BREAK CAME AND WE WENT OUR SEPARATE WAYS FOR the holidays, but you called me during that break, which let my family know that I hadn't just made you up. I was reading the book, *Orthodox Theology*, when you called. It must have been for Bob Webber's class. I was both surprised and terribly pleased that you called.

After we returned to school, one of the first things I remember doing together was watching *Anne of Green Gables* in full with some of the other Wild West couples. You held my hand during the movie and I was surprised at the public display of affection in front of your friends. I've always loved the touch of your hands—from the very first time until now. Though it is more familiar now, it is no less sweet and precious. I am even more thrilled by it because now I know the depth of love that is behind the touch. Then, there was the thrill and tentativeness of something new but not certain.

We started dating then. I remember meeting your parents for the first time and wondering if they liked me—a normal feeling I suspect for new girlfriends.

It took a while for you to tell me that you loved me. I think, as with most things for you, you deliberate long and want to be sure of something before you'll say it or do it. It has taken me a long time to believe that you really love me. I'm sorry for my insecurity that caused you so much consternation. I was not sure of myself; hence, the difficulty in believing that you could and did really love me. I believe it now. You have proven yourself over and over to me, especially in this past year. Your love is deep and is rooted in your own sense of being loved by our eternal Creator. It was only when I came to understand how much I was loved by God that I could begin to see love elsewhere, despite the fact that it was there all along.

Thank you for loving me and for expressing it so freely and so often. It gives me a strong sense of security to be loved so much, especially during these difficult days.

It brings me joy to write of my own love for you. I have had to learn how to love and don't feel that I've done very well at it. You are so worth loving, and I have come to admire and respect you so much as a person of real goodness and integrity. Thank you for leading our family down a good path of putting God and His work first, of giving yourself fully to Him even though you don't always feel His presence.

One of our most memorable times during dating was our trip to Colombia, to visit your parents. I remember exploring Bogota a little bit, and Rachel and Tavi being there. I remember a side trip up into the mountains outside of Bogota and lunch at a little restaurant. It was just the two of us and we went by bus. We stayed at Gloria's house.

It was my next trip, when we were engaged, that took us to Valledupar. We met at a hotel after I flew in, but we had the problem of my not having a visa. You had to sneak me into Colombia from Venezuela. I did a lot of drawing on that trip because I was helping your parents with their literacy program. I enjoyed doing that. I remember Theresa and the iguana and her dance in the bathroom to get out of his way!

The Indians didn't know what to make of me. I didn't have enough hair and I was too thin. We went to that coming of age party and had to dance. We tried dancing together and couldn't quite get our feet to work with the music.

I remember late talks on the balcony after your parents went to bed and visits to the rooftop to get some relief from the heat and enjoy the view.

I enjoyed visiting Colombia and experiencing a little bit of your life there. I sang at church one Sunday and also tried to jump off that bridge but didn't have the courage. I did manage to attract quite a crowd, though.

March 31, 2006 ✍ *Lynette's Memories*

I'M SITTING AT THE KITCHEN TABLE WATCHING THE DOWNY WOOD-pecker and the rain drizzling down. It's a dark, wet day, but we're warm inside. You're sitting at the table listening to your Bible tapes. I'm remembering several hunting trips to Wyoming with your family. We had the camper and your mom did a great job with meals. How beautiful the sky was in the early morning hours when all the stars shone bright and you felt as though you could reach up and touch them. We looked all over for a moose and then one day we came upon a mother and her young one. You asked Wayne where to shoot it. You brought the mother down and the little one was left to survive on her own. You didn't want your mom to know about the baby, knowing that she would feel bad. The carcass was hung in a tree and we spent more time looking for a deer for Wayne.

There was another hunting trip with Matt and Erica. Erica and I walked through the woods trying to flush out deer for you. You got a spike bull that time. I had a hard time watching that beautiful animal die, but the meat was very good and tender. I got a license to hunt the first trip, but I never had the opportunity to shoot at anything. It's just as well because I would have had a hard time with killing anything. I enjoyed your pleasure at hunting, though, and enjoy the out-of-doors and camp. Your parents always made the trip so easy for us.

Just after we started dating, Valentine's Day was upon us. I wanted to do something special for you, so I made a cheesecake and brought it over early morning and set it up on a table in the yard with a candle. We sat outside and ate cheesecake and all my baked goods. That delights me. You say mine are so good that it's spoiled your appreciation of other baked goods. You don't know how much I have appreciated such praise from you. I love baking for you and satisfying your sweet tooth.

THIS BRINGS ME TO A SAD PART OF OUR JOURNEY TOGETHER—OUR break-up. I initiated the break-up because it seemed to me you were not serious about me. I still loved you, though, and I missed you so much. You went to stay at Dodds then, passing the days there until your trip to China and around the world came up in June. You started doing things with Crystal Dodds and I was very jealous. You took a trip to Colombia somewhere in there, and came one night to say goodbye to me. You knocked on the bedroom window in the wee hours of the morning and I let you in. You left by the front door. When you returned from Colombia, you brought me a beautiful black leather jacket, which I still have after fifteen years. I was so touched that you would bring me a gift even after we had broken up.

Just before you left for China, we attended Rachel's wedding in Memphis. I was invited and went so that I could say goodbye to you from there. After the wedding I left with Jed Park, who took me to meet my family that was traveling in the South. I was so heartsick at our parting because I didn't know if I would ever see you again.

We were apart for seven months. We kept in touch, though not frequently. I didn't know where you were, but I got a phone card for you so you could call me whenever you wanted to. I was an emotional wreck most of the time you were away. I still loved you and I missed you terribly.

Then one day you came back. Your cousin Laurie called me to tell me you were back. This was January of 1992. I knew then that you were back in the area, but I didn't know how or what you were thinking about me. You came to the door one day, and I was so happy to see you again.

I was ready to continue our relationship and so were you. On February 29, after Katherine and Doug's wedding, you proposed to me on the front steps of the Wild West house. You had a beautiful ring for me—I didn't even know you were looking at rings—and the proposal came as a complete surprise to me.

You wanted to get married in June because that was when your parents would be back from Colombia. That meant we had four months to get ready. It was a frantic period. During that time we made the trip to Colombia which I wrote about earlier.

Since our church wasn't big enough to hold a wedding in, we had to find another church to use. We found a Lutheran Church in Glen Ellyn that was willing to rent to us, but we had to find somewhere else to hold the reception. We thought to hold that at someone's house and printed that address in our invitation, but two weeks before the wedding, as we were looking for somewhere to spend our first night, we came across this wonderful bed and breakfast in Geneva, and I knew instantly that that was where I wanted the reception held. The garden was lovely and there was a pool there. We were able to book the place on short notice and simply handed out sheets with a change of address at the wedding itself.

In preparing for the wedding, one of our issues was the wedding cake. I wanted a real showpiece and had found a picture of one in a magazine. I had learned of a place that would make it for $300. When you found that out, you were very upset and said it was too expensive and wouldn't even be enough to feed everyone. I cried and said something to the effect of you not caring about my need to have a beautiful cake. You said you could make it for much less. So, I let it go and you and your mom did a magnificent job on the three layers. I had Pat Swindle make the flowers and had birds to go on top of the cake. It was so beautiful and I was so proud of you for doing such a great job. You made that same cake again for Doug and April's wedding later that year.

Our wedding and rehearsal dinner were amazing. We had the rehearsal dinner at the Wheaton College dining hall with about 75 people. I had put together a slide show of our lives and had Tim help me put it together with music. Others did skits on our relationship. We were all dressed Wild West for the occasion and had a great time.

The next day was Sunday. Our wedding was in the afternoon. We had a rehearsal for the wedding the evening before and everything had gone smoothly. Our processional music was from the movie *Henry V*, "Not unto us, O Lord, but to Thy name give glory." That was our wish for our marriage, and it was a wonderful beginning.

We each had six attendants and they processed down the aisle as couples with that wonderful music being sung by a men's chorus in the background. We had a trumpet as well. You walked alone down the aisle, as did Fr. Doug. We also had two banners in our procession. I walked down with my father and met you at the front.

We had met earlier for pictures so I had already seen you that day. How handsome you were in your tuxedo. I was so proud of you. During the wedding it was as though I was passing through a dream. I was getting married! I felt the uncertainty of what marriage would be, but I also felt the joy of being with you. I feel that joy now has grown from a small seed into a glorious tree. Our marriage has become such a beautiful thing. You said you would remain faithful "in sickness and in health" and so it has proven true, for I am desperately sick and you have remained steadfast, filling our lives with joy each day as you draw strength from our Lord. You are a marvelous husband, so true, so worthy, so noble, so good. I delight in you and what you have become over the years of our being together. I have been shaped by you in my thoughts and character. I'm sorry the process has been so slow and I have caused you many heartaches along the way.

I'm so glad I married you that day. You have been such a good companion on this journey of life.

Our wedding concluded with earnest "I do's" and we went out to our bed and breakfast for our reception. As people lined up for food, we met them and greeted them all. There was a tent there from a wedding on the previous day and tables and chairs. My mom and dad had decorated bird cages for each table. The food tables, too, were beautifully arranged and decorated, and the food was good—some of it even gleaned, like the smoked sausage—but the cake was the highlight of the evening—your creation!

You rolled up your pants and sat with some of your groomsmen dangling your feet in the pool. I came and sat on your lap.

We cut the cake and shared a bite. I think you smashed it into my face. We were relaxed and enjoyed visiting with people. We stayed so long that we didn't have a bang-up departure. We just slipped out through the gate and went to our car for a drive. Since we were staying the night at that bed and breakfast, we just made a pretext of going away. I remember that we drove to Bobbie Spense's house. Then we went back to our bed and breakfast for our honeymoon night. You kept worrying about the Wild West guys coming and discovering us there. They never did, despite the fact that they seemed to have an idea that we were planning to stay there. . . .

The rest of our honeymoon was so fun and so interesting. I enjoyed our time at Mansion Hill Inn despite the fact that you were not feeling well. The place was so sumptuous and I felt very pampered to be there. I have to say, though, that our return visit last year was a magnificent experience, such a wonderful time of bonding in every way. I think it was deepened by my repentance, my recognizing my willfulness over the years, and my acknowledging my lack of respect for your headship. I thank God for opening my eyes to so many of my weaknesses and for paving a path toward real love and companionship. Mansion Hill Inn will always serve as a touchstone in our lives—part of our beginning and part of our healing.

Back to our honeymoon—I enjoyed so many aspects of our travels—our lazy days of exploring Antigua, its historic aspects and its good food and coffee. It was fun to rent a car and drive through the hills to Chichicastenango. I can't remember exactly where we had that nice hotel room. Was it there or somewhere else in the district I enjoyed the bazaar and shopping for carpets. Our biggest delight, though, was Tikal, which we flew to. Our room was nothing to speak of there, but the ruins were incredible. How fun it was to explore those mysterious edifices and imagine them a thousand years ago, alive with markets and bazaars, temple worship and most likely infant sacrifices. Our favorite thing was to sit on a high point in one of the temples at dusk and watch the toucans with their brightly colored beaks fly by. In the background we heard the screeching monkeys bid farewell to daylight and welcome night time. The jungle definitely came alive at night with a whole different community of creatures. For us, it was time to retire.

You did scare me quite a bit with your fearlessness. You didn't mind running up the steeply sloping staircases that ran up hundreds of stairs into the upper chambers of the temples. And there were no railings. I couldn't do it. You were not bothered at all by the narrow walkways that bordered those upper chambers and dropped dozens of feet into the trees below. I've always been afraid of such things. Today this fearlessness emerges especially in the mountains of Albania, where you have spent so many hours navigating our Land Rover over roads that some people would call by names other than "roads." You have always made us feel safe with you. Not that I haven't asked you to slow down sometimes, but that doesn't come from a lack of confidence in your driving. It grows out of my own fear of heights.

August 10, 2006 ❧ *Lynette's Memories*

I'M WRITING FROM CAMP AT ST. JOHN VLADIMIR MONASTERY. I haven't written for a while because of being occupied with other things in Albania. Last night you told me over drinks at the coffee shop up the road that Katie Zahasky at Mayo said I had very little time left to live—possibly a few weeks. The news came as a shock and made me cry. Now I feel a desperate urgency to finish the things that I started earlier in the States. Things I want you to remember me by. I'm recording some songs, which some of the girls have asked for. I want to finish this book of our memories together, and I want to complete a photo memory book for Katherine. Tristan's is almost done, for which I am very grateful. I pray that God will give me the strength and wits to complete these things.

We left Tikal after two splendid days and went to Belize to enjoy some time at the seacoast. Taking the advice of a local, we went out to one of the islands and rented a little room. There wasn't much to the island, but the beach was beautiful. In the night, however, a storm blew in a swarm of sand gnats, which we didn't know about. In the wee hours of the morning we both started to get bitten quite badly by these tiny black insects that we could hardly see, but we were covered with them. We tried all sorts of things to try to escape them. We put on our own bathing suits and jumped into the sea, leaving only our heads above water. Unfortunately, the mosquitoes were out in a thick fog and they tormented us to the point where we got out of the water and ran back to our room. Then we tried standing in the shower and running water on ourselves. That helped for a while but we knew we couldn't stay in the shower forever. Our final attempt actually did work. We got dressed and jumped back into bed under just the top sheet and then sealed the sheet down on all sides. At last, we had cut ourselves off from the gnats. But we couldn't really spend the last two days of our honeymoon under a sheet, so we got off that island as quickly as we could and went to one of the biggest, well-touristed islands, got a hotel room with an air conditioner and made ourselves very comfortable.

Those last days of our honeymoon were quite blissful. We enjoyed a number of really fun outings. We went snorkeling and spear fishing and had lunch cooked for us on a quiet beach under palm trees. I bought a bikini—my first ever, and very self-consciously wore it on our outings. We went for boat rides and just generally enjoyed the water. Our bodies were completely sunburned, and this, coupled with the bites, made us pretty uncomfortable.

Our trip back to Guatemala City to catch our plane to the States was very convoluted. We caught a tiny little plane from our island to the mainland of Belize. From there we made the milk run through Central America, stopping in almost every country until we arrived in Guatemala City. We saw far more of Central America than we had ever hoped to see, all the while restless in our seat because of sunburn and bites. (I had about 300 of them.)

After arriving back in the States from our honeymoon, we set up house in Winfield. We had rented part of a home that had been designed to house aging parents, but the parents didn't want to live there. It was a nice space for us with two large rooms, a bedroom, bathroom, and kitchen, plus a back porch, which served as our entrance. For the most part our rent was paid in labor. You worked for Judy, remodeling her house or building her furniture in exchange for rent. I think it was a good arrangement for both sides. You did really good work for her and I think she was pleased.

We enjoyed using the tennis courts across the street and tried to increase our skills in that field. I took great delight in seeing the deer that often dallied in the field across the street.

Those three years spent in Winfield were mostly years of transition. We wanted to be missionaries, but were trying to reconcile that with being Orthodox. We just couldn't seem to figure out what, if anything, the Orthodox were doing in missions. You felt very strongly that you couldn't be Orthodox if you couldn't do missions with them. We asked questions of many prominent Orthodox people about what the Orthodox were doing in missions, and no one seemed able to give an adequate answer.

It wasn't until I met Christine Kouros and Betty Sellas that we finally found some people who had gone on several short-term trips with the Orthodox Christian Mission Center. Through these young women I was able to meet Fr. Couchell, who at that time was director of the OCMC. Through him we discovered how to "apply" to the OCMC. The mission center was very much in its infancy then, and we had to pay a dear price to help in its growth process. You know all that so I won't write about it here, but that long, painful process was good preparation for us in learning how to work in a truly "byzantine" context. After more than ten years, however, we are still trying to learn how to unwrap the layers and layers of complexities and inconsistencies of the Byzantine mindset.

By the grace of God, and through the help of Fr. Peter Gillquist and Fr. George Scoulas, we were eventually accepted as candidates with the OCMC. It was in May of 1995 that we received that memorable call from Fr. Luke Veronis, asking us if we could come to Albania in four months to teach at the Resurrection of Christ Theological Academy. We looked at each other and said, "Yes," and then I said, "Where is Albania?"

I want to back up a bit and write some more about our time in Winfield. Those years you worked for Pat Lewis in construction and remodeling. Your days were long and tiring and often you came home around 6 or 7 PM and just crashed on our living room carpet. In winter you worked in harsh, cold weather and would tell me afterwards about running around the tops of ice-covered walls. Summers were hot and sweat-drenching. You had to be careful about dehydration and sunstroke or you'd get those dreadful headaches, which you have only in recent years learned how to manage. Those headaches used to make you terribly ill with vomiting and pain all over. . . .

Those years have paid off well for you because you gained many skills in the construction field, especially in plumbing and electricity. These have been very valuable in solving problems in Albania.

I was working at Wheaton College when we got married, and I was very satisfied with my job in graphic design. However, in volunteering as the designer and illustrator for *Touchstone* Magazine, I felt it might be much better if I devoted more time to that project. I proposed therefore, that *Touchstone* hire me part-time and that I try freelancing for the rest of the time. *Touchstone* agreed to my proposal, and I began to drive into Chicago two days a week to work on the magazine. This was in the days when we were still running calque and pasting up the pages on board. The illustrations I did were created from home and then photographed and pasted up. It was a long and tedious process, but I was very happy working for *Touchstone*. I can't say that I did very well in the area of freelancing.

I'm not sure how much more I will be able to write, nor how lucid I will be. I'm dying now; I have only a little bit of time left. I'm sorry because I could have written more faithfully. I'll try to go on . . .

CHAPTER 7

Return to Her Adopted Homeland ⁊⁊

IN JANUARY, LYNETTE AND NATHAN BEGAN DISCUSSING THE POSSIBIL-
ity of returning to Albania. The onset of her depression and subsequent
period of darkness postponed that possibility. As she realized that her
health was continuing to deteriorate and that death appeared imminent,
Lynette didn't want to just sit around waiting to die. Following Easter and
the slow journey out of depression, Lynette and Nathan began discussing
anew the possibilities and consequences of returning to Albania.

Lynette, however, knew that her mother did not have much time to live.
In July 2005, doctors thought her mother Marce would only live for a few
months at best. She surprised everyone, though, by surviving for a final
family reunion over Christmas, and then living on into the spring. Lynette
strongly wanted to be present for the end of her mother's life, but simultaneously she realized that her own life was ebbing away. Unbeknown to
Lynette or Nathan, Lynette's cancer had already begun to metastasize into
her liver. Had they known this fact, the decision to leave American medical care and return to Albania would have been much harder to make.
Yet under the providence of God, this fact remained hidden, allowing the
Hoppes to make their decision to return to their adopted homeland. As
Lynette would often say, "When I die, I want to die in the saddle. I want to
be active until my final days, instead of lying in a bed waiting for death."

With this understanding, Lynette and Nathan made the decision to return to Albania on May 17, 2006. Of course, other factors contributed to this major decision. Lynette knew that Nathan would continue to serve as a missionary after she died, and thus, she wanted to help her children transition back into life in Albania while she was still alive. As she and Nathan discussed where he would bury her, she desired to be placed somewhere where her children would have easy access to visit their mother's grave. She also had a strong desire to see her Albanian family and be active in ministry once again.

May 27, 2006 🕮 *Website Posting*

I'M SITTING AT NATHAN'S DESK IN ALBANIA AND AM LOOKING around his office. Everything is so familiar—the computer, the book-lined cabinets, the maps on the walls. It's as though we were never away. Our old habits are still in place, too. In the kitchen, I still keep walking over near the stove to throw things in the trash, but the trash can has moved. The last residents moved it, but I haven't caught on yet. The children are rediscovering their old toys and all the creatures that live in the courtyard—the ants, the snails, the lizards. This morning they found four snails of different sizes and made up a family: a father, a mother, a sister and brother. The snails went into a box called "home" and were doused with leaves to eat. The children are playing as though a day hasn't passed since they last went hunting for bugs in this place.

The sounds are familiar, too: the ringing of the doorbell, the neighborhood children calling to each other, the chirping of the sparrows in the orange trees next door, the whine of the water pump, the click of the electricity coming back. We are home and it feels so comfortable.

We knew we were back the first morning when our crippled neighbor, Maro, who is 76 years old and scoots herself around on a small stool, came banging on the gate early in the morning before we were awake. "I'm sick," she said. "Open the door." It was so familiar.

People have been stopping by to greet us, welcoming us with sincere joy and enthusiasm, and bringing gifts of chocolates, flowers, and ice cream. We feel loved and needed. Everyone is offering help, whether it is for house cleaning, meal preparation, shopping, or baby-sitting. My housekeeper is back with us, and she is a huge blessing. I couldn't do anything without her help before, and I am in much greater need of it now.

We've jumped right into the work. Our first Saturday was spent driving to the seminary to see the university students who were attending their spring conference. We went with them to the beach for the afternoon. The kids played in the water and built sand castles while we visited. It was a glorious afternoon. I loved feeling the sea breeze tangle my hair as I listened to the girls express their needs and concerns over coffee at an outdoor, seaside restaurant. I understood most of the conversation in Albanian and was glad I had not lost all my facility in the language.

Nathan is holding meetings to organize the children's camps in Kosovo this June and is working to hire more help for the national children's office so that day camps can be held around Tirana this summer. We feel the urgency to try to accomplish something while we are here, but things take time. Nothing is ever simple.

We thank God for the opportunity to be back. I have been feeling quite well and have been able to rest a fair amount. Tristan and Katherine are still adjusting to the time zone. They are falling asleep late and rising late, but that will change gradually. They don't have to get up for school now, so I'm not worrying about the late hours. Tristan is a bit fearful at night and we would ask you to pray for him, that he would overcome his fear and be able to fall asleep more easily.

We are especially in need of your prayers here. We feel ourselves to be on the front lines. Satan held this place in his grip for many years under the old regime, and he does not relinquish his territory without a fight. Thank God, he is already defeated, but he opposes mightily the work of our Lord. Pray that we will be faithful and will do the will of God in all things with grace and joy.

June 7, 2006 ❧ *Website Posting*

WE ARE APPROACHING THE END OF OUR THIRD WEEK IN ALBANIA. How rapidly the days are passing, and how much we feel the urgency to do something with the days that we have. Nathan is working with the leaders of our National Children's Office to organize four camps in Kosovo, which will begin the third week of June and continue through the first week of July. He and 25 young people, most from our seminary, will be away for two weeks. I have considered carefully whether or not I can manage by myself with him away, and I think we can do it, with the help of a few friends who have promised to look after me. He will be an eight-hour drive away and accessible by phone, so that if need be he can return to us in a day's drive. I am assisting this work by creating logos to be used as theme pieces for T-shirts, banners, and craft projects.

I have been feeling fairly well, thank God, and have been so pleased to have had the energy to visit the seminary and see the students, attend discussions with university students in their newly purchased student center, catch up with old friends, and participate in two weddings.

The children are very happy here and are delighted to be playing once more with their old friends. We are giving thought to their education for this fall, should it be that we are able to stay longer than the summer. We visited a very good school organized by the Protestant missionary community in Tirana and would be very pleased to have our children attend this school. We would appreciate your prayers for this. It appears that the school does not grant Orthodox missionaries the same discount that they give to the Protestant missionaries, and the full price is extremely high for missionary budgets such as ours. Nathan is going to appeal to the board to see if they would reconsider this policy. If they do not, we would have to pay the same fees as those for the diplomatic community.

There are many difficulties associated with life and work here, both within the church and without, and we are encountering a lot of discouragement among our fellow workers. It is hard not to get discouraged along with them, as the difficulties are very real and very distressing. We want to try to rise above these stumbling blocks, looking to Jesus rather than giving in to the circumstances, and becoming, by the grace of God, a source of encouragement to those around us. Please pray that we would have the strength to do this.

One of the struggles that all missionaries have is how and when to help the many people that come to our door asking for help. This is never easy, nor simple, and the poor oftentimes are very demanding and persistent. We need love and wisdom to see in these sufferers the face of Jesus, and not become frustrated by the many requests and needs that confront us.

Another program that is being organized by our National Children's Office is four-day kids' clubs. We are planning to hire a newly married young couple from our seminary to implement this program, which will consist of games, singing, crafts, and Bible stories. These will be held at different locations around the city. We held the first of such programs at our own home with the neighborhood children two years ago, and this continued in our absence last year with fellow missionaries who were staying in our house. We hope to hold eight such clubs this summer, including the one at our own house. The plan is to have ongoing contact with these children during the school year by organizing weekly activities for them, perhaps in the same locations. Please pray that we will be able to find eight places to hold these clubs.

We have such an overwhelming sense here that without prayer, all of our work is in vain. We must abide in the Vine, who is our Lord, for without Him, truly we can do nothing, at least nothing that counts for the Kingdom of Heaven.

Thank you so much for praying for us. We are so happy and so blessed to be given the opportunity to serve once more this Church and people whom we love. May God grant us many years. We appreciate also your financial support, which makes it possible for us to be here.

June 16, 2006   *Website Posting*

I SPOKE WITH MY SISTER BY PHONE LAST NIGHT. SHE HAS BEEN caring for our mom this past week and said that mom is failing very quickly now. She is so weak that she can hardly walk. Her mind is becoming more confused and she is struggling with anxiety. After speaking with my sister, I was overwhelmed by sadness. Throughout the dark hours of the night, I wrestled with the thought that perhaps

I should not have left my mom. The realization that I would not be present with her to say goodbye hit me hard, and I wept at the travesty of that first sin which brought death and separation into our world.

We knew that in returning to Albania we had put our hands to the plow, as it were, and should not look back with regret or longing. We felt strongly in coming back that we were following the will of God, and we have since had this confirmed many times over, but this does not erase the sadness of being separated from my mother as she approaches death. It does, however, allay any fear that we made a mistake in coming back to Albania.

God, in his goodness, granted me a great consolation. It seems that my 96-year-old grandmother so desires to see her daughter one more time that she is undertaking the long ride from Montana to Minnesota to visit her ailing child. My aunt and uncle will drive her, and they will be arriving sometime today (June 15). Additionally, on Saturday, my mom's brother and his wife will arrive for a week-long visit. This means that perhaps at death my mom will be surrounded by her family, as well as having my sister and my father present. My joy at the prospect of this unexpected reunion lifted my sadness considerably.

I have been enjoying many good days here. God has given me strength and energy, for which I am extremely grateful, as it allows me to participate in many different activities. One of these, which occurred at the beginning of this week, was the graduation ceremony for our fourth-year seminary students. Although we were away for three semesters, Nathan had played a significant role in the lives of these students during their first two-and-a-half years in school. He had been demanding as a teacher, but his efforts to push his students academically and spiritually had been appreciated. These graduates are a very promising group of young people, and Nathan hopes to hire several of them for ministry with university students and children.

I have been attending the weekly meeting of the university students on Tuesday evenings. Despite the fact that the students are in an exam period, many are still taking time from their studies to come for fellowship and to hear a speaker. I was asked to speak this week on what I have experienced through my illness, something I was glad to share. In preparing for this talk, I read through all of my old updates that had been posted to the website and in doing so, relived many of the same joys and struggles I had experienced at the time I wrote. I was reminded again of the grace and goodness of God in our lives over the past 18 months and the generosity of so many people through their faithful prayers and giving.

Fr. Luke Veronis arrived in Albania two days ago for a nine-day visit. He is here to unite in holy matrimony a young man from his church in Massachusetts to one of our young women here, a match orchestrated by him and his wife, Faith. It is wonderful to have Fr. Luke back. He addressed our mission team last night and encouraged us in our ministries to focus on relationships more than on projects. It was a very good reminder of where to put our efforts. I think of this often for myself. Since I don't have much energy, I can only do a few things. Trying to discern what is most valuable is not always easy, but I know that people are always important. I am reminded of Jesus' reply to the man who asked what was the greatest commandment. "To love the Lord your God with all your heart, mind and soul" was his reply, and then he added, "and to love your neighbor as yourself." This is a good guide for my life here. I must pour out my heart in devotion to Christ and then allow his love to flow back through me to others. It sounds simple, but I know I get in the way sometimes and block the current of that love, especially when I am tired or frustrated. The needs of people rarely come at convenient times.

June 28, 2006   ❧   *Website Posting*

(The Death of Lynette's Mother)

"Precious in the sight of the Lord is the death of His saints."

Psalm 116:15

WHEN THE PHONE RANG JUST AFTER MIDNIGHT LAST SUNDAY MORNing, we didn't at first guess that it was someone from home calling to say that mom had passed away. For the entire week prior to this phone call, I had been calling every day to see how mom was doing and to say a few words to her directly. The last words she had spoken to me a few days earlier were almost incomprehensible because her throat was so dry. She hadn't had food or drink for about four days by then; just a few drops of water squeezed out of a sponge into her mouth to quench her thirst. Swallowing was difficult, and she seemed to choke on what few drops of liquid she took. None of us could believe how tenaciously she clung to life, ready to go, yet unwilling to depart. Now, here it was, the phone call telling of her departure from this life.

Several times during that last week, I sang to mom over the phone. Mom had always liked my voice, and singing hymns and other Christian songs to her enabled me to give something from afar. My sister, who put the phone on "speaker" whenever I called so that mom could hear, said that mom responded to my voice and seemed to be soothed by my singing. One of the songs I sang each time was a hymn called "Finally Home," which speaks of that moment when we reach out and touch the hand of God and find ourselves home. It's a beautiful hymn, and mom had requested that it be sung at her funeral. I sang it to her as she lay dying in the hope that it would comfort her and give her peace in her suffering. When my sister called with the news of mom's death, she asked that I sing that song one last time. Though mom was gone, it would bring comfort to everyone who had now gathered around her to say goodbye: my father, my sister, the eldest of my three brothers, the youngest and his family, my grandmother, two aunts and two uncles. And so I sang,

> *When engulfed by the terrors of tempestuous seas*
> *Unknown waves before you roll.*
> *At the end of doubt and terror is eternity,*
> *Though fear and darkness seize your soul.*
> *But just think of stepping on shore,*
> *And finding it heaven,*
> *Of touching a hand and finding it God's,*
> *Of breathing new air and finding it celestial,*
> *Of waking up in glory and finding it home.*

It is hard for me to comprehend that mom is gone, and because of this, I have not yet grieved her passing. The last time I saw her (about five weeks ago), she was getting up each day and sitting in her chair. She was still able to hold conversations and participate in our afternoon tea parties. I did not see her fade away, nor did I see that last week of suffering as her body broke out in painful bedsores. I did not say my goodbyes to her at her bedside; I said them over the phone, and I did not see them carry her sheet-swathed body out of the house and realize, with a shock, that she would never stand at her door to receive visitors or family as she had done so often before. Her earthly life is over, but I cannot grasp that fact.

The wake will be held this evening, the funeral tomorrow, and the burial on Thursday, but we will not be present for any of these events. I cannot travel alone any more, and it is too hard to travel as a family right now. I was blessed to have a year-and-a-half with mom before she died, something I would not have had were it not for my own illness. How strange it is that I went home to live with my parents so that my mom could help me in my illness, but within six months she was diagnosed with advanced cancer, and I began to help her in her illness. God's ways are incomprehensible.

Our joy and comfort are that mom is with Jesus now, and she is part of that great "cloud of witnesses" that surrounds us. We feel that her prayers for us, which were always made while she lived, will continue even more fervently now that she is in heaven. We, the living, together with those who have died in Christ, constitute the body of Christ, the Church, which is alive and vibrant. We know that we will continue to feel mom's presence, especially during the Divine Liturgy when we come together to join that magnificent worship in heaven, in which mom now participates with joy.

Though we feel great joy for mom now, there have been some painful lessons to learn in the process of watching a loved one die. One of the petitions in the litanies of the Divine Liturgy is "for a Christian end to our lives, painless, blameless and peaceful." I have puzzled over the "painless" aspect of this prayer, wondering if it meant physical painlessness. I'm not sure whether it does or not, but I saw in the case of my mom that she struggled with intense emotional pain at the end because of some things that had happened in her life. I think these things were unresolved for the most part during her life, and I cannot know for sure whether they were resolved at the very end.

It was difficult to watch her struggle with these things and wish so much that she could be completely at peace. The lesson is that we must be reconciled with everyone before we die; we must forgive and receive forgiveness as much as is possible, or all the unresolved pain and conflict will emerge at the end when we can no longer hold up our guard. This multiplies the suffering that almost always accompanies the dying process. When we pray, then, for a "painless, blameless, and peaceful" end to our lives, we need to know that we are praying that we will resolve relational conflicts while we are still able to, so that it will be possible for us to die in peace.

You would think that being around a loved one that is dying would bring out the best in everyone, but the truth is that it brings forward what everyone actually is. All pretenses and good intentions are ripped away in the face of the intense stress that accompanies the dying process, especially when it drags on for months. It is very sobering and humbling to see ourselves as we are and not as we wish we were. I have seen that it is possible to have all of the right Christian words, and yet to remain untransformed and to be dominated by bitterness and anger from the past.

I have been asked many times if facing death causes one to strip away automatically all that is superficial and "unredeemed" in oneself. Perhaps it happens that way for some, but in my case, I have had to be very intentional about it. I have been very disappointed with myself for not being more transformed through my illness. I still struggle with many of the same flaws in my character and habits, and see that I must still "work out my salvation with fear and trembling" moment-by-moment, day-in and day-out. What is different now, however, is perhaps a sense of urgency. I don't know how much time I have, and I feel the need to share the love of Christ with everyone around me.

Yesterday, I spoke by phone with my youngest brother, and he shared with me that after mom died, her brow, which for many days had been deeply furrowed with pain, suddenly smoothed out, and her mouth, which had hung open for days, broke into a broad smile. He said that they were all amazed to watch this transformation of her countenance, and even the Hospice nurse who was present said that she had never seen such a thing happen before. All who were present at mom's bedside were deeply comforted by what appeared to be a manifestation of mom's joy at meeting her Lord face to face. Also, as mom lay dying, rain had been pelting down outside. After she drew her last breath, the rain slowed and a brilliant rainbow broke out across the sky. My brother said that, again, here was a sign to them that mom was being received with favor in heaven. Hearing his words, I was greatly comforted. Thank God, mom was at peace in a place of joy.

Nathan left for Kosovo this morning (Tuesday, June 27). Last Wednesday, he had taken a group of 25 of our Orthodox young people to Kosovo to hold camps for about 1,800 children from Muslim villages. After arriving, settling in and getting the first camp going, he hopped on a bus and came back to Tirana to be with me in the event of my mother's death. George Russell, a fellow missionary, very kindly drove to Kosovo to stand in for Nathan while he was away. I was so happy that Nathan was with me when I received news of my mother's death. It would have been extremely difficult to bear this without him at my side. Since his arrival home, however, things have arisen that demanded his presence again in Kosovo, so he left after spending three days with us. Please pray for these Kosovo camps and for our young people.

Regarding my health, I have been feeling very well for the entirety of our stay thus far. I did have a bit of a scare last Friday. I woke up in the night with terrible pain in my shoulder and was convinced that the joint was disintegrating. I was afraid that I wouldn't have the use of my arm any more. Thank God, our American co-worker, Dr. Charles Linderman, called the next day to see how I was doing, and when I told him "not well," he stopped by to see me. After examining me, he said that the problem seemed to be an inflammation in the shoulder area, not the disintegration of the bones. I was very relieved to hear that, and have been taking Advil since then as an anti-inflammatory drug. The pain is lessening, and I am feeling much better. Thank you for your prayers. God has been very good to give me such comfortable days and so much energy.

Nathan will be away for the next week-and-a-half. Please pray for us as he is away. Also, most of our other team members have left or will be leaving for the States or Greece this week, and we are feeling quite alone.

Please also remember in your prayers the soul of my mother, Marci, as well as me and my family as we rejoice that mom is with Jesus now, but also grieve that she is no longer with us. God bless you.

July 25, 2006   *Website Posting*

TWO DAYS AGO, I HAD BLOOD DRAWN AT OUR ORTHODOX CLINIC IN Tirana. Dr. Linderman, the American doctor on our team, picked up the results yesterday and brought them to me to discuss the outcome. Amazingly, my hemoglobin, which was what I had been most concerned about, had actually gone up to its highest level in a long time. For this, I was extremely grateful, recognizing in it the grace of God. I would not have to go to Greece or somewhere else for a blood transfusion. (Albania's blood supply is considered unsafe.) All the other tests came out within normal limits except for the liver function indicator, and this was quite alarming. These results indicated that there was cancer activity in the liver, something that hadn't been detected before, or so we thought. In looking over my test results from Mayo Clinic, however, Dr. Linderman said that the last tests I had in the States just before leaving for Albania showed an elevation in the liver function indicator. These had not been pointed out to me at the time, perhaps because we did not meet with a doctor. Nathan observed that perhaps that also was the grace of God, because had we seen those results before leaving we would have had a much more difficult time choosing to come. We have seen again and again how critical it has been for us to be here at this time because of the summer ministries, but also because of a number of serious issues that have arisen and needed our intervention.

It is interesting to be seriously ill and live in a society that refuses to talk openly about illness. Here, when someone asks how I am doing, I almost always say, *mir*, which means, "well," because if I say, *ç'ka* ("so-so"), or *jo mir* ("not well"), I will always be contradicted and told, "no, you *are* doing well." Then I'll be scolded for not thinking positively or reminded that God, of course, will do a miracle. In

Albania, terminally ill people are never told that they are seriously ill, even up until the point of death. They are always told that they will get well. When death comes then, family and friends fall to wailing and crying, as though death had come as a complete surprise. The Orthodox, for the most part, act in exactly the same manner, wailing and weeping as those who have no hope. It is very distressing to observe such things.

How does one balance faith in God's power to heal and acknowledging that very likely, if one has cancer, one will die from the disease? I think one can hold both things at the same time. As I have said before, I firmly believe that I will never get so ill that I will be beyond God's ability to heal me. At the same time, I see that my disease is progressing and I ought to take measures to be prepared to die, perhaps even soon. The fact that I probably have cancer in the liver now makes my death seem even more imminent. With Nathan's help, I am trying to focus not on the painful path that may lie ahead, but on the joys and responsibilities of today. I know I have written about this before, but with each new phase of my illness comes the need to learn many of the same things over again. I hope with each new phase, however, that I am learning the same thing at a deeper level, but I am not sure I can really judge such things.

For example, I remember that God loves me with a depth that I cannot even fathom. This ignites in me an overwhelming sense of joy and the desire to respond to Him with my own love. What I see differently now, however, is that God loves everyone with that same unfathomable love and that I ought to try to see that love in them—especially in those whom I find unlovely or who have wronged or offended me in some way. This forces me to look at them differently. How can I malign someone whom God loves so deeply? I think my comprehension of God's unimaginable holiness also is growing, perhaps with very small steps. I really have such a desire to grasp more of his holiness because I think it is the key to humility. How can I be flippant or arrogant or selfish if I see God in his holiness? As the responses of others reveal, all one can say in the presence of God's holiness is "I am unclean!" This also gives meaning to why we say, "Lord have mercy," so many times in our prayers. What else can we say?

* * *

My mom's death still haunts me. Sometimes I have strange dreams about it. I do not think that I have fully grieved for her. She died during the middle of the Kosovo camps, and although Nathan was with me when we received the news of her passing, he had to return a few days later to Kosovo because of some serious issues that had arisen with the media. While he was away, I had to discipline my mind strictly so that I would not break down with no one around to support me. I didn't know what I would do if I broke down. All the time Nathan was away, almost everyone else from our mission team was also away or left after his departure. It was a strange feeling to be almost alone here, desperately in need of support and floundering a bit to find it. I was able to speak with my sister and brothers on the phone during that time, and that was a big help to me in processing mom's death. The children and I also spent two days with the Linderman family at St. Vlash, about an hour's drive from Tirana, and that was a precious time for us, and good support for me.

It was much harder to be absent from mom's funeral than I ever thought possible. I think we made the right decision in not going home for it, but I realized, perhaps too late, the importance of being able to say farewell to a loved one, and the need to be together with other family members at that time. I don't think I will be able to fully grieve for my mother until I have returned to her house and seen that she is no longer there to welcome me.

I told Nathan last night that I feel a bit homeless right now, despite the fact that we have lived in our present house for almost six years. He said that his mom felt that way after her mother died because there was no longer anyone "to go home to." I suspect that I will feel this way for some time.

* * *

The children's camps in Kosovo, which occupied so much of Nathan's time and attention in June, went very well. Under Nathan's direction, twenty-five of our young people organized camps for 1,250 children in three different locations. As I mentioned in my previous update, George Russell also went to Kosovo to assist with our team, particularly during Nathan's absence. He had such a wonderful time there that he ended up staying almost the entire time. Our staff members wore T-shirts printed with the name of the Orthodox Church of Albania, and this caused a big stir in town. Several newspaper articles were printed, accusing our group of doing religious propaganda in the schools. Nathan and the other leaders of the camp were able to meet the mayor of the town as well as leaders from the government to explain our presence there and what our program was. He also met with several reporters, who ended up publishing very positive articles about our camp program and the role of the Orthodox Church of Albania in reaching out to these Muslim children. Nathan was extremely pleased with how our leaders handled a very volatile situation during his absence, but our young people were extremely relieved to have Nathan back. At the end of our group's time in Kosovo, relations with the town and the media were very favorable. A very positive article, complete with four large photographs, was published recently in a local Albanian newspaper. This favorable publicity comes at a critical time when the Church is suffering through some very negative press, something that has brought much grief to the Archbishop.

My summers in Albania have always been spent preparing for and attending our girls' camps, which are held at a monastery about an hour's drive from Tirana. My primary responsibilities have been to organize and direct the craft project and also to give talks as needed on the camp's theme.

This year, our craft project is making hemp bracelets and necklaces decorated with beads. We've just completed the junior high girls' camp, and so far the craft project has been a big hit. The girls loved making the bracelets and wearing them around camp or keeping them as gifts to give to others. I was so pleased by their enthusiasm and hope to have similar results in the second and third camps. I will be giving a talk on the camps' main theme, "Be not overcome by evil, but overcome evil with good," a fantastic passage in Romans 12, and I would appreciate your prayers as I prepare over the next week for this.

We have a very tangible example at our camp of trying to overcome evil with good. At present, the "overcoming with good" has yet to be realized. Let me explain.

From the very first summer that our camps have been held at this monastery, we have had trouble with our water supply. In the beginning, the village in which the monastery is located complained that we were using too much water and depleting the supply for the local residents. All of this was very strange because before we started holding our camps at the monastery, our church did a project to provide the village with plenty of water. The project was successful and should have solved the water problems for the entire village. In our case, however, it didn't seem to work as we were continuing to run out of water and had to buy it from a neighbor.

Last week, during our first camp, we ran out of water again. Fault was placed on a group of workers who had mixed concrete using water from the monastery's reservoir and had spread it around a new bathroom that was being constructed outside the church. Simple math showed, however, that the amount of water needed to mix the concrete was minimal compared to the size of our two water tanks. The workers couldn't possibly have used up the water. For the first time in all my years at camp, Nathan was with us this year. Knowing of his skills in plumbing and electricity (and math!), and being confident that there ought to be an adequate supply of water for us and the village, I begged him to get involved in solving this persistent problem. What he discovered, after insisting that the main water line near our pipe be dug up, was that the valve between the main water line and the 3-inch pipe that runs to the monastery's reservoir was almost completely closed. This meant that our tank was never able to get an adequate supply of water to fill. Someone had turned the valve almost closed and then had buried it so that no one would know of its existence. All the evidence pointed to an employee of the monastery, who is brother to the one whose water we have purchased each summer to make up for our shortage.

The sad thing about this case is that this man who closed the valve watched our girls suffer by having no water to bathe in, and saw our kitchen piled with unwashed dishes and marred by a filthy floor. He saw all this and did nothing to relieve the suffering around him, knowing that he had the key (or rather, the valve) to relieve it—and all that to win a few dollars. The ironic thing is that, in the first place, the water he sold to us was a gift to him from the Church.

What do we do in this case? There is nothing to be gained by accusing this employee, as he would deny any guilt. There is nothing to be gained by firing him because there is no guarantee that the next employee would be any different. All we can do is open the valve and keep an eye on it until the camps are over. The monastery does not have any permanent residents. We need water only for the girls' camps, which run for about six weeks of the year. The rest of the year, anyone who chooses can close the valve, and it would not be a problem for us.

Regardless of what we do, we need to remember that God deeply loves this man whom we think guilty. Perhaps God will have more pity on him because he is poor and acts out of his poverty. May God help us also to have pity on him and any others that we feel have "wronged us" (or the Church, as in this case).

What does it mean to overcome evil with good? That is a question to be answered many times over as we face evil in this world. Evil has no scruples, and we may get hurt in the process of trying to do good. We cannot forget that Christ, who is the Good One, was killed for doing good. Of course, Christ's death was necessary because it was through this that evil was overcome. Nonetheless, evil rebelled against the good that it confronted in Jesus, and appeared to have "won" when it crucified the Lord. Thank God, it was otherwise.

* * *

We are hoping to put our children in an English-speaking missionary kids' school this September. For some reason, the policy of the school is to charge non-Protestant missionaries at the diplomatic rate, which is 60% more than rates charged to Protestant missionaries. We are going to try to appeal to the board on this and would ask for your prayers. The school is a good one and we would be very pleased to have our children enrolled in it. I am not up for home-schooling the kids any more, so that isn't an option this year.

We continue to be very grateful for your prayers and support, which make our work in Albania possible. Things seem to be particularly challenging and discouraging right now, so we appreciate your prayers even more. God bless you.

Overcoming Evil with Good

THIS WEEK, WE HAVE BEEN DISCUSSING A PASSAGE IN ROMANS chapter 12 that describes for us what a Christian should look like, or, in other words, it paints "a portrait of a Christian." This does not mean that all Christians will look exactly alike—some will be more advanced than others and will resemble more closely this portrait; others will have farther to go and thus will not look very much like it. But all should be striving to become more and more like it.

The part of the portrait that I have been assigned comes in the last verse of the chapter and in many ways summarizes the passage. "Do not be overcome by evil, but overcome evil with good." This may seem like a very simple statement, but the truth is that evil sometimes can be very difficult to identify. Remember that the devil often disguises himself as an angel of light. Therefore, it is easy for us to be deceived, especially if we are not paying attention to our spiritual lives.

Let's start with a question. How can we learn to recognize evil? Since we may not immediately recognize evil when we confront it, especially if everyone around us seems to think the evil is fine, then we must train ourselves to identify evil, or we may not see it until it is too late and we have gotten ourselves entangled in it.

I think the keys to learning how to recognize evil are given to us at the beginning of this chapter—chapter 12 of the book of Romans. I want us to look at these keys now. I see four of them. The first two are found in verses one and two. Let's read them now.

"I appeal to you therefore, brethren, by the mercies of God, to present your bodies as a living sacrifice, holy and acceptable to God, which is your spiritual worship. Do not be conformed to this world but be transformed by the renewal of your mind, that you may prove what is the will of God, what is good and acceptable and perfect."

A Living Sacrifice

The first key, then, is to present our bodies as a living sacrifice. What exactly does this mean? In the eleven chapters of the book of

Romans that precede this passage, St. Paul describes everything that Christ has done to bring about our salvation through his death and resurrection. Now he stops and says, "Therefore, brethren . . ." Or we might put his words this way, "Now let me tell you what your response should be to the incredible things that Christ has done: 'Present your bodies as a living sacrifice.'"

This image of the sacrifice comes from the Old Testament, when the Jewish people brought animals or birds to the temple to be laid on the altar and burned so that they might have forgiveness for their sins. When Christ died on the cross, the need for animal sacrifices ended because Christ was the final sacrifice for sins. In the Eucharist we participate in the sacrifice of Christ on the cross and are then given Christ's body and blood to feed our souls.

In response to this great work of Christ as our sacrifice for sins, we are called by St. Paul to put ourselves on the altar as a living sacrifice, which is holy and acceptable to God. This doesn't happen one time only; we must present ourselves over and over again in love. In so doing, we say with all our heart, "Lord, I give myself to you," and we give over control of our lives to Christ. This is called our spiritual worship.

So, the first key to recognizing evil, then, is to present our bodies to Christ as a living sacrifice. This means to place ourselves in his hands and his care, to come to him continuously, giving ourselves completely to him.

Be Transformed by the Renewing of Your Mind

The second key to recognizing evil is given to us in verse two. St. Paul goes on to say, "Do not be conformed to this world, but be transformed by the renewal of your mind, that you may prove what is the will of God, what is good and acceptable and perfect."

The second key to knowing how to recognize evil has two parts. The first is to not allow ourselves to be conformed to this world. What does this mean? It means that we must not allow the world to shape what we become. We cannot allow the attitudes and behaviors of those around us to turn us into something that is not Christian.

Nathan spoke the other night about one of these areas—that is, the area of sexual relationships. To emphasize this again, I urge you not to let yourselves be formed by what your friends say, or what the TV or movies portray, if these are contrary to what the Holy Scriptures say. To be different from your friends is very hard because you want to be accepted by your friends and don't want to be identified as different. If your friends are influencing you to do or say bad things, find different friends. I know that it is easy to say this but very hard to do, but you must take it seriously, for friends do have a great deal of influence over us. To not be conformed requires that one be a little bit tough. Each of us has been created as a unique person, and only when we pursue a relationship with Christ are we able to become that truly unique person.

The second part of this key is to be transformed by a renewed mind. It is only through the grace of God that we can be changed into this portrait of a Christian, and this comes by allowing ourselves to be transformed by Christ. As we are transformed we will begin to see what is the good and perfect will of God. In this case, the will of God is not so much knowing what God wants us to do, but knowing what he wants us to become. Our mind can become renewed through prayer and studying the Scriptures, but also through exposing ourselves to people who are more mature in their faith. We learn from their experiences and in turn become transformed by their examples. We also can be transformed by participating in the Eucharist because it is a channel of God's grace to us and brings healing of soul and mind according to our faith. We learn to recognize evil by becoming familiar with what is good. Evil doesn't have its own existence. It is simply the absence of good, and since God is good, it is, in a sense, the absence of God.

The process of being transformed is something that will occur throughout our lives. It is not something that we will ever finish; therefore, we must recognize our need to be continually transformed into the likeness of Christ, we must pray for it, and God will show us in what ways we need to be changed. This is a work that involves the grace of God plus our own efforts. As we make efforts to become more like Christ, we free him to shower us with his grace. If we make no efforts, then his work in us is stifled and suppressed.

I am always disappointed with myself when I see how much I still need transformation, especially in the area of patience with my children. When the children do not obey, or fight with one another, it is very easy for me to get upset with their behavior and to speak with them impatiently. I know that I need to continue to pray for transformation in this area, and also to work much harder at it. Before I say anything to correct my children, I need to ask God for patience; I need to remember that they are still children and will behave immaturely. I also need to be more consistent with them and to follow up on them more closely. For example, if I tell them not to do something and they do it anyway, there need to be some immediate consequences, but sometimes there isn't time or I don't feel up to disciplining them. In neglecting to follow through, however, I teach them that it is okay to disobey because I, their mother, am not going to do anything about it anyway.

The second key to learning how to recognize evil has two aspects, one negative and one positive: first, do not be conformed to this world, but second, be transformed through a renewed mind.

The Third Key Is Humility

In verse three, St. Paul bids his readers "not to think more highly of themselves than they ought, but to look on themselves with sober judgment." We need to recognize in ourselves that we are capable of doing any or all of the most terrible things. We must not think that somehow we are above doing wrong. Even the best or the most spiritual among us, if he or she is not vigilant about his or her soul, can do great wrong, usually beginning with small things. Rarely does one fall suddenly into terrible sin. It usually happens slowly over time, by giving in in small areas. We must be very sober and see this in ourselves. Also we must be careful not to judge others and to be quick to see that we could do the same things that we think are so bad in them. If we train ourselves to think of the holiness of God, we will be very sober in our judgment because we will know that compared to Him we fall very short in goodness.

So, the third key to recognizing evil is humility—not to think more highly of ourselves than we ought and to remember always that we are capable of falling into evil ourselves if we are not vigilant in caring for our souls and seeking the grace of God in our lives.

The Final Key

The fourth key to recognizing evil is found in verse five. "We, though many, are one body in Christ, and individually members one of another." The body of Christ referred to here is the Church. We need the church—we need each other as Christians. We cannot stand alone. This is why the church is given to us, so that we can stand together. Think of a single thread—how easy it is to break a single strand of thread, but if you put together many threads and make a rope, you have something very strong that can hold together against great pressure and weight. So it is with us. If we stand together with many others, we are much stronger than if we stand alone. In this way, in the Church, we can stand together to resist evil. But each one in the Church must be seeking good individually so that we bring together good to stand against evil.

Also, in our churches we will find those who have more experience in walking with Christ and more wisdom about what is good, so they can help us learn to recognize that which is not good in our societies and in our lives. We must be humble and listen to their counsel, which is for our good. Unfortunately, here in Albania, I see that there is not a strong sense of community in our churches. We do not look for our support from the Church; we look for it from our friends, who do not always lead us on a good path. Or we look for it from our families. I hope and pray that our churches in Albania will grow into strong communities that will serve as lights in an evil world, and that within these churches we will have strong youth groups that will help encourage young people to walk on the path to Christ. You can begin to help build communities in your churches by forming friendships with those within the church and striving to form a group of youth that can support each other.

Our fourth key to recognizing evil is to stand together as Christians and to gain wisdom from others in the church.

Now we are prepared with our four keys, which are (1) to present ourselves as a living sacrifice; (2) not to be conformed to this world, but to be transformed by a renewal of the mind; (3) humility; (4) to stand together as Christians and gain wisdom from those more mature.

We need to ask another question at this point: What is evil? Evil is the absence of Good. To overcome evil we must make a practice of doing good. Evil is darkness. Therefore, even the smallest light can overcome darkness. We must be lights in this dark world. Try an experiment sometime. Go into a room at night and take a candle and matches with you. Turn off all the lights so that the room is absolutely black, then strike the match and light the candle. See what a difference one candle can make in a dark room. You can be that one candle that lights up a very dark place, as long as you choose to do good.

We have our four keys to recognizing evil, so let us take a second look at our verse from Romans 12, "Be not overcome by evil, but overcome evil with good." To be overcome by evil is to give in to the power of evil and to let it take control of us. This rarely happens quickly. Usually it happens gradually over time as we give in a little bit at a time. Often we know that we should not be doing what we are doing, but we justify it by saying, "This is just a little thing. It won't matter this one time." But the truth is that it does matter because it leads us to a bigger thing and a bigger thing until we are completely overtaken, and then we are trapped and cannot get out, or we don't want to get out.

We are commanded instead to overcome evil with good. One of the most important ways in which we can overcome evil with good is to forgive. I see here in this society that it is very difficult for people to forgive each other. That explains the presence of the vendetta, in which for generations people are afraid to go out of their homes for fear of being killed in revenge for something their family has done. This is a terrible evil, but it could be overcome by good—the good of forgiveness—if both sides were willing to let go of their desire for revenge and instead to forgive.

Most of our overcoming evil will occur in small ways: for example, not taking offense with someone who has just spoken harshly to us, but rather answering with a gentle voice. Another example is not allowing ourselves to get involved in gossiping about someone else, especially if the talk is very unkind. Many people's lives have been hurt through gossip. We can simply reply to someone who is gossiping, "We don't know that these things are true. Let us try to speak kindly about this person."

There are many other small ways to do good in the face of evil. For myself, I have the evil of a serious illness. The good I try to do in the face of my illness is to be patient with it, and to accept that God is working all things for my salvation. I try not to complain nor to blame anyone else for my troubles.

I want to conclude with a story that tells of some people who forgave and what happened afterwards. This is something that happened in 1956 in Ecuador, South America. There were five missionary families that went to Ecuador to try to reach a group of Indians in the jungle with the love of Jesus. Few foreigners had ever had contact with these Indians, and the Indians were very suspicious of outsiders. To initiate contact, the five husbands would fly into an area where these people were and drop gifts down to them. This continued for some time. Then one day they decided it was time to try to make closer contact, so they landed their plane and slowly began to try to form a friendship with these people. They did this a few times, then one day, after landing their plane, the missionaries realized that something was not right, but it was too late. The Indians came at them with spears and killed all of them. As you can imagine, this was devastating for the missionary wives and children. Nevertheless, by the grace of God, the families forgave the killers. Later at least two of the wives returned to live with the Indians and through their love and forgiveness won them to Christ. This story illustrates that by the grace of God, it is possible to overcome evil with good—in this case, the good of forgiveness.

Most of us will not be called upon to overcome such terrible evil through such incredible good, but we will have many opportunities to overcome evil in small, everyday ways. Let us always seek to do good and to become more and more like the "portrait of a Christian."

August 14, 2006   &   *Website Posting*

WE'RE IN THE MIDDLE OF OUR THIRD GIRLS' CAMP AND THINGS SEEM to be going smoothly. Today we lost two girls, who said that they were unaccustomed to being in such a closed environment with so much religious activity. Their reason for leaving was a bit difficult to comprehend, but the girls must not have realized that this was a Church camp. Everyone else seems to be in high spirits, including me. This is the first summer that I have attended all three camps, but the time has been very precious. Nathan has had a lot of work to do in Tirana this week, but he has made the effort to be with us almost every night. This has necessitated doing a lot of driving late at night on a terrible road that winds through the mountains. Last night he left Tirana at midnight and ran into dreadful fog and couldn't move faster than 20 mph. The road, with its many sharp turns, has few guard rails, and no lines painted on it. I couldn't sleep until Nathan arrived, but thank God he made it safely.

Nathan's work has involved overseeing an OCMC short-term team from the States. Part of the team is focusing its efforts on the children's home and helping with the orphans there. The other part of the team has organized and is now implementing a seven-day English camp in Tirana. The program, which is being attended by 40–45 children, is going well, and the team has taken to it with a great deal of zeal and energy. We thank God for their helpful and serving spirits.

My craft project of making hemp bracelets and necklaces with beads continues to be a hit with the girls. As the ages of the girls has increased with each camp, their skills have increased as well, and they are able to learn more complex designs as well as complete the projects faster. At the end of this camp, the girls will probably go home with their arms and necks dangling with numerous bracelets and necklaces.

Each summer we realize the importance of these camps in feeding the girls spiritually. They have so little Christian teaching, if any, in their homes, so we want to take advantage of the time to plant and water spiritual seeds in their hearts and minds. Nathan and I will both give talks at this camp as well as have discussions on various relational issues.

The third week of August will see the start of another series of children's camps in Kosovo. Nathan, for the most part, will spend his time with me, but he may go up with the group and open the camps, then return after the first few days. If the camps start smoothly, then our Albanian staff can carry on by themselves without Nathan. These camps are extremely challenging and intense, as shown by the camps early this year, in which the press and government got involved, but our Albanian staff does a very good job of overseeing them. Despite this, it is still important for Nathan to be there if he can. For certain, George Russell will accompany the group to Kosovo, and his help will be much appreciated.

I had a CT scan made of my thorax and abdomen the day camp started. The results were startling. The liver had grown dramatically. We were all surprised because the blood counts from my previous tests three weeks ago had indicated very early stages of cancer activity in my liver. The only reason I went in for a scan last week was because I was beginning to feel swelling in my abdomen, which was accompanied by difficulties in breathing and eating, and I wanted to have these things checked out.

My blood tests yesterday indicated that the liver counts had more than quadrupled, indicating that the liver is failing rapidly. The doctor said it was likely that I had only weeks to live, not months. It was all very sobering.

I'm not sure how one copes with such bad news. I cried some, of course, thinking about leaving my husband and children, but the Lord also gave me a tremendous amount of grace to be joyful in a time of crisis.

As I have reflected back on the past three months—the duration of our stay here and the "incubation" period of my liver cancer—I am amazed that I have felt so well, that I have almost been unaware of anything going on in my liver, so I have felt no anxiety about it. I have been able to prepare for the camps without any interruptions. Camp ends this week and it will probably be the last formal ministry I will do on earth, but I'm so happy about it. I have loved doing these camps, knowing that it truly is important in the lives of these girls.

I have had this overwhelming sense that God is allowing me to stay in the saddle until the end. It appears that I am being allowed to fall off my horse at the last minute and won't have a long, drawn-out illness like my mother had. If this is truly the case, I'm so thankful for the opportunity to be active until the end, but we'll see what God actually has for us.

One thing that is proving to be rather challenging is the question of where to be buried. Nathan is really taking this to heart. We had wanted me to be buried at St. Vlash, the natural choice for us because we are connected with the school there and really love the place. I asked the Archbishop, but he felt that it would not be appropriate. Others have asked and been refused, and if I am granted permission, others will ask in the future and will question why I was allowed and they are not. It is rather complicated. I have resigned myself to this reality, but now, where do we go? The major cemeteries are large, crowded, miserable places. Today we will look at the village cemetery just outside the monastery grounds of St. Vlash. This might be close enough, and most certainly the land was a part of the former property of the Church as all of the land surrounding the monastery and school was at one time, but it hasn't been returned to the Church, and probably never will be.

You ask, how am I feeling spiritually? and I answer, very well, thank God. This is manifestly the result of God's grace. Both Nathan and I feel ourselves overwhelmed by the amazing grace that God has given to us. We could not be so joyful without his help. I pray that this will continue to the end. Who knows what will happen when I begin to feel poorly, but for now, I am happy and feel a great sense of joyful anticipation at my home-going. God is with us and will continue to be with us until the end.

Nathan spoke with the children a little bit last night about what may be coming in order to prepare them a bit for the end. They were surprisingly peaceful. Tristan said, "If mommy does die, then she'll be with Jesus." Then they asked if I would be here for Christmas. The truth is that because I do not look or act sick, they can't really get their little minds around my going. The truth is that we can't either.

One exciting thing for me is that so many people want to come and see me before the end, including members of my own family, my best friend and her daughter, who is also my goddaughter, and several priests with whom we are very close. Here, also, we have our dear co-workers who are ready to help with the smallest detail. Dennis and Constance Luisi, new missionaries with the OCMC who are from our home parish, are planning to arrive on 8 September, and they will be so attentive to any needs we may have. The Archbishop, too, has offered whatever help we may need. From him, we have asked for a hospital bed for such a time as I may become bedridden.

We are hoping to find a reclining chair as well, but these are not available in Albania and it may be very hard to find one. I know my mom spent a lot of time sitting in her recliner, so that she would not have to be in bed all day long.

Running through my mind is, "What do I need to do with my last days?" I have this urgent sense that I need to complete some projects—writing letters to leave with the children for the special events in the future—birthdays, graduation, weddings, first babies, and so on. I'm also doing photo memory books for them. Tristan's is almost done, but I have yet to start Katherine's. I have recorded some songs at the request of some of our young people here who like my singing. I'm also writing a book for Nathan of our memories together. Please pray that I will have both the discipline and the wits to complete these projects. I really would feel bad in the end if I didn't complete these.

When I first got news of my pending departure, I was frantic, thinking I needed to do some kind of "ministry," but I soon realized that there was no value in ministry at this point. What I have done until now is what I have done. What I have become, is what I am. To try to have some kind of dramatically different prayer life is simply an attempt to "win his favor" and would actually be rather artificial. I am allowing myself to simply relax in the love of Jesus, to enjoy him in a new way, to think about joining him soon.

I have so much peace in thinking that there is nothing I can do to win over Christ. All I can do is throw myself into his arms and know that it is only through the work of Christ that I can be saved. I feel that I am ready to die a "painless, blameless, and peaceful death" even as we pray every liturgy. I may have a lot of physical pain, but in spirit I feel no pain, other than the pain of leaving those I love.

August 15, 2006 Letters for the Children

[In these final days, Lynette took time to write and dictate several letters for her children to read at future dates. She wrote the following letters for her children's next birthdays. She also wrote letters for their graduation days and weddings.]

For December 9, 2006

To my beloved Tristan on his 9th birthday,

I just want you to know how much I am missing you on this your special day, your 9th birthday. Your grandmother is here with me and so is your great grandfather. Never forget that we love you very much and are praying for you.

I will never forget what great models you used to make from Legos and K'nex, such as trucks, airplanes, helicopters and other wonderful things. You surprised us all with your incredible talent. Don't be anxious about learning to read, it will come.

My prayer for you this next year is to learn to love Jesus more, to get along with your sister, to help your Dad as much as you can, to pray for your Mommy and know that your Mommy is always praying for you.

I will be praying for you and always watching over you.

I love you,

Mommy

For April 12, 2007

To My Beloved Katherine on her 7th birthday,

On this special day in your life, know that we are remembering you from Heaven. Your grandma is here with me and so is your great grandfather. Never forget that we love you very much and are praying for you all the time.

I will always remember snuggling together almost every morning, playing games together, doing crafts, reading books, going to the beach, and getting your hair braided at Henrietta's.

My prayer for you for the next year is for you to learn to love Jesus more, to get along well with your brother, to help your Daddy in any way possible, to remember to pray for your Mommy and to remember that your Mommy will always pray for you.

I wish I could physically be there with you, but we have to trust that God knows best. I will always be watching over you.

I love you,

Mommy

CHAPTER 8

Entrance into Eternity 🙰

LYNETTE FULFILLED HER DREAM OF BEING ACTIVE IN MINISTRY RIGHT up until her death. In fact, for a month previous to her demise, she vigorously involved herself in the arts and crafts projects and in giving several talks at each of the three girls' summer church camps held at the St. John Vladimir Monastery. During this time, she also took the time to sing a number of songs on a CD for her children, while writing some letters for future events in the lives of Tristan and Katherine. Exactly eleven days before she died, she even offered a powerful and inspirational talk to the girls about her journey with cancer and preparing for death. Interestingly, it was precisely on this day that her motor skills began to fail.

August 16, 2006 Talk at the Girls' Camp

The Final Journey

Lynette's Last Talk at the Good Shepherd Girls' Camp

IT'S A GOOD DAY TO GIVE A TALK BECAUSE EACH DAY I FEEL MYSELF failing more and more. Today I realize that it is hard for me to focus on anything at all. I have fallen asleep in so many things, even in the middle of some conversations. So if I fall asleep in the middle of my talk, don't worry because Nathan will take over.

Maybe you find it very strange that I would give a talk like this. Here in Albania, nobody talks about the subject of death or serious illness. People don't even tell those who are sick that they are really sick. The problem with such an attitude is that people don't have time to prepare themselves for death. If we tell the truth, we all really need to prepare for death and get ready to meet our Maker. This ultimate meeting will either be a very joyful thing—for those who believe in Jesus Christ—or a very terrifying thing for those who are not prepared. So it is a blessing to know that we need to prepare.

The truth is that we will all die one day. No one can escape from death. I have thought of this fact often for myself as I have prayed for healing. Of course, I would love to be healed at this moment in life. Yet even if I am healed, I realize that I will still die one day. I can never escape death. None of us can!

Let me give you a little history of my own illness. About 20 months ago I found out that I have cancer. I had no clues whatsoever before that time. One day I was giving a lesson in graphic design and I felt a terrible pain under my arm. When I explored under my arm I felt a very large lump. I immediately called my fellow missionary, Dr. Charles Linderman, and asked if it was something that I should worry about. He told me to come into his office immediately and he would do an ultrasound and a mammography, as well as examine me.

You can't imagine my shock when, from those tests, I discovered a huge lump in my breast. How could I have possibly missed this? Thank God that Nathan and I were very peaceful at that time. I think God showered us with so much grace because suddenly our whole life was turned upside down.

Dr. Charles told us to go to America within one month. So we needed to close up our house, make arrangements to find a good clinic in America to go to, and say goodbye to all our dear friends here. To tell you the truth, I thought that I would get my treatment— an operation, radiation, chemotherapy—and we would be back in Albania in six months. Well, was I mistaken!

When we got to the States and I had surgery, along with other tests, I discovered that I was much worse off than I ever imagined. The cancer had already spread to my spine, where there was a big tumor. And once cancer spreads, it is very difficult to control. My cancer gradually began to spread more and more. Over the last year and a half that we've been in America the cancer has really gone throughout my body. Of course, I have a lot of pain, but I control it with medication.

Well, in March of this year, Nathan and I started to talk about the idea of coming back to Albania. I had a little bit of a quiet period, and I really had a longing to come back to Albania. Actually, I forgot to say that last summer I had a longing to return to Albania and we did visit in October. But I really thought that that visit would be the last time I would ever see Albania.

Well, in March we started talking about returning to Albania. The strange thing was that for the first time in my life, I fell into a period of depression and anxiety. I have never experienced such things before. It was so strange for me. It made me really anxious because I didn't know what I would feel next or what would come to me next. At the same time, my mother was dying from liver cancer.

I said, "How can I go back to Albania because I don't know how I will feel, and also my mother is dying." So we prayed much and we decided to go ahead and come. I knew that my sister would take care of my mother. My sister was wonderful! My sister and my father told me, after my mother died, that it would have been extremely difficult for me to be there at my mother's death. And she really believed that it was better for me not to see what my mother suffered.

So just a few weeks ago, after a blood test, I found out that the cancer had gone into my liver, which is a very bad sign. Since then, my liver has grown so fast. I feel like I am pregnant. I can't eat very much or even breathe very easily because of the pressure. Thus, it's a difficult time physically, even though I still don't really feel sick. I know that sounds funny, but I don't feel bad. I think this is just the grace of God for me. It's like He's allowing me to stay on my horse until the very end. Some day I'm just going to fall off. To me this is just a wonderful thing, because I saw with my mother, who died of liver cancer, that she had six months in bed. It was so hard because she could hardly move and go to the bathroom. I just feel so much the grace of God in so many areas.

Thank God! Thank God!

I want to go back a little to over a year ago when I started to pray very seriously about healing. At that time I offered prayers to St. Nektarios for healing. I don't know if you are familiar with these prayers, but there exist some beautiful prayers where we ask St. Nektarios to intercede for us. The interesting thing about those prayers, however, is that most of it is prayer for healing of soul. There really is only a little about healing of body.

As I started to pray these prayers, I realized that it was more important to be healed in soul than in body. Thus, I started to ask God to show me what it meant to be healed in soul. Over the last year, I have focused my attention much more on the healing of soul than on body. I think the healing of soul has come to me in different ways. I prayed to God to show me this, and he surely showed me areas that needed healing. I'll give one example.

When I had a scan last summer which showed that the cancer had spread throughout my body, I started to realize how willful I had been in my relationship with Nathan. I had acted independently so often with him, making decisions without consulting him. I didn't realize how much this hurt him and our relationship together. Now this came because I had made some decisions about my treatment for cancer without consulting Nathan. My decisions were something that actually hurt me in the treatment process. I realized I hadn't done a good thing for myself, but I felt, "This is my body, so why can't I decide about it myself." I realized as a wife, however, that I needed to consult with him, especially in important things like my treatment. Now Nathan is not the type to say, "This is what you are going to do and you have to obey me." He likes us working together on all things. But I like to do things on my own.

When I realized my own willfulness, though, I confessed to him about my sin of making independent decisions, and since then, our relationship has just blossomed so much! I have seen our love for each other grow so deeply. And this has been such a blessing to us. Nathan often says to me that even though this is a difficult time for us, at the same time it is one of the most beautiful times we have together. And I am very grateful for that.

I could give many other examples of the healing of the soul that I have experienced over the past year, but I want to talk about another aspect of preparing to die.

The truth is that there will be many ups and downs in this process. Sometimes as Christians we think that life should be an upward journey of having more and more joy all the time. The truth, however, is that sometimes we will really struggle with life. We must accept this as a part of our journey. Sometimes we won't even feel like praying, but we must do it anyway, or at least seek others to pray for us.

Sometimes I would feel like all I can do is cling to Jesus and beg Him not to let me go. He will always hold on to us. He will never, never abandon us. We can't trust in our feelings ever! Our feelings are an extremely unreliable judge of how we are.

When people ask me how I pray now, I tell them that my prayers are much more about just enjoying my relationship with Jesus more than any structured, formal prayers. I like to just sit and think about Him, about being with Him.

In the Divine Liturgy every Sunday, we offer a prayer where we say in the litanies, "For a Christian end to our lives, painless, blameless and peaceful." As you can imagine, I have paid special attention to this prayer every Sunday. I've always thought, "What does it mean to die 'painless, blameless and peaceful'?"

Does it mean that we can actually pray to not have any pain at the end? I think that it may mean physical pain, but I think it means more about the pain in the soul. I have a wonderful mother who has been such a great example to me. I would never want to say anything negative about her, but I did learn much about watching her die. I'm not sure that she died a painless death, and I think that it was because she had some unresolved issues in her own life.

I think that if you want to have a "painless" death, it means that you must be reconciled with all those around you. I think that my mother had some unresolved things with those around her. So, this painless part of dying requires that we really think through carefully about those who have hurt us and try to heal ourselves in this way. So that would be the "painless" part.

As for the blameless part, this is a part that all of us as Christians can fear as we are dying. We are afraid that we haven't done enough to make God happy. The truth is, however, that we can never do enough. Jesus has done enough. For us to think that somehow we can do enough good works is our pride speaking. Or it is a temptation from the devil, who fills us with fear and whispers, "You aren't good enough."

So for myself now, I just feel so much joy at the idea of facing Christ because I know that He has done everything for me. It is His work that has prepared me to face him. I don't need to be afraid. In fact, it's a very, very joyful thing.

So we have painless, blameless, and peaceful. I think the peacefulness comes from knowing who it is that we will meet. Jesus says, "I go to prepare a place for you so that where I am you may be there also. Be not afraid." So we have every reason to be at peace, because He will be there waiting for us.

There is a verse in the Psalms that says, "Precious in the sight of the Lord is the death of his saints." At first that verse can sound so strange. How can death be something precious? But it is because He is awaiting us. He is prepared for us. And this is such a great thing of joy for us.

I said that a few days ago the doctor told me that I only have a few weeks. Who knows, really; we cannot know anything for sure. They take their guesses from the signs. But thank God, thank God that I feel "painless, blameless, and peaceful."

In the end, I can say that I have never felt that God has given me something terrible. Even during those times of depression and anxiety, when I did feel like He was absolutely nowhere, I learned to cling to what I know is true. I learned not to trust my feelings at all. I have to trust in what I know about God—He is good; He is love; He is always with us.

[At this point, some girls offered comments and asked a few questions. Nathan, sensing that Lynette was tiring, answered in her stead:]

This is why it is very important during our lives to be spiritually prepared for our journey through life. If we remain unprepared spiritually, we won't know how to face a crisis. Don't think that crises are only for others. Don't believe that we can live however we want, and only when we get older, we can begin to focus on spiritual things. Athletes don't prepare on the day of their contest, but they begin much before the actual contest. In like manner we have to be ready, preparing from now for our spiritual journeys.

Something that has been a great strength for us has been the big family we have here in Albania and in America. There are days when we are both weak, and we don't feel we can face the day, and yet, this is when the Body of Christ comes to our rescue. Countless people are praying for us and have supported us.

How difficult it would be to have Lynette die and know that she isn't with Christ. It would be very dark indeed.

Whether we want it or not, whether we presently have a sickness or not, we will all die one day. Therefore we have to live in a manner prepared to face death.

Remember, whenever we celebrate the saints, we do so on the day that they died. Through their death they have entered into a full union with God and live in His presence forever.

[At the end of the talk, all the campers stood and sang "Christ is Risen!" See page 269 for a free download of this recorded talk.]

August 18, 2006 ❦ *From Nathan*

LYNETTE HAS BEGUN TO SLIP AWAY FROM US. A FEW WEEKS AGO when we learned that the cancer had begun in her liver, we believed that it was at an early stage and that we would still have some time together. Since then, things have progressed very rapidly. Ten days ago a scan showed that cancer had completely taken over her liver and caused her liver to expand to fill most of her abdomen. Since then, she has begun to show signs of liver failure, with these becoming acute in the last 48 hours. She is extremely tired, sleeping throughout the night and most of the day. She has begun to lose her motor skills; things like drinking out of a glass have become very difficult. She has spilled her water on herself many times in the last two days. It is becoming difficult for her to think and speak clearly. The doctors say that her time is now very short. Those who are planning to come and visit are accelerating their travel arrangements in hopes of arriving while she can still communicate.

We returned from the girls' summer camp yesterday. The evening before we left, Lynette gathered her strength and mental faculties to spend about one hour speaking to the girls about the end of life and preparation to meet our Lord. This was a beautiful time in which the work which God has done in Lynette shone out so clearly. Death is almost never talked about here in Albania, and terminally ill people are not told that they are dying, so we pray that Lynette's testimony will help these young women to prepare for a Christian end to their lives.

We continue to be so grateful for the companionship of each one of you on this difficult journey. We have been so wonderfully sustained by you in so many ways. I asked your prayers especially for these last days and hours which we have with Lynette. Though we have known it was coming for a long time, the end has come suddenly and there are still many things which we would like to finish. Please pray that she will have at least a few hours of strength and clear thought and that we will use these moments well. Also pray that those who are coming to visit will arrive in time.

Pray for the children and me, that we will have a sustaining sense of His presence. My eyes are full of tears as I write but I also have a strong sense of joy. The jewel which I have been privileged to hold a short time is slipping away from me, but I know that she will be held in far more worthy arms until we are reunited. I am so blessed in these days by her joy and her faith and her love. She is truly an icon of Christ to me, which is sustaining me.

August 21, 2006   ❧   *From Nathan*

DEAR FRIENDS,

Thank you for your tremendous outpouring of love and support in these difficult days. Lynette's situation has stabilized slightly since I last wrote. We realized on Friday evening that her dramatic decline was exacerbated by rising levels of pain medication in her blood. Her failing liver was not removing the medication from the bloodstream effectively and we were continuing to give her normal doses. We dramatically reduced her medication, and she was much more alert on Saturday morning and able to make significant progress on some of the letters which she wished to write for the children. About noon she began to have a terrible itchiness across most of her body which made it impossible for her to sleep or sit comfortably. We initially thought that this was another common symptom of liver failure which is very difficult to treat. Late Saturday evening a hospice doctor from the United States who has helped us a great deal on this journey called to see how Lynette was doing. He suggested that the itchiness might be a withdrawal symptom from her pain medication. Thank God the itching went away very quickly after we restarted the pain medication. We are now working to find the balance, giving her as little medication as possible so that we do not make her excessively sleepy and further compromise the liver, but enough to prevent withdrawal symptoms and pain.

Though the itching is gone, Lynette is still finding it difficult to get comfortable. This is primarily because of fluid buildup in her body, which has filled her abdomen, causing her to look and feel seven months pregnant. She also has difficulty lying on her back because of the cancer in her spine. We are very blessed by friends in the States who had a contact in Albania that owned a recliner (these are normally not available here). This chair was delivered to our home this evening; hopefully it will help Lynette find a comfortable way to sit.

It now looks like Lynette will probably survive long enough to greet her family and friends who are coming this week. She is making slow but steady progress on her letters and picture books for the children. Pray that she will have clarity of thought for this process. She is working with one of our fellow missionaries who is writing for her. This is a real struggle because she wants to pour all her creativity and love into these projects but clear sustained thought is now very difficult.

We have been very blessed by the community of love around us in Albania. Each day many people stop by to express their love and help in any way they can. They have provided food, taking care of the children, answering the door, answering the phone and anything else I have asked. This leaves me free to sit by Lynette's bed and focus on her. These days and hours together are a great joy to us as we savor the love which has grown between us over the years. It is truly a blessing that God has left her with us a little while longer. Through your prayers and notes you are also part of this community of love. Lynette has so enjoyed each of your messages that I have read to her. Please forgive me for not responding individually to your expressions of love.

August 24, 2006   &la   *From Nathan*

DEAR FRIENDS,
Rejoice in the Lord always!

I have been meditating on this exhortation this morning as I move quietly around Lynette's room, arranging things and cleaning up, and then as I shower and get ready for the day. Her condition has deteriorated over the last 24 hours. Fluid is accumulating in her abdomen much more quickly than hoped. Her speech and motor skills also show a significant decline from yesterday. How then can I rejoice? But I do feel a great sense of joy. It is a great honor and joy to accompany my dearest friend to the gates of Paradise. It is a joy because our Lord is with us and we are drawing near to Him. It is a joy because our love for each other continues to grow and deepen through this time of trial. As Lynette's body fails, her spirit is soaring. She radiates peace, joy, and love to all those around her. This journey is also a joy because of the love of the body of Christ which is enveloping us. We are so blessed by all of the family and friends who are making the great effort to come and visit us. The Lord has worked out many challenges of scheduling in a very high-traffic season and the complications of renewing expired passports. Lynette's three brothers have already arrived, as well as our dear coworkers Fr. Luke and Faith Veronis and the priest of our home parish, Fr. Pat Reardon. Each one is such a blessing to all of us. We are also so grateful to all of you who have reached out to help in so many ways, with encouraging e-mails, letters, and financial help for those who are traveling to see us. To name only a few.

We also continue to be blessed by the loving support of the community here in Albania. I am amazed at all of those who have come together to care for us so beautifully.

LYNETTE'S PHYSICAL CONDITION CONTINUED TO DECLINE TODAY. She now has great difficulty saying even a few words. Swallowing is also difficult. She is in a deep sleep the vast majority of the time.

It is a great blessing that her family members and best friend had all arrived by yesterday and were able to have meaningful conversations with her.

Today has been a blessed day of prayer, fellowship, and singing. We have rejoiced together in a great gift of our salvation and have been blessed to live this day in the company of one who is finishing her race. She continues to be filled with peace and joy. For several hours this evening all sat around the large recliner in which she was resting. For much of the time she seemed to be completely asleep but often her countenance would be illumined by a bright smile of joy. Occasionally her eyes would open and she would say a few words to us, but mostly she simply rested as we sang and praised our great God. Fr. Patrick anointed her with myrrh from one of the weeping icons.

Walking to the gates of Paradise with a dying person also has its more earthy side. I just heard Lynette moving and so ran to see how I could help her. She needed to roll on her other side, which she is unable to do by herself now. Before moving her I swung the bag for her catheter, which was installed this afternoon, across the bed. Urine poured out because the valve had not been closed properly last time we emptied it. I moved Lynette to the recliner so that I could change the sheets and clean the featherbed. Thankfully she immediately fell soundly asleep again in the recliner, allowing me time to prepare the bed for her. Thank God she is again resting quietly on clean linens. This is only one of the menial tasks which caring for a person who is becoming increasingly helpless requires. I am grateful for each one, because it is one more opportunity to express my love for her before her departure.

A team of 15 Albanian young people leaves tomorrow morning for Kosovo to run a four-day day camp for 450 children in a Muslim village. This will be the first time in the five-year history of these camps that a team is going without me. Please pray for these young people. This work in Kosovo is very challenging physically, emotionally and spiritually. I will deeply miss the dear friends that make up this team during this difficult time, but I am extremely pleased that they are able to carry on the ministry even if I cannot be present. We are very blessed by such competent and zealous Albanian coworkers that are such a joy to work with.

꽃

On August 27, 2006,
Lynette Katherine Hoppe passed away.

꽃

September 6, 2006   꽃   *From Nathan*

DEAR FRIENDS,
It is with deep sorrow and great joy that I write to you regarding the falling asleep of my beloved wife Lynette Katherine. She passed quietly and peacefully from my arms to the arms of our Lord Jesus at 5:14 P.M. August 27.

Saturday and Sunday were beautiful days. On Saturday she had increasing difficulty speaking and at times struggled to find a comfortable position to rest in. We moved her frequently from side to side and from bed to recliner. For much of the time she was only semi-conscious. Throughout the day people came to bid her farewell, some staying only a few minutes, others sitting by the bed longer. For each one she had a bright smile of recognition and often a few words, though at times it was difficult to understand what she was trying to say. The Archbishop came and sat with us for almost an hour as we sang hymns and shared remembrances about Lynette's life. His visit was a true blessing to us. Though we could rarely understand her sentences, we all had the sense that she was filled with peace and joy at her eminent home-going. At one point she said "Death . . . is so beautiful." The words "wonderful," "beautiful," and "joy" often stood out from her garbled sentences.

Lynette settled down quietly to sleep on Saturday evening. We passed a quiet night with me snuggled close beside her enjoying the beauty of her presence. On Sunday morning she woke up, sat herself up in bed and said she wanted to move to her recliner. I settled her comfortably there and spent a blessed morning with her while others went to liturgy. I read many e-mails of encouragement that you had sent aloud to her. I also sat holding her hand and spoke quietly to her, telling her how much I loved her, what a joy she has been to me and how wonderfully she has enriched my life. I asked her again to forgive me for all the ways in which I have failed her. I asked her if she had heard our singing around her the night before. She said yes and that she liked it very much. I asked her if she could open her eyes and tell me that she loved me. She said, "No, but I feel it." Those were truly blessed hours with her, of tears, but also of great joy.

Just after noon three priests came to give her Holy Communion for the last time. The afternoon was spent quietly with different friends and family members surrounding her, holding her hand and talking quietly to her. About three o'clock we noticed that her breathing was becoming more labored and her pulse faint. We realized that the end may be coming soon. We called Fr. Pat, who had gone to rest for a few minutes, and other friends and family members. We sat around Lynette's chair and sang and prayed and cried. The atmosphere in the room was a strange mixture of great joy and deep sadness. We were witnessing a home-going, a birthday of the fulfillment of a life in Christ, but we were also experiencing the pain of separation and loss. Each of us kissed her and said goodbye, telling her how much we loved her. Tristan and Katherine also came in to say goodbye to their mother. When Katherine kissed her Lynette, she said some words which we could not understand but they were filled with recognition and love.

At about 4:30 P.M. her breathing became much more difficult; she was struggling for each breath. Then gradually her breathing smoothed out and became slow and easy. For about 15 minutes she lingered with us quietly and peacefully and then slipped away. It was one of the most beautiful things I will ever see. Fr. Pat started the Trisagion service for the departed with her last breath.

LYNETTE RESTED QUIETLY IN OUR HOME FOR 40 HOURS AFTER HER death. The house was filled with joy and peace during that time. A few minutes after Lynette passed from this life, the Archbishop arrived to pray and grieve with us. He placed a beautiful olive wood cross in Lynette's hand and sang the Trisagion prayers for the departed. I then spent a short time alone with Lynette. She had fallen asleep but she was still very much present. I again spoke to her of my love and how I would miss her. I took a beautiful delicate pink rosebud from one of the vases of flowers and placed it in her hand next to the cross. The flower added a splash of color against the white linen in which she was clothed. I had intentionally dressed her in white in her last days, thinking of the spotless white robes of baptism. Through her final confession and absolution she had returned to that state of innocence before our Lord.

After placing the flower in Lynette's hand I sang "Rejoice in the Lord always and again I say rejoice" and "This is the day that the Lord has made; I will rejoice and be glad in it." I was filled with a profound sense that this was a time for joy and that it was my privilege to rejoice. Lynette and I have grown immensely in our love for one another over the past 20 months. What had been a deep and sincere love grew much deeper and richer through her illness. We had found one another in a much more profound way just as we were being separated. In this new deeper experience of love I was able to surrender her to the embrace of our Lord with joy. My tears also flowed, tears of sadness, tears of loss, but not tears of despair.

In the first half hour after Lynette's death, an amazing thing happened to her countenance. All the lines of care, distress, and pain were smoothed away and a beautiful smile appeared. There was no external intervention to arrange her face. A profound beauty shone forth. The photographs capture only a fraction of the joy and peace that radiated from her.

I left the room and began to make phone calls, to inform different ones who have supported us so faithfully on this journey that Lynette had fallen asleep in the Lord. As I was doing this, Lynette's sister and several other women who are very dear to her began preparing her body. They washed and anointed her with holy oil before dressing her in a beautiful pale yellow gown.

During this time I was also working on arrangements regarding the funeral. The normal custom in Albania is that the burial take place within 12 to 24 hours. This is necessary because embalming and refrigeration are not available. Because a number of people were planning to travel from the United States and Kosovo for the funeral, we wished to delay the burial an extra day. In order to do this I thought that it would be necessary to send her body to the morgue for refrigeration. I was not at all happy about this but it seemed unavoidable. When our dear friend Prokopi, who blessed us by making many of the funeral arrangements, went to pick up the casket, they asked if he would like a refrigeration unit to go with it. We had no idea that this was available in Albania. This unit with a glass top fit over the top of the casket, making it possible to refrigerate the body as it lay at rest in our home. This was a great blessing to us.

As word spread of Lynette's home-going, people began to arrive at the house to give their condolences and pay their respects. Metropolitan John of Korca left immediately from his seat upon hearing the news to make the 3½-hour drive to support us at this time of loss. Dear friends and family members divided the nighttime hours into shifts and held continuous vigil, reading Psalms and singing at Lynette's side. Every person who came was profoundly struck by the beauty of her countenance.

After a very emotionally intense day, the Lord graciously granted a good night of rest to the children and me. On Monday morning I went to the village cemetery of St. Vlash to choose the grave site. They granted us a beautiful plot slightly removed from the other graves and next to a cemetery flowerbed, which we will be allowed to develop as we wish.

When I returned home, Metropolitan John came with several priests to sing the Trisagion service. Fr. Martin Ritsi arrived from the United States in the afternoon. He had left home 15 minutes after receiving my call regarding Lynette's passing in order to catch the last possible flight which would bring him to Albania in time for the funeral. He was a great blessing in helping to coordinate the service.

I rose early on Tuesday morning to spend precious time taking leave of Lynette before visitors began to arrive. With a few of those who had kept a vigil through the night and at times by myself, I passed about 90 minutes sitting or standing by the casket gazing on the beauty of her face. At times tears flowed, but the large resurrection icon and the joy and peace of her countenance were constant reminders that he has trampled down death by death and granted life to those in the tombs.

Throughout the morning many visitors had congregated around her body singing "Christ is risen" and other hymns of joy and victory. At about 10:30 A.M. the refrigeration unit was removed from the casket, giving family and loved ones the opportunity to kiss her brow and say farewell. Tristan and Katherine made beautiful cards with love notes for Mommy. Tristan placed his in the coffin, but Katherine wanted me to keep hers to help us remember Mommy.

The funeral procession of three buses and many cars departed for St. Vlash about 11 o'clock. When we arrived, there were already many people there who had come independently. Lynette's brothers and other willing hands carried the casket from the gates of the monastery into the church, where a huge resurrection icon was placed at its head. The service was conducted beautifully in English and Albanian by the Archbishop, assisted by Metropolitan Ignatius of Berat and Metropolitan John of Korca together with a number of priests from Albania and the United States.

As we emerged from the church for the short walk to the cemetery, a brisk wind was blowing. It had been threatening rain that morning as we drove to St. Vlash but now the threat was gone as only the wind, which cooled and invigorated the procession, remained. Lynette always liked a stiff breeze and it was appropriate for her final journey. The choir sang "Christ is risen" and other joyful hymns as we carried her body to its resting place.

At the graveside the final prayers were said and dirt was sprinkled on the coffin. Then it was lowered into the ground. I was very struck by the fact that the lid was not nailed or screwed on. It was simply set in place. I do not know if this is normal practice in Albania, and at first I thought it was an oversight which needed to be rectified; then I reflected that that box is only her temporary resting place. Therefore it is appropriate that the lid be left loose to facilitate the resurrection.

As the dirt was filled in over the coffin we stood and sang, "Amazing Grace," "It Is Well with My Soul," "Christ Is Risen!" and many more. Tears flowed but joy was in the air. As we left the graveside a line formed of people coming to offer their condolences. I greeted each with "Christ is risen!" I truly had the sense of celebrating her heavenly birthday together with these dear friends. The love and kindness in their faces was a true blessing to me.

After the burial the archbishop hosted a luncheon for more than 150 of the guests at the seminary dining room. It was a beautiful event at which the spirit of joy and celebration continued. Lynette's family members and other guests spoke briefly, giving greetings and thanking the Albanian people for their love and hospitality.

September 10, 2006   Fr. Patrick Reardon

I WENT TO ALBANIA, AS MOST OF YOU KNOW, TO BE WITH ONE OF the parishioners from our little church in Chicago, Lynette Hoppe, whose family has served as missionaries in that country for the past nine years. Lynette was dying, and she had asked me, when I spoke to her by phone just days before, to come and help her die. This being one of the things that priests do, and Lynette being one of my favorite parishioners, I hastened to comply.

I was blessed to be with Lynette and her family during the closing days of her life. In addition to her husband Nathan and her children, Tristan and Katherine, Lynette was surrounded by her father, her older sister, and her three younger brothers, along with Gaye Buchanan and her daughter, Lynette's goddaughter, Rebecca. Gaye herself (the wife of Dr. Tom Buchanan, a *Touchstone* senior editor) has been Lynette's close friend since their college days at Wheaton. Fr. Luke and Faith Veronis, formerly missionaries to Albania, likewise ministered to Lynette during most of that time.

On each of the closing days of her life, including the Sunday on which she died, Lynette was strengthened with the Sacred Viaticum, faithfully carried to her by the priests from the cathedral. The Archbishop also came by to pray with her.

All of us prayed with her constantly during that time. Lynette was blessed to come from a strong family of evangelical missionaries to Africa. Her father, sister, and brothers led us in singing scores of classical Protestant hymns over the several days, many of their lines assuming new dimensions in my mind by reason of the context. We also sang Orthodox hymns from time to time, including the Cherubic Hymn. (I recalled that St. Elizabeth the New Martyr died while singing that hymn down in the mine shaft where she had been thrown by the Bolsheviks.) The Psalms and other parts of the Holy Scriptures (2 Corinthians 4 & 5 come prominently to mind) were read to Lynette over and over, as we prepared her to meet the Lord.

The final crisis came on Sunday, August 27. By mid-afternoon it was obvious that this was Lynette's last day on earth. Her family and the other American missionaries to Albania filled the room where she sat propped up on a reclining chair. Although she struggled for breath, Lynette did not fight death. She demonstrated the faith, serenity, and deep trust in God that we had always seen in her. On one of the days when I counseled with her last year, I encouraged Lynette not to let the memory of the sufferings of our Lord depart from her mind, and she told me that this had been a great source of strength to her. I rather suspect that this was the subject of that dear soul's final conscious thoughts.

I gave Lynette final Absolution and stayed right at her ear during the final hour or so of her life, praying the Jesus Prayer and gently saying other things to fill her with hope. When Lynette's breath and pulse stopped at 5:14 PM, I placed the Church's stole on her head and prayed the ancient admonition, "Go forth, Christian soul, out of this world . . ." Then we all started singing the Trisagion for the Departed. When we finished, I read everybody the First Epistle to the Thessalonians 4:13–18. They all gave it a hearty "Amen!"

Something happened about thirty minutes after Lynette died that I have never otherwise seen. Dead already for 30 minutes, Lynette began to smile. Everyone saw it. She was buried with that smile. It was certainly the death of a holy one, precious in the sight of the Lord.

Two days later three bishops, many priests, and hundreds of the faithful laid our sweet Lynette to rest, still wearing that smile. You may see pictures of the funeral at prayforlynette.org.

YESTERDAY EVENING MARKED FOUR WEEKS SINCE LYNETTE'S DEATH. Sunday afternoons have become a special time for me. 5:14 P.M. is a moment of sadness and a moment of joy. My dearest friend passed from my life and was born to eternal life.

Many have asked how we are doing. The answer is that I think by God's grace and through your prayers we are doing very well. I am seeking to live each day in joy. And I feel that I have been given joy as a gift from our Lord. I expected these weeks after all of the guests left, when we were beginning to settle down to figure out normal life, to be very difficult. And they have been hard; we have felt Lynette's absence in new painful ways, but we have also felt her continuing presence with us.

I am currently in Serbia representing the Orthodox Church of Albania at the official dialogue with the Catholic Church. It's been an interesting experience in many ways, including meeting many distinguished people, serious theological work, and state dinners with the prime minister and the president. One of the real pleasures of these experiences in the past has been telling Lynette about them when I return home. I have repeatedly felt a twinge of pain and sorrow realizing that I have no one to tell. On the other hand I have the sense that she is present with me experiencing these things with me now.

In addition to the pain of Lynette's absence I have faced two temptations, one regarding the past, the other the future. I am tempted to regret many things. To regret many things which were left unfinished, to regret that I did not love her better, to regret that in the many thousands of photographs I have taken I do not have better ones of her, and so on. I am also tempted to face all the pain of the future without her at once. I try to firmly reject both temptations. I am grateful for all that God gave us, and I trust him for the future. I try to accept the gift and the challenge of each day as it comes. God gives the strength for what he requires when he requires it. In his book *The Screwtape Letters,* C. S. Lewis says that only the present exists. Past is gone and the future does not yet exist. When we live in the present we live in reality, and that is where we meet God because he is the source of reality. The evil one seeks to entice us to live in the past or the future precisely in order to rob us of the joy of experiencing God in the present moment. I cannot change the past and I do not know what the future will be, but I can live the joy of God's presence in this moment.

Tristan and Katherine seem to be doing very well. They of course miss their mother very much, but they also have a childlike faith. They know that she is with Jesus and that she is doing fine. We talk about her often and we pray for her and we ask her to pray for us. She continues to be part of our family. I think that an important process of preparation happened for the children over the last year and a half as I became their primary caregiver. This has meant that there was no dramatic transition for them and that they had full confidence that I would be able to take care of them. This sense of personal security has helped them to face the personal loss. We have all slept together in one bed since Lynette's death. I think that this has been a source of comfort to all of us.

It has been such a blessing for us to be in Albania at this time of challenge and joy. Our close community of fellow missionaries and dear Albanian brothers and sisters has given us a large family of love and support. Many people have stopped by our home regularly. They have helped with practical issues like meals and the care of the children, but most of all they have wrapped us in an embrace of love which has carried us through the pain. You also, around the world, have been part of this great hug of the family of God. I have so deeply appreciated each of your e-mails and cards and packages. I hope you will forgive me for the fact that I have not thanked you individually, but please know that I am grateful. I have heard from some that they were reluctant to write because they thought we must be overwhelmed with messages. There have been many, but I would welcome many more. You are all a tremendous source of encouragement to me.

The children started school on September 6. They are attending an international Christian school which primarily serves the Protestant missionary community. It seems to be a good environment for them where a number of their friends already attend. I am very pleased with both of their teachers. Please pray for them, especially for Tristan, that this will be a successful school year. I think that they will face many challenges in adjusting to life without Lynette, and I hope that the school community will be a support in this process. Tristan is not very enthusiastic about school; his learning style is not very compatible with standard educational methods. He feels that school really takes too much away from playtime. Please also pray regarding the tuition which we are being asked to pay. Because we are not evangelical Protestants we are being charged the diplomatic rate, which is 2½ times that of other missionaries. It is very difficult, both because it is a great deal of money, and because of the negative spirit between Christians which it implies. I hope to meet with members of the board this week. Please pray for love and understanding, and that this will be an opportunity for a growth in teamwork between Christians in Albania.

I plan to visit the United States with the children for two weeks at the end of October. When we came to Albania in May, we did not know what the future would be or how long we would be staying in Albania. There are many loose ends that need to be tied up in the US. I am also looking forward to seeing my family and many other dear friends. We will be making brief visits in Minnesota, Arkansas, and Chicago.

I will not be teaching at the theological Academy this fall. I want to have time to be close to the children. I also need some time to sort through the chaos created by our irregular lives over the past 20 months. I will still be kept very busy with the children's ministry, the University Ministry, and work in Kosovo, among other things.

Again, thank you for your love. Thank you for your prayers. Thank you for all of your letters and acts of encouragement. You have truly been a blessing to us.

October 10, 2006   ✣   *From Nathan*

The Forty-Day Memorial Service

THE NUMBER 40 HAS ALWAYS BEEN IMPORTANT IN THE HISTORY OF salvation and judgment. The number is found some 100 times in the Bible. It appears first as the number of days of rain in the flood.

Isaac and Esau were each 40 years old when they married. Moses spent 40 years in the desert preparing for his ministry and 40 days and 40 nights on the holy Mountain. The spies spent 40 days exploring the land. Israel spent 40 years in the desert. David and Solomon each reigned for 40 years during the golden age of Israel's history. Our Lord Jesus fasted for 40 days in preparation for his ministry. He lay for 40 hours in the tomb before his glorious resurrection and he sojourned 40 days with his disciples before his ascension.

We also in a special way remember and pray for our loved ones for the first 40 days after their death. We remember them and pray for them in time although we know that they have already passed into eternity. We ask the Lord to give them rest in his presence, knowing that he does so based on his mercy and finished work of Christ on their behalf, not based on any merit of our prayers. We remember our loved ones to our Lord because we love them and we love him and he loves them. We continue to be one community together with those who are in heaven and those of us still on earth. We sense that they are that great cloud of witnesses around us cheering us on as we continue to run our race (Hebrews 12). We are so grateful that they continue to pray for us, to bring us before our Lord. God is not the God of the dead but of the living; all are alive in Christ.

It is difficult to believe that 40 days have already passed since Lynette fell asleep. Like the other steps on this journey, the celebration of 40 days has been a beautiful experience of the love of our community and the permeable barrier between time and eternity. We had two commemorations, one on Sunday the first of October, anticipating the 40 days, at the cathedral in Tirana, and a second on Thursday the fifth at the monastery of St. Vlash.

In Tirana the archbishop led the Trisagion prayers at the end of the liturgy. A beautiful white koliva was prepared by the women of our missionary team. Our mission team and other close friends gathered at our house for coffee and refreshments after liturgy.

Thursday Bishop Ilia held a special liturgy at St. Vlash with the students of the theological Academy in memory of Lynette, which concluded with the Trisagion prayers and the distribution of koliva. After liturgy we planted a cypress tree outside the church. This tree will be a beautiful memorial for Lynette. It replaces one of the ancient trees which had formed a rectangle around the church, of which only a few remain.

After the planting of the tree we processed together to the cemetery, where Metropolitan John of Korca led the Trisagion prayers. Flowers were laid on the grave and we concluded by singing "Christ is risen from the dead, trampling down death by death, and to those in the tombs bestowing life." The celebration was followed by a hearty breakfast, together with the students, in the seminary dining hall.

"O God of spirits and of all flesh, who has trampled down death, and made powerless the devil, and given life to thy world: Do thou, the same Lord, give rest to the soul of thy departed servant Lynette, in a place of brightness, a place of verdure, a place of repose, whence all sickness, sorrow, and sighing have fled away." *From the Trisagion prayers*

As always, we are very grateful for your prayers. The children are doing well and seem to be coping well with Lynette's death. Please continue to pray for Tristan as he is really struggling with school. He is very bright and likes to learn, but the standard educational model does not work well for him. He will be a late bloomer on reading and writing, which makes the classroom environment difficult. In addition to the real challenges he faces, he also resents the fact that school takes up so much playtime. Please pray that his friendships at school will deepen and that his reading and writing skills will improve quickly; also pray that I will have wisdom and patience to help him in this process. This is an area where we very much feel Lynette's absence.

Please pray for our visit to the United States. We will be leaving on Thursday evening (October 12) for about 2½ weeks in the US. We have a very packed schedule which will involve a lot of traveling. We will be visiting family and tying up many loose ends left from our time in the US. There are many things to pack up, insurance papers to file, and much more. This will be a very poignant time, especially as we return to Lynette's parents' home, where we spent much of our last year and a half together. Pray that this would be a healthy step in our grieving process, and that we would be able to treasure the sweet memories, even as we grieve.

Please pray for the university and children's ministries for which

I am responsible. Both will begin programs for the new academic year in the next few weeks. I am very grateful for excellent coworkers in both these ministries. Pray that we will be able to effectively communicate the Gospel and build Christian communities in which children and students grow in Christ.

Thank you again for your love and support.

November 23, 2006 *From Nathan*

The Feast of Thanksgiving

Give thanks to the LORD, for he is good; his love endures forever.
(Psalm 118:1 & 29)

IN THIS SEASON IN WHICH WE CELEBRATE THE FEAST OF THANKSgiving, I am surprised to find myself more deeply and truly thankful than I can ever remember being. It is surprising because from a worldly perspective I have the least reason to be thankful. Lynette's death was less than three months ago and my heart is still very tender. It is such a comfort to know that indeed the Lord is good and that his love endures forever.

Lynette and I spoke about this several times as we faced together the fact that she was dying and would be leaving us. We talked about the fact that since the Lord is good and his love endures forever that this means that what he is doing in our lives is an expression of his goodness and love. It is not simply that he is using us for some other purpose but that he is working in us for our salvation in his great love for us.

Since he called Lynette home at this time, it is clear that her road is finished, and that this was for her salvation, but it is also clear that her home-going is God's expression of love and care for the children and me. Therefore we must look to the future with joy and hope, not sadness and despair. The spirit of thanksgiving and the spirit of joy walk hand in hand. There is of course pain and sadness, but I have found that this can truly be a bright sadness if I choose the path of thanksgiving and joy.

This is the gift which God has given, not the product of personal strength or fortitude. It is my choice whether to accept it and live in it, or to reject it and wallow in despair. I am so grateful for each of you, your prayers and your expressions of support and encouragement, which make the journey so much easier. As I consider the way that the Lord has cared for us through you, I realize that I do have many, many reasons to be thankful. The loss of Lynette is of course very painful, but the love that each one of you has shown and continues to show to us has eased the pain and made the burden light. It is truly a wondrous thing to be part of the body of Christ.

The last five weeks have been very busy. On October 12 we flew to England, where we spent two days visiting the Essex monastery and continuing to the United States on the 14th. This was a wonderful quiet moment of rest and reflection between the fast-paced schedule of Albania and the whirlwind of our visit in the US. We arrived in Minnesota late on Saturday night and attended liturgy the next morning at our beloved parish in Rochester. It was so wonderful to be home with these dear friends that supported us over our many months of treatment at Mayo Clinic. That evening the Evangelical Free Church in Plainview, where Lynette's parents attend, held a memorial service for her. It was a beautiful time of celebrating her life and God's goodness to us.

I spent the next several days trying to gather things from the house which we would need as we returned to Albania. This was the most painful period of grieving through which I have yet passed. As I sorted through much of our life together over the past two years, the pain of Lynette's absence was intense. I spent many hours simply weeping, as the house was so full of her but yet she was not there. We face a dynamic tension in the face of death and in the certain knowledge of Christ's victory over it, and in a case like Lynette's, a definite experience of that victory, but also in the deep emotional reaction of our humanity against this violation of our human identity. We were not made to die and therefore we revolt against it.

Over the past 14 years, and especially in the past two years, I have grown together with Lynette as one person. It is very painful to have part of myself cut away. At the same time, I do rejoice with her because she has experienced the final victory over our enemy, and I rejoice that we will be together again, but in the meantime I suffer the true pain that is the consequence of sin in our world. Tears are also a wonderful gift from our Lord in this journey. In a strange way, though shed in great pain, they wash away the pain of loss and leave behind quiet gratitude for the fact that Lynette was and is part of my life. I have reflected many times on the tremendous blessing that I had to be married to her for 14 years. I cannot be bitter that it was not longer, and I am grateful that I had the privilege and the joy.

From Minnesota we drove the 14 hours to my parents' home in Arkansas, where we spent six days. It was truly a blessing to be with them and other close friends and family members who had not been able to come to the funeral. One of the highlights of the visit for Tristan was several fishing trips with my dad. From Arkansas we headed to Chicago. Early the next morning we flew to Denver for a quick overnight visit with dear friends who are missionaries in Central Asia and who are only rarely on the same side of the world as we.

We returned to Chicago late Saturday night in time to be at liturgy at our home parish of All Saints. It was truly a joy to worship and share and cry with this dear family, who with so many others have been such a source of strength and support to us. I had two more whirlwind days of visiting friends and family around the Chicago area and packing. I also did a two-hour interview for Ancient Faith Radio (www.ancientfaithradio.com) regarding Lynette's journey with cancer and our work in Albania.

I left for Albania on Wednesday, November 1, arriving the evening of the second. I spent approximately 10 hours in Albania before my 5 A.M. departure the next morning for Bratislava, Slovakia, where I represented the Albanian Orthodox Church at the official dialogue between the Orthodox Church and the Lutheran World Federation. I finally returned home at midnight on Wednesday, November 8. The children had remained in the US with Lynette's sister in order to visit Fr. Luke and Faith Veronis and their family in Massachusetts. They returned to Albania the same day I did with Fr. Pat and Denise Reardon, who were coming for a visit. It was very good to be home together again. The children were too exhausted to go to school on Thursday but returned on Friday. I think their reentry process has gone fairly smoothly. Their teachers have been very understanding and helpful with our special needs at this time.

I ask your special prayers for the children and myself again this coming weekend as I will be traveling to Kosovo. We will be leaving very early in the morning of November 23, Thanksgiving day. I will be leading a group of twelve young people attending the feast day of St. Stephen of Decani at that monastery. We will also be meeting the directors of various schools and arranging the schedule for the camping program next summer. Please pray for safety in travel as the mountains we must cross are often covered in deep snow at this time of year. Also pray that our presence at the monastery would be a blessing and that our meetings with school and government authorities would be successful. The children will not be going with me so this will mean another five days of separation. Please pray that the Lord would comfort, sustain and fill them with joy.

As always, thank you for your love and prayers and all the other ways that you so lovingly support us.

February 27, 2007   *&*   *From Nathan*

Six-Month Memorial Service

DEAR FRIENDS, THIS WEEK WE CELEBRATE SIX MONTHS SINCE Lynette's death and transition into the presence of our Lord. They have been six good though at times very challenging months. I would again like to express my deep gratitude to each of you who have prayed for us and supported us in different ways during this time.

People often ask how the children are doing, and I must still say that I am surprised at how well they seem to be doing. They do not seem in any way traumatized or damaged. They have the normal challenges and difficulties of young children, but they are happy and well adjusted. Tristan continues to struggle with some aspects of school as he has always done, especially his reading and spelling. Katherine is doing very well in school and enjoys it very much.

I have become more aware in recent weeks of my limitations as a single parent. I think I am doing well in caring for the children in meeting their basic needs, but I feel very inadequate to add those special touches which make life interesting and fun. I am trying very hard to organize my schedule to be with the children after school and on weekends, and we enjoy our time together. I am very grateful for the excellent support we have, especially from our missionary community here. The children have a number of close friends that they love spending time with. I have a great deal of flexibility on occasions when my responsibilities require me to be away from the children. There are always people who are willing to watch the children and they are delighted to be with their friends.

My own grieving process continues to progress. There are still many sad and poignant moments, but in general I am finding that the sharp pain of Lynette's loss is being replaced by a deep gratitude for the time that I had with her. A picture of us together hangs on my wall, and it no longer brings tears to my eyes to look at it. I remember the joy of the event with her.

I spent several hours a few days ago looking through the files on her laptop computer for the first time. (The computer had needed repair and has just recently been returned to me.) I felt her presence very strongly as I read different talks she had prepared and letters she had written, but that presence brought pleasure, not pain. I know that grieving has its seasons and the sharper pains will probably return, but I am grateful for the current stage. Please keep praying for us as the journey is not over yet.

I have begun the process of preparing the permanent marker for Lynette's grave. In Albania this is traditionally a large stone slab which is placed over the grave approximately one year after the burial. I have wanted to make this something special which would be a witness to her life and faith.

Lynette always loved mosaics and had wanted to learn this art for many years. She planned to begin studying it if the Lord had granted her healing from her cancer. She enjoyed a close friendship with a very talented mosaic artist here who has done numerous pieces for the churches around Albania. I have commissioned this artist, whose name is Edward, to do a mosaic of the resurrection and one of St. Katherine for Lynette's grave. He is very excited about this project and is enthusiastic about doing something which will be a real tribute to Lynette.

We suffered a major disappointment this month when we were informed by the board of the school where the children attend that they will not recognize us as fellow missionaries. The school is organized jointly by several Protestant missionary organizations. The mission of the school is to serve the Protestant missionary community. Non-missionaries pay about 2½ times the tuition of missionaries. I had petitioned the board to be recognized as a fellow missionary, both because I believe it is important for all of those who are serving Christ here in Albania to recognize and support one another and because the additional cost of the non-missionary tuition is very substantial. After two meetings with members of the board I believed that we had come to a mutual positive understanding, but then I received a letter from them informing me that they were resolved to maintain their policy of treating Orthodox missionaries as non-missionaries. I have been deeply saddened by this decision.

I will resume teaching Patrology at the Resurrection of Christ Theological Academy after Easter. Deacon Hector, who had been teaching these classes in my absence, will be returning to the United States for the birth of their baby. I am looking forward to being back in the classroom and in daily contact with the Church fathers, but I am wondering where I will find the time. It has been a real challenge to restrict my working hours in order to make sufficient quality time with the children. There are many challenging and exciting things happening with the children's and university ministries for which I am responsible, as well as many other areas. I am increasingly convinced that the most important area of ministry is investing in the development of people. I am very blessed with an excellent staff of coworkers: please pray that I will be able to inspire and lead them well. I have and will be doing a fair amount of speaking at a variety of events on various topics. These include: training events for my staff and volunteers, the girls' Winter Camp, the Tirana women's group weekly meetings and a conference for the diocese they are organizing, two weekly Bible studies, regular talks at the University weekly meetings. These opportunities are both a joy and a great responsibility. I ask your prayers that I will inspire those to whom I speak to draw closer to Christ and live life more fully in him.

I want to close by thanking each of you who have supported us financially and in prayer. I apologize that you have not received individual thank-you notes. This was something that Lynette had always done and I have not yet been able to do.

August 27, 2007   ❧   *Georgia Gillman*

One-Year Memorial

THIS PAST SUNDAY THE LITURGY WAS FILLED WITH A SPECIAL GRACE. The Archbishop remembered Lynette's name during the Liturgy, and afterwards he said a few words with much love about Lynette to all the people before they started the memorial service. After Raimonda and a few of us finished passing out the koliva [boiled wheat used for Orthodox memorials], about 20 of us drove out to Shen Vlash Monastery. It was a beautiful day and you know how lovely the place is where she is buried. When I got there I was amazed by the grave stone. I had heard that it was going to be with mosaics on both sides, but it was so wonderful to see! It's taller than six feet and when you walk up to it on the back side is the mosaic of the Resurrection and it says *"Une jam ngjallja dhe jeta"* ["I am the Resurrection and the Life" (Jn 11:25)] at the bottom. Then on the other side is the mosaic of St. Katherine, below which is [Lynette's] "Orthodox" name and the dates of her birth and death.

The Archbishop read the trisagion prayers—some in English and some in Albanian, and then said some more words at the end. He quoted (among other things) St. John Chrysostom, who said, "You honor the martyrs and saints by becoming like them," and thus encouraged us to remember Lynette's goodness and the depth of her spiritual life, while trying to become like her.

Afterwards we had lunch at Shen Vlash, and at the end the Archbishop invited us to tell our own memories about Lynette. I told a story about how she had encouraged me and given me some wise words about loving the children at the school. People from the camps, the university, the women's group, Petrach, and others also shared their memories.

The most beautiful words came from Tefta. Tefta said two days before Lynette died, when she was so weak she couldn't talk very much, Tefta had gone to spend some time with her. Lynette invited her to sit and they drank several glasses of water together. After a period of time, Lynette asked if she was bored by just sitting and drinking water.

"No, of course not," said Tefta. After another silence Lynette asked, "Tefta, tell me, how did the Albanian mothers endure? So many of them suffered and were even imprisoned. How did they endure that? I want to know so that I can endure like them."

Tefta said that before answering she just sat there shocked—how could someone in so much pain be thinking about the suffering of others, and seeing the others' pain as greater than her own?

The other thing Tefta said was that when her own brother died only a few months after Lynette, she told him, "It's OK. You have a friend waiting for you there." And Tefta said that she was able to face his death better because of the way she had seen Lynette die with faith.

Archbishop Anastasios encouraged Isidori to collect all of these stories and use it for a program on the Church Radio. And he encouraged all of us to not only remember her deeds, some of which may have been left unfinished in her lifetime, but to continue her work and be willing to suffer as she did. Not just words, but action.

I miss her very much. She really was peaceful and God-bearing in a way that is hard to explain, but could be felt easily. May God grant us all to have her peace and strength.

CHAPTER 9

The Legacy

L YNETTE TOUCHED THE LIVES OF COUNTLESS PEOPLE THROUGH HER inspiring life and her holy journey towards death. People from around the world prayed for Lynette and even wrote her letters of support and love. Many expressed how her writings on her website and witness itself touched and encouraged them in a unique manner. Those who knew her best—family members, lifelong and fairly recent friends, and her co-missionaries— testified to her saintly transformation. Following are a variety of reflections that reveal diverse perspectives on Lynette's life and death.

Faith Veronis   Co-missionary & Friend

Albania Changed Lynette

I FIRST ENCOUNTERED LYNETTE THROUGH HER MISSIONARY RESUME: graphic designer, theologically trained, visual artist, writer, musician, seamstress, and gourmet cook. Indeed, I was quite eager to meet Lynette, while curious to see if this missionary could live up to her impressive list of accomplishments. Needless to say, she was everything and more. After years of serving together as OCMC missionaries and forming a friendship that would unite us as sisters in Christ, I would add to her resume, "and uses all her gifts for the glory of God."

Luke and I first met Nathan and Lynette at a Missions and Evangelism Conference in Brookline, Massachusetts. At this conference, the Hoppes talked with Archbishop Anastasios and my husband about the prospects of serving as missionaries in Albania. I distinctly remember having lunch with this attractive and reserved couple. They listened so attentively as my enthusiastic husband gave them an earful about the Albanian mission. As I observed their attentiveness and questions regarding their future mission plans, I quickly realized this couple was not seeking to be long-term missionaries, but lifelong missionaries.

Luke and I tried to mentor Nathan and Lynette in the early stages of their ministry in Albania, but we quickly realized that we also had much to learn from two MKs (Missionary Kids) who grew up in the mission fields of Uganda and Colombia. Even though they both were blessed with a variety of mission experiences and knowledge, they still began their work in Albania with humility, patience, and careful reflection. They adjusted to the culture and church conditions in a sensitive manner. They readily learned from the other American and Greek missionaries, as well as the emerging Albanian leaders. They did not feel compelled to rush into any ministry since they were in no rush to complete their ministry. Albania was to become their indefinite home.

I felt it a privilege to work with Lynette. Whenever you asked her to do something, she did it in a spectacular way. I can think of so many instances but will share only a few. Soon after the Hoppes arrived, I hosted a Valentine's Day party in my home for some missionary and Albanian couples and asked Lynette to bake a dessert. She and Nathan arrived late at the party because she became so stressed out about her dessert. She was a gourmet cook trying to bake under Albanian conditions. She wanted to impress us with her delicious cream puffs but found it hard to bake when electricity could leave suddenly for hours at a time. Still, the cream puffs were among the most delicious I ever tasted, and the perseverance and perfection she showed would become lasting traits of Lynette's style.

I tapped into Lynette's artistic background for our arts and crafts program at summer camp. Each summer we ventured into the village of St. John Vladimir on the outskirts of Elbasan for six weeks to run three camps for hundreds of girls. Lynette always chose the most beautiful projects, including mosaics and wood paintings. Although they were never easy projects, Lynette assured me that the girls would be able to complete them, while learning perseverance and beauty. The girls loved the projects and took pride in being able to complete them. I also enjoyed the challenge of attempting these art projects, some of which still hang in my home today and remind me of camp and Lynette. Archbishop Anastasios liked one of her mosaics so much that he even hung it up at the entrance to our Archdiocesan Center in Tirana. After we left the mission field, it was a natural choice for Lynette to serve as the spiritual guide for the Girls' Camp. Her love and dedication to these young girls was evident in the fact that she chose to spend the last weeks of her life there.

The Kosovo War in April of 1999 revealed another side of the Hoppes. In response to the 500,000 refugees who flooded into Albania, I chose to focus on helping mothers who had just given birth and had nothing for themselves or their newborns. The hospital nurses came to know me as the "bag lady from the Orthodox Church." Daily I would bring bags of clothing, diapers, food, and medicines to the two maternity hospitals in Tirana.

One day I asked Lynette to come with me. She was so moved by the plight of these women that she and Nathan immediately decided to house a family, instead of allowing them to take their newborn back into a refugee camp. They hosted a family of four in their small apartment for a month or two. They developed a beautiful relationship with this family, which they continued to cultivate even after the war. In fact, this was part of the impetus for an ongoing ministry that Nathan runs in Kosovo to this day. And this Kosovar family was not the only family the Hoppes hosted as refugees. When a fire seriously damaged our home, the Hoppes graciously hosted us for two weeks, which turned into a time of wonderful bonding for us and our children.

When our family departed from Albania after ten years of service, we received such a wonderful farewell from many Albanian friends, along with our dear missionary community. I distinctly remember at our farewell meal how one of the missionaries thanked us for all we had done, and then thanked us for leaving them in the good hands of the Hoppes. Nathan and Lynette became, and deservedly so, the new team leaders of the OCMC Albanian missionaries. They also agreed to support many of the ministries in which we were involved. As we stayed in touch with many of our friends during our first year back in the States, we would often hear people express their appreciation for the leadership of Nathan and Lynette.

Although we worked together in various ministries, what bonded me most with Lynette was motherhood. As a pregnant mother in Albania, I was thrilled to learn that Lynette was arriving with her three-month-old Tristan. We would be able to raise our children together in the mission field. Our boys are only nine months apart and our girls only three months apart. As our children bonded with one another, we bonded even more. Our children shared home-schooling experiences and just loved playing with one another. In fact, to this day, our oldest son Paul will still remind his school friends that Tristan is his best friend. Tristan and Katherine have visited our Massachusetts home on several occasions during Lynette's illness and after her death. It warms my heart to see how strong our children's friendship remains despite their long distance from each other and contrasting life experiences. My husband and I often say that our children will be connected to missions more through the friendship they have with Tristan and Katherine than by anything else.

Some people in America have asked me what Lynette was like as a mother and how she handled her illness and pending death knowing that she was leaving behind two precious children. I believe that Lynette approached motherhood as she approached her Christian walk—with patience, gentleness, kindness, and love. She adored her children and loved reading to them, singing to them, and just being with them. Her birthday parties for them were highlights for all children who attended. And our children still talk about Lynette's legendary annual St. Nicholas Day celebrations.

In several phone conversations I had with her during her illness, Lynette expressed gratitude that her children seemed peaceful. Tristan and Katherine are good-natured children who get along with others easily. When they did fuss, Lynette would tell me she was firm, telling them to toughen up and prepare for more difficult challenges that life will bring. I often use Lynette's words about toughening up with my own children when they whine.

On one occasion late in her illness, she shared how Tristan had overheard a conversation regarding his mother's possible death. When he became frightened and saddened, she took him by the hand and led him to her icons. She told him if she died, he could come before these icons of Christ and the Virgin Mary and feel her presence. She would be with them, praying for her family. Naturally, it saddened Lynette that she would not see her children pass through different stages in life, but she accepted this with grace and faith. She was not a possessive mother. She felt very comfortable sharing her children with others. Even towards the end of her life, I firmly believe that Lynette trusted that God would provide for her children through Nathan and the many others who loved their family. And she believed that she would be connected to her children through her prayers and their prayers.

Like my husband, I encouraged Lynette to write some notes for her children before she died. I remember Lynette's response was that she wanted to write a novel for her children. The setting was Maine, with Tristan and Katherine as the main fictional characters. She had a plot and story line. That was Lynette—letters were too simple, she wanted a novel for her children. Of course, Lynette's problem was that her days were filled with projects for the present. Lynette appreciated each day, and would rather spend time sewing a ballerina tutu for Katherine or mother-daughter Christmas dresses, or simply watching Tristan build a Lego model, than writing a note for the future.

In the end, Lynette left a living legacy for her children. Tristan and Katherine will only have a few written memories from their mother, but whenever they meet the countless people Lynette touched through her life and death, they will hear plenty of stories about the special woman their mother was.

I thank God that this book will also act as a legacy for her children. When I think of this book, though, I have to chuckle. Lynette worked so diligently and patiently over a seven-year period to produce her book, *Resurrection: The Orthodox Autocephalous Church of Albania*. It was a miracle that Lynette was able to travel to Greece to oversee the final details for its publishing right after she discovered her cancer. Had she discovered her cancer a few weeks earlier, the book might never have reached publication. During the remaining twenty months of her life, she could have never realized, though, that she was authoring still another book—one that would share her journey of cancer and death. I know she would be humbled, yet grateful for the opportunity to preach once again about God's love through suffering, death, and resurrection. I just remind my husband that this book must be beautiful, since Lynette only did things in a beautiful manner.

When Lynette shared with us that she and Nathan had decided to return to Albania and spend whatever time God gave her there, we concurred with their decision. For Nathan and Lynette, returning to Albania meant returning home. We knew the Albanians and missionary community would embrace the Hoppe family and offer Lynette all the love and care she needed until her death. We stayed in touch with the Hoppes following their return, and marveled at Lynette's activity. It was almost as if Albania reinvigorated her.

Three months later she told me that the cancer had spread to her liver and she might have only a few weeks to live. She was on her way back to the camp to offer a final talk and then hoped to return to Tirana to host a neighborhood children's camp in her home. I asked her if she felt up to all that. She responded that she preferred to fall off her saddle rather than to just sit around, waiting to die. That was my spunky and determined friend Lynette.

A few days later, we received the tearful call from Nathan informing us that Lynette was in her final stages. I knew that Luke would travel to Albania to say goodbye. I desperately wanted to go, but hesitated to leave my four young children. I am not very good at separating from my kids, but my husband encouraged me to join him. I felt badly thinking that Lynette was departing this earthly life from her children, and I hesitated to leave my own for five days.

In the end we decided to leave our children with our parents, and flew to Albania. I thank God I was present with Lynette during her final moments of life. I will never forget sitting around her bedside with friends and family. Although Lynette's speech was beginning to falter when we arrived, she could still communicate fairly well.

Her limited conversation remained full of gratitude and joy. When I thanked her for all that she meant to me, our children, and to so many others, she responded, "Faith, Albania changed me."

I pondered these words for a long time. I understood what she meant. All of us who have served as long-term missionaries in Albania can relate to Lynette's words, "Albania changed me." For Lynette especially, she was able to take all of her experiences and interactions, both good and bad, and transform them into something beautiful in God's eyes. I believe as she was researching for her book, she interacted in a personal and spiritual way with the history, the culture, the environment, the people, the church, the poverty, the corruption, and all the suffering of Albania—and saw God's hand present. In her later years, she realized that those she set out to serve—the youth, the women, the poor and marginalized—had all in return made significant imprints on her heart.

Albania changed Lynette. And Lynette changed Albania. All for the glory of God.

Sherry Daehn ⟶ *Lynette's Sister*

Returning to God

THE FIRST THING I THINK OF WHEN I REMEMBER MY SISTER IS HER thirst for knowledge and her desire to know God more intimately every day. She was a voracious reader of many types of books, but the most important books she loved to read daily were her Bible and various books on the lives of saints. She wanted the love of God to radiate through her and from her to everyone she came in contact with . . . and it did.

She is the only person in my life that I have always been able to talk to . . . about anything. She never judged me even though I turned away from my faith for many years. I like to believe that we grew even closer together during the last twenty months of her life during her battle with cancer.

I know that her love, support, encouragement, faith, and her deep commitment to living her faith in all aspects of her life is the catalyst

God used to bring me back into a living, growing relationship with Him. I shared my feelings of anger towards God for allowing her to get cancer. She shared with me how her cancer was drawing her closer to God and how he was using it to reach others. She shared how she could see God's hand in everything leading up to her diagnosis and that she realized that, even though she would be sad to leave her husband and not get to see her children grow up, God had worked things out for others to take over for her in her absence. Her absolute sense of peace about it was incredible to witness.

The day she realized how completely, deeply, and irrevocably God loved her was a turning point for her and me. I am so appreciative that she shared the experience with me, and looking back I realize that it was also another event that opened the door of my heart just a little more to listening and hearing God's voice calling me back to Him.

Growing up, Lynette was always a good sport. She was always happy. The few years we had to grow up together were great fun. Even when we were punished for something, she managed to turn our punishment into great fun so we forgot we were being punished.

There was a certain rivalry between us too. If I learned something, she had to learn it and learn it better. We all had to take piano lessons, which I tolerated, but she excelled at. I decided I wanted to learn to play the guitar, so she had to also, but had to be better than I. I loved to sing and joined a choir; she had to also, and took voice lessons and became a well-known soloist. I gave up and realized that the fine arts were just not for me, but they were for her.

After she finished college, she decided to pursue her Master's degree at Wheaton College just outside of Chicago. I used to have to take week-long classes in Chicago, and we would work it out for me to go down the weekend before and after my class and stay with her. She introduced me to fun new restaurants, how to "glean" for food from grocery store dumpsters, Giordano's and Gino's pizza, and the best movies ever (*Princess Bride* and *Willow*). We had great fun together on those weekends, and I believe those times were the beginning of us becoming very good friends besides being sisters.

Once she and Nathan went to Albania as missionaries, I was always so honored when she would ask if I could get things for them to send along with someone who was going to Albania for a visit, or drive down to Chicago, pick them up, and bring them back to Minnesota. Those times were precious and allowed me extra time with her and Nathan and the children.

I love my sister and miss her dearly, but having the hope and knowledge that I will spend eternity with her in the presence of our Holy and Eternal God makes the pain of missing her easier. I am so thankful that God put us together in the same earthly family.

Lynn Holm &c *Lynette's Father*

A Girl of Faith

THIS HAS BEEN A HARD THING TO DO—WRITING ABOUT LYNETTE. She has made such an impact on my life as her dad.

She was born on Mother's Day and has been a special gift ever since. She was such an easy child to raise. If she did anything wrong, all you had to do is look at her sternly and she would be crushed. Friends would ask us if we would have a boy, were we going to name him Lynn. Neither Marce nor I wanted that to happen. So it was a joy to name her Lynette—little Lynn. She has really lived up to her name.

Being artistic myself, I wondered if we would have a child with that trait. Before she was three and before we left for Uganda, East Africa, she displayed that trait by drawing on the wall in one of the rooms of our house. So we knew we had to channel that into the right place. Later, as she showed more ability, we asked a British lady in our church in Kampala, who was an art teacher from the Royal School of Art in London, if she would tutor her. The lady was delighted. She helped her draw a lot of pixie drawings which might still be in some of our things somewhere.

Lynette was a great help to me in illustrating my sermons. The last thing she did before she left home after high school was to draw me the "praying hands" for a message I was preaching. That will always be a special drawing and memory as I put it on a stand on the platform that Sunday morning in Windom, Minnesota.

She and her girlfriend in high school did a lot of duets together and Lynette did a lot of solos. This was true in her high school programs. Then when she went to Moody, this expanded, and we went down to hear her perform with such humility. When she had a solo part in the *Messiah*, it was just her commitment to using her musical ability for the glory of God. That followed in her schooling at Northwestern College in Minneapolis. There she sang in *The Mikado* with a young man from our church in Lake City, Minnesota. That performance is still a fond memory of so many. So many times she came home to Lake City and sang solos, and many would cry with tears of feeling the Lord singing through her.

We had taught all of our children that we never had problems in our home. They were prayer projects. One of the first for Lynette came in the first term of our service in Kampala, when she came running from the back of our house there, tripped, and fell, hitting her forehead on the cement threshold of the back door. The fall split her forehead open, and Marce had to hold it shut while I drove to the Mission doctor. She had that scar on her forehead the rest of her life, but kept it covered with her bangs. When that happened we all gathered around her, and I said, "This is not a problem but a prayer project. We will ask the Lord to take care of Lynette and heal her and that she would have no after effects."

Lynette always wanted me to pick out a life's partner for her. It was too hard for her to do. I had to remind her many times that I hadn't found one I would give her to. So when she brought Nathan to meet us, I was so glad. Here was my kind of a guy. He has never failed to live up to that first impression, and I am so glad we let the Lord work that all out.

There are too many wonderful memories around tea parties and gourmet meals. Lynette learned well from her mother. They were very close. When I would go down to Moody Bible Institute's annual pastor's conference around Memorial Day, Marce would go with me. While Lynette was at Moody and then later when she was in graduate school at Wheaton, Marce would go and stay in the house where Lynette lived with Gaye and her other two roommates. I felt it was special for Marce and Lynette to have those times together and let their hair down.

The last memory is when Lynette came to me in May 2006, before Marce went home to be with the Lord. She came to ask if it would be OK for her and the family to go back "home" to Albania. She was feeling better and stronger, and her blood count had stayed up. I assured her that she could. I told her, "We know how you love the Albanian people. We loved the Ugandan people and still do." She told me that no matter what happened, if she did get worse, she wanted to die there and be buried there. We understood that. I gave her our blessing, knowing how hard this would be on Marce. But I also could see how hard it was on Lynette to see her mother deteriorate more each day and week. I assured her that the Lord would take of her and He would be here for her mom. I knew it would be hard for me, but I am glad I learned, as in all the other hard things in my life, that God's grace would always be there in adequate supply. I was also thankful later that she was not here to see her mother's last moments. It was also a confirmation of Lynette's faith to see her leave under such a situation.

I pray that the Lord will get all the glory for what He did in and through Lynette's life. I am greatly humbled to have had a daughter like her. She was a very special gift from the Lord. Her brothers and her sister are special gifts also, making me blessed beyond measure.

Dr. Tom Miller ✧ *Hospice Doctor*

A Most Gracious Death

NATHAN AND LYNETTE HOPPE CALLED ME ON OCCASION TO ASK FOR some medical advice during various difficult situations that arose during her fatal illness. The voice on the other end of the phone always seemed calm and confident. That was true during the most desperate times, even as Lynette was aware that she was approaching death.

They struck me as people who were prepared for this ordeal. I don't mean there was a premonition of what Lynette was about to face before she got her diagnosis. Rather, I had the impression they already had been living a life that could absorb this otherwise senseless tragedy and shock. I had the feeling that they already had been turning to God for meaning and hope and had been disciplining their lives to keep an open heart to learn how their own agenda and strength could interfere with His plan. That is why Lynette could say, "I have experienced such delight in the nearness of God these past few months, and this makes my illness so worthwhile."

I have been a hospice physician in North America for the last four years. The most common response to a terminal diagnosis I encounter, no matter what the person's age, is an expression of feeling wronged. Americans have the illusion of being in control. We believe that the world is ours to manage. Our advanced practice of medicine nourishes this illusion with stories of medical miracles and promises of recovery from all that ails us. But I have seen that this stance interferes with our ability to handle suffering. As the late Christian philosopher Ivan Illych once said, "Only pain that is perceived as curable is intolerable." And as a friend and medical colleague, Ray Armstrong Downing MD, added: "In an age of medical miracles, all pain in America is perceived as curable, consequently all pain is intolerable." Have we lost our ability to tolerate suffering?

As people feel wronged when they deal with terminal illness, the suffering is so intolerable that they go to great lengths to get out from under it. Most try to manipulate God into a miracle. Many stick all of their hope to the next medical treatment offered them. Some travel to foreign lands at great expense to seek some cure they heard or read about. And when these efforts can no longer offer what they promise, there is an existential loneliness—a feeling that the universe has failed them and their life has had no meaning. There is no way to make sense out of suffering, to put it into any meaningful context and let it open the heart to God and his work to get us ready for the next step.

In her writings and in our sporadic phone conversations, I could see Lynette struggling with the temptations that face us all during the crises of life. For a while she thought that her illness could be kept at bay by her own efforts to eat right, exercise, and rest. Though these things were doubtless a great help, she came to the end of their helpfulness when her illness advanced despite her straining. She understood her efforts were "willful, arrogant, selfish and independent."

Despair and depression would trouble her profoundly and cause her to suffer deeply in her spirit. It affected her outlook and her energy. She prepared to accept even this, however, as a way to deepen her faith. She eventually absorbed it and moved on.

Lynette, along with friends and family, prayed for a miracle, but resisted the temptation to demand one, or to expect it because of her own goodness, or believe that God would not let death happen to her because of her age, her importance to her family and her mission. "We are walking along a path that takes us from that self-serving desire of wanting God for my healing to the place of loving God for himself alone."

As a physician whom Lynette and Nathan occasionally turned to for advice, I sensed this faith and confidence in the Lord's loving hand. I didn't need to soften my words unnecessarily or sidestep the tough issues. I could talk to them openly about what I was able to see from a distance.

Lynette maintained more energy and purpose at the very end than I usually see in people who die. It had to be the result of her preparedness to die to sin every day and to see God's hand in her life. This preparation doubtless was occurring long before her illness. I sense that she had been trained in humility. She had learned to see through the "selfish, arrogant" route with its promises of healing. When setbacks occurred, she understood them not as an injustice, but looked for God's hand, and took it, and grew toward his purpose and love. Consequently, she had one of the most gracious deaths that I had ever known about.

May we all prepare our lives in such a way that we die to sin daily and train ourselves to depend on God.

Fr. Nick Kasemeotis 🕇 *Parish Priest*

An Unexpected Blessing

BEFORE I EVEN MET NATHAN OR LYNETTE, I HAD NUMEROUS PHONE calls from priests letting me know the Hoppes were in Rochester for medical treatment at the Mayo Clinic. We get several hundred

Orthodox visitors over the course of a year, so two more wasn't a surprise. What did surprise me was how many people called to let me know they were here. Nathan and Lynette were very unassuming about their reputation. When I had a chance to talk to Lynette about the severity of her condition, I remember my strong reaction. There is an impulse to ask God "why" when one sees people like Lynette and her family. After all, here is a family who left all the comforts and luxuries of life here in the States to go off to do what few people would do, and in return Lynette gets terminal cancer. This can challenge our faith and sense of fairness.

Of course, we all had the hope that a miracle of healing would take place for them. This involves mixed thoughts and feelings. We all hope and pray for physical healing, but what about the disappointment when the miracle does not happen? It seemed that in each Holy Unction service we offered, we asked God one more time to heal her. Unfortunately, this was not the case this time.

When I finally got to spend some quality time with Lynette, I heard the typical religious phrases like "We accept God's will" that I often hear from sick people. I have been a chaplain at Mayo for twenty-three years, visiting thousands of sick people, and unless people are saints, I see how people try to hide a great deal of fear, pain, and frustration. Only after they deal with such issues can they find a real acceptance of their condition. In the case of Lynette, and I might be wrong, but I feel that I had met a saint. Don't get me wrong. During their seventeen months in Rochester, I did hear about her pain, worries, and concerns. Yet they were always in the light of her acceptance.

The Paris Trip

It quickly became apparent that these were very special people, and special people deserve our best. One day I had lunch with Lynette and Nathan and asked her if there was something that she always wanted to do but never had a chance. After her somewhat persistent "I am very content," we finally established that she did have a dream of going to Paris. Things moved into motion as they arranged for the appropriate care for their children. I contacted Fr. Harry Pappas at St. Mary's in Minneapolis and Fr. Rick Andrews at St. George in

St. Paul about raising the needed finances, and both helped greatly in sending funds from their parishes. We passed a tray in Rochester, announcing our plan to send Nathan and Lynette to Paris. By this time the parish had gotten to know the family well and we set a record by collecting well over $1300. (Normally our trays for Archdiocese-mandated causes bring in about $200 to $500 at most.) Our collection simply revealed the love and respect that our parish had for Lynette and Nathan. I prayed that her health would hold out.

They finally left for Paris, only for us to watch on the news about riots throughout the city. And the riots lasted the entire week they were there. Had we sent two saintly people into danger? I was sweating back in Rochester, only to be relieved when they got back and told me that the riots had not affected them.

Time to Leave Rochester

In trying to show our love for the Hoppes, we not only sent them to Paris, but we offered a membership to our Rochester Athletic Club, along with other fineries of living in the States. But we worried whether we were spoiling them. Would they really want to go back to Albania?

Of course, the Hoppes did not let the "good life" get to them. As Lynette would say, "I'm not going to wait around and die in Rochester." As much as they had become a part of our parish, and we hated to see them go, we also realized that we were only a small part of their lives. We just thanked God for the blessing to have met them. Although we met Lynette when she was ill, we witnessed how the "sick" can teach the "healthy." I often see how a sickness can really define who a person is. This is what happened in Rochester. For that we are grateful!

The Hoppes also blessed me and our parish by teaching us in a very real way what Orthodox missions is all about, and what strength, hope, and faith in the face of terminal illness are all about. Nathan and Lynette are truly gifted people.

I must also say that I was amazed to see how Nathan put aside his calling and vocation to be with his wife during a very long period of illness in Rochester. This is something that Lynette greatly appreciated. They dealt with her sickness, struggles, and ultimate death with one mind.

I began by saying that we receive several hundred Orthodox visitors to Rochester for medical attention every year. Very few visitors have an impact on this parish like that of Lynette, Nathan, and the children. I am glad that she was able to get back to Albania before her death. The Lord called her to the place where she and her family had dedicated their lives. We miss her, Nathan, and the children. May our Lord "remember her in His kingdom." There are not many like her.

Joel David Holm ❦ *Lynette's Brother*

A Lover of God

WHAT WAS SAID OF THE BRILLIANT WRITER JOSEPH CONRAD's identity aptly applies to another brilliant writer, Lynette Hoppe.

> *She was traditional yet modern.*
> *She was flexible yet stable.*
> *She was wise yet naïve.*
> *She was independent yet dependent.*
> *She was stoic yet epicurean.*
> *She was well rounded yet focused.*
> *She was particular yet accommodating.*
> *She was passionate yet calm.*
> *She was international yet homey.*
> *She was complex yet simple.*
> *She was brilliant yet absent-minded.*
> *She was heavenly minded yet down to earth.*
> *She had expensive taste yet was generous to the poor and needy.*
> *She was public yet private.*
> *She was a communicator yet quiet.*
> *She was American yet Albanian.*
> *She was a saint yet a sinner.*
> *She was being yet becoming.*

Yet with her complexity, Lynette had a profound and growing love for Christ and love for people.

As a family member you often don't appreciate your siblings until later in life. With Lynette this first happened to me when we were in college together. We both attended Moody Bible Institute when she was in her third year and I was in my first year. It was during that year a real friendship developed between us that was more than just being siblings. I began to realize and appreciate the depth of my sister's wisdom, talents, and love for Christ. Twenty-six years later I still remember some of her sayings, such as "Leaders are readers" and "God takes serious Christians seriously."

The depth of Lynette was confirmed and really brought out by her battle with cancer—from her first response to her last breath. As is well known, these types of experiences really bring out who we are. What came out of Lynette was a deep love for Christ. Even with Lynette's ups and downs emotionally, spiritually, psychologically, and physically, her depth was seen in her pursuit of and walk with Christ to the end. This pursuit of and walk with Christ is a process. As has been said, the Christian life is about becoming—becoming who God has already declared us to be, or to put it differently, our sanctification attaining to our justification.

I can illustrate this with several things she said during her battle. First, in a conversation with her after more than a year of fighting cancer, she said something to the effect of, "Each step of the journey, each intensification of the cancer, means I have to apply anew the gospel, the truth of God's word, to that experience. It's like I have to relearn the things I have already learned." As someone else has said, "We can't live on yesterday's faith." As Lynette's illness intensified, she had to, and did, apply her faith afresh to those situations and learned anew the truth of God's word.

Second, after hearing the news that she had cancer, she wrote home to say:

I am doing well, despite the news. I think people here can't believe that I haven't collapsed or gone to pieces, but the truth is that I have no reason to. . . . When the pathologist showed my test results to our American doctor here, he said, "She's a good woman, isn't she? Why do the bad test results always come to the good people?" I can answer his question (though, I'm not sure about the "good woman" part). I do not believe that something bad has happened to me. I see this cancer as a manifestation of my Lord's desire to draw me nearer to himself. He wants all of me and not just a half-distracted nod in his direction now and then. I am honored to be entrusted with such a gift. I just hope I am worthy of it. . . . My prayer is not for healing, but for the grace to walk with courage and joy through whatever I may encounter. I don't want to become ill-tempered and whiny. I want to shine through this and gain that for which it is intended: a deeper love for God and a closer walk with him.

Such is the legacy of Lynette to me. She had a deep love for God and a close walk with him. As a result, she greatly encouraged me to do the same. I'm grateful to have known her as a sister and as a friend.

Metropolitan John (Pelushi) of Korca

A Death That Glorified God

THERE IS AN ALBANIAN PROVERB THAT SAYS, "IF YOU WANT TO know what kind of person someone was, look at the way he died." The saints repeated the same thing. Even if people were considered holy during their lives, the way they faced death was an important testimony to their holiness and the grace of the Holy Spirit upon them. Dostoevsky even attests to this in his story of the Staretz Zosima. Facing death offers a very serious and real proof of faith, because it reveals how deep and strong one's faith is. One facing death finds no place for pretense and must take off all the masks he has been wearing all his life.

The way Lynette faced death showed who she was. I remember her call to me right after the doctors diagnosed her with cancer. Although troubled, instead of fear I sensed in her voice the strength of her faith and hope in everlasting life. Only a living faith and a strong hope in everlasting life could overcome the fear of death.

It looks easy when somebody else faces it. Those few minutes that make an athlete a champion are the result of thousands of long hours of training and effort. The same happens in facing death; facing it becomes possible because of long hours of spiritual preparation and training. A human soul is cleansed, enriched, and strengthened only when in communion with the ultimate reality—that of eternity. The deep sensations and virtues cultivated from a life in communion with the Divine, even when we are not completely conscious of this struggle, reveal the greatest preparation in facing the final passage, the most important event in everybody's life.

Lynette prepared for this passage for a long time. Her entire life was truly a preparation. The deep experience of faith had enriched her soul, had cultivated sensations that never leave, because every experience of holiness leaves unforgettable traces in the human soul. Endowed with artistic talent and with sensitivity, nurtured and strengthened by Christ's love, Lynette felt God's presence, and it was this presence that would transform her and enable her to feel it everywhere, in any situation or circumstance she would find herself in.

The cultivation of virtue is a spiritual treasure that is indispensable in making somebody able to rejoice in their daily existence, as well as to face every difficulty. It is a treasure, valuable in good times and bad times, in mourning and happiness, in the cross and resurrection. It is "the real leaven" of life. This was true for Lynette. She could rejoice in her daily life as well as when she faced a very difficult test. When God is present in the smallest details of our everyday life, certainly He will be even more present in the hour of one's greatest trial. This happened with Lynette. Though young and with two little children, facing death didn't make her "drown in despair" because nothing can take away the joy given by God, regardless of how tragic the events might seem in our eyes.

Lynette was a good friend in the fullest sense of the word. True friendship brings joy and the joy of authentic friendship brings communion. True friendship may even be compared with a Sacrament. Just as God transmits His invisible grace through the visible objects of the Sacraments, in like manner friendship can become a vessel transmitting God's grace and unspeakable joy, leading a person to experience a full life. Unfortunately, though, we live in times that have weakened the understanding of friendship, transforming them, at best, into partnerships, and thus taking the joy out of life. One of the reasons that people of our day have lost the natural human sensation, and with it the ability to rejoice, is because they have lost communion with the other world, with the divine. Communion with the holy is often realized through the relations we have not only with each other, but even with the entire universe.

Lynette found it extremely important to practice God's teaching in her daily life. When we don't practice these lessons in our daily lives, then these teachings won't have any value for us. In order to get well, it is not enough to simply believe in the effect of the cure. If we don't inject the medicine into our body, it will do us no good. The same can be said for faith. If we don't practice it in our daily lives, the faith we possess loses its value. Lynette carefully tried to live her faith out in every detail of her life. Although she constantly expressed concrete love for others, regardless of their social position, giving so much to the poor and those in need, she always felt guilty that she didn't do more. Every time she complained to me about this, I inwardly rejoiced because I knew that she truly did help others in a significant way. I was happy for her experience of God, for her humility, for her sincere generosity which came from her communion with God. In order to keep her pride in check, though, I would not tell what I really thought. However surprising it seems, this is how it typically happens. Those who do much and offer their best often accuse themselves of never having done enough, while those who do little tend to justify themselves for what they haven't done. Humility and an authentic sense of unworthiness come from a vibrant communion with the living God.

Lynette always considered her relationship with God—not an abstract relationship, but a very personal relationship with a personal God—of utmost importance. She took God seriously. A holy and wise man once said, "We can't separate people into good and bad, but into those that take Christ seriously and those that don't." Lynette's love for God, her humility and sweetness, her strength and the dignity with which she faced death came from this vibrant relationship and burning desire to live with Christ. Her moving writings and letters during her martyrdom of cancer testify to this.

Lynette, together with her husband Nathan and the many other missionaries who have served in Albania, tried to share Christ's love and teachings. The unique aspect of Lynette is how she preached Christ not only with her life but more so with her death. Her death glorified God. It reminds me of the words of the Evangelist John, who writes about the revelation of Christ to Peter describing the way he is going to die, "This he spoke, signifying by what death he would glorify God" (John 21:19). To glorify God with your life is a great thing, but it's even greater to glorify God with your death. This is the fulfillment of a Christian life, when death itself points to the glory of God.

In a culture where death creates incredible pain and desperation and where so many people simply try to avoid it by not even mentioning it, Lynette's life stands as an incredible witness of how a Christian views life and faces death. The Good News and *Kerygma* of the Church is that the Lord defeated death, and death itself is not the end; life does not end in sadness or forgetfulness but offers a passageway into a deeper joy and fuller encounter with God. We proclaim these words all the time, but when someone preaches them with their lives, they have a much greater impact and credibility. Our Lord Himself didn't preach the Good News only with words, but empowered them and gave them life through His death and resurrection. *By death he conquered death.* Lynette's way of facing death became her greatest preaching and teachings as a missionary in Albania, and thus truly inspired the many people throughout the world who accompanied her on her road to Calvary. She especially touched our Albanian youth by her life and death, as they witnessed with their own eyes how a true believer trusts Jesus Christ as they face death. Death itself, the greatest and most common enemy of everyone, is transformed into glory through Jesus Christ.

When I met Lynette for the last time, she was clearly in agony. She lay in bed pale, yet with a bright grace and a palpable divine peace shining from her face. She had her eyes closed, with little strength left in her body. After she thanked me for visiting her and being there, the very last words I heard from her mouth were, "What a wonderful thing!" She repeated these words two or three times. I wanted to ask her what was she feeling or watching while she was saying this, but I couldn't since she seemed exhausted. I don't know what she felt or what she saw with her soul's eyes in those final moments, but what I am sure of is that she abode in a deep spiritual communion with her Lord. Her face radiated continuously the grace of another world.

The following day, on Sunday afternoon, Nathan called and told me that Lynette had passed away. Although I expected and knew that her departure would be a matter of days, the news of her death shocked and saddened me. In this state of sadness I opened the Gospel, wondering what word our Lord would give to me. I have a very old French Gospel, the first Bible I ever read, to which I have a strong emotional attachment. The Bible was opened and I read: "*Tes péshés te sont remis. . . . Ta foi t'a sauvée. Va en paix!*" "Your sins are forgiven. . . . Your faith has saved you. Go in peace!" (Lk 7:48, 50). Deep down I felt and believed that these words were for Lynette, and a comfort and brightness filled my soul.

May you rest in peace, our dear sister, and pray for the people and the church you loved so much.

Fr. Alexander Veronis

President Emeritus, OCMC Mission Board

Missionary Par Excellence

WE ENCOUNTER CERTAIN PEOPLE IN LIFE WHO LEAVE THEIR MARK on our souls forever. One such person for me was Dr. Victor Rambo, an American ophthalmologist who gave fifty years of missionary service in India. Dr. Rambo possessed a love for Jesus Christ which radiated in his person. "Learn to be givers in life, not just takers," he would often say. He lived a very simple personal lifestyle. He did not own a car or a home. He trusted in God to provide his needs.

Lynette Hoppe reminded me of Dr. Rambo when I first met her. She exuded a passion for missions. Lynette and her husband Nathan believed wholeheartedly in the promise of Christ, "You shall receive power when the Holy Spirit has come upon you; and you shall be my witnesses . . . to the end of the earth." Their subsequent life of missionary service gave strong evidence of God's power working in their lives.

From the beginning of their relationship with the OCMC, Nathan and Lynette made it clear that they intended to become lifelong missionaries. They were willing to go anywhere to serve the spread of the gospel in a cross-cultural setting. The OCMC commissioned the Hoppes to go to Albania in spring 1995, but it was then decided that Nathan should first attend an Orthodox seminary. By late spring 1998, they finally left to serve in Albania, the poorest country in Europe. Lynette admitted later that she did not even know where Albania was! Her desire was to live the Great Commission (Matthew 28:19) and it did not matter where.

In the way of preparation for the Hoppes' service, Archbishop Anastasios (Yannoulatos), a charismatic missionary-professor from the University of Athens, was leading the restoration of Orthodoxy in Albania since the collapse of communism in 1991. He would become Lynette's spiritual mentor during her missionary service in Albania, a blessing she always cherished.

Archbishop Anastasios is a Christ-centered spiritual leader who had rendered ten years of exemplary missionary service for the Orthodox Church in East Africa (1981–1991). Prior to that he taught world religions at the University of Athens and was a scholar on Islam, the dominant religion in Albania.

A spiritual renaissance was already occurring in the Orthodox mission in Albania when Lynette and Nathan joined the mission. They immediately immersed themselves in the mission's ministries and contributed a great deal with their many talents.

Presvytera Pearl and I had the pleasure on three occasions to host Lynette and Nathan and their beloved children, Tristan and Katherine, as guests in our home in Lancaster, Pennsylvania. We also visited their home in the Albanian mission during three visits to Albania. We marveled at the person of Lynette. Refined, gracious, hospitable, humble, artistic, articulate, devout, knowledgeable, talented, quiet yet vibrant, peaceful, accommodating, soft and feminine . . . these are adjectives that quickly came to mind when meeting this remarkable missionary.

Lynette possessed the faith, simplicity, and single-mindedness of notable missionaries like Dr. Rambo. She identified with the poor as did Mother Teresa of Calcutta, welcoming gypsies and street people into her humble home. Lynette strove always to make Jesus Christ known to others and to share his love and teaching, death and resurrection. "What you have heard from me through many witnesses entrust to faithful people who will be able to teach others as well. Share in suffering like a good soldier of Jesus Christ," the Apostle Paul wrote to his disciple Timothy. They are words by which Lynette Hoppe lived and died.

Lynette epitomized the "virtuous wife" described in Proverbs 31. This brilliant Christian woman had chosen the perfect career. She loved the Lord Jesus and the gospel. She adored her husband and children. She displayed compassion for the beggars she met on the streets of Albania. She quoted the Bible effortlessly as she lived it. She knew how to live simply and accepted the deprivations found in a poor nation.

Lynette accepted such inconveniences without complaining because her vision focused on Christ. "Christ is by far and away our greatest treasure in life, and anything that stands in the way of gaining Him must be sacrificed."

Lynette proved to be one of the best missionaries ever to serve under the OCMC!

Gabriela Bezhani   Albanian Co-worker

Our Albanian Missionary

WE HAVE WITNESSED MANY MISSIONARIES WHO HAVE COME AND gone. Lynette was special among all of them. I remember her as a quiet woman, a loving mother, a respectful person who was kind to everybody. I have never seen Lynette angry in all the eight years that I knew her. Her calmness and patience always attracted my attention. Her talent in art and decoration was seen everywhere. She had a beautiful voice, and I remember the girls at the camp always asked Lynette to sing for us. Among all the songs she sang, "Amazing Grace" was the one we always asked for. She was a loving mother, sensitive to the needs of others, a wonderful example of a Christian mother and wife.

Lynette was an example in many things, but the most powerful of all was the way she dealt with her illness and the fact that she accepted death willingly. When Lynette and Nathan learned that she had cancer, they shared the news with everybody in the community. This was a strange thing for most of the Albanians because we never tell somebody that he/she is ill until the very end. We never think of their right to know and prepare themselves for it.

What made a great impression on me during that first stage in her illness was the fact she was peaceful and not angry at God. Lynette talked at our girls' camp about death and described to the girls this first stage by saying: "God showered us with so much grace." I never heard Lynette asking why God gave her this illness, but she said, "That's what God has for me now."

Throughout her illness she possessed an inner peace which she reflected in her face and beautiful smile. Her newsletters, diary, and all her writings were an inspiration for all of us. Many people were amazed at the way she accepted her illness. She never saw it as a bad thing but as a good thing given to her by God so that she might draw closer to Him through her illness.

She never lost joy in the journey home. This was an impossible thing for almost all the Albanians who knew Lynette. How was it possible that she had so much joy even though she knew that she was dying?

The psalmist says: "Precious in the sight of the Lord is the death of His servant." Lynette was God's faithful servant. She knew that Christ had gone before her to prepare a place for her. She also said: "I feel so much joy from the idea of facing Christ . . . it is His work that has prepared me to be in front of Him."

For most of the Albanians death is the end of everything, the greatest despair. That's how they would react toward it. But Lynette's example was completely different. It was a real blessing for me to work and be so close with Lynette and see all her steps in this journey. Lynette prepared herself to go and meet the Lord. This is one of the things that too many Albanians don't do even when the chance is offered to them by God.

Lynette's example taught us many things. She taught us how to accept God's will in our lives, how to see it as a gift given to us for salvation. I remember Lynette saying about her illness: "This is good because it is given to me by God and God is good. I might not fully understand it but I'm sure that this is good." She taught us how to conquer death because she was with Christ, who by death trampled upon death and upon those in the tombs bestowed life. Lynette's life was bestowed by Christ and she knew it; that's why she had inner peace, no anxiety or fear of death. Two weeks before she passed away she gave a talk at the girls' camp on death. She knew she had only weeks to live and yet she was filled with joy, peace, and love that I have never seen in somebody before. She inspired the girls to think and be prepared for death. "One day we are all going to die," she said. "We should be prepared for death because we will meet our Maker."

I had to say goodbye to Lynette three days before she passed away because I had to go to Kosovo to organize a camp for children there. I remember her looking at me and asking when we were leaving. She had an inner peace and the grace of God was upon her. As I greeted her I thought of the fact that that was our last minute together here on earth, and I cried. She had taught me so many things. Actually I had always seen her illness and example as a lesson that God was teaching me through her. And I'm grateful to God and Lynette because I really believe that I learned so many things from that.

Another thing I won't forget in my life is Lynette's burial. There was sadness but not despair. The light of Resurrection was present everywhere. Actually this is the opposite of what happens in Albanian burials (whether they are Christians or not). In the Albanian burials you'll see a deep despair and a hopeless mourning. The way we deal with death is like there is no Resurrection. The troparion of Resurrection is not sung in our burials, but Lynette's burial was accompanied by the Resurrection troparion and many other Christian songs, whether sung by her in a CD or by her friends and family members that were present there.

It made a great impression that Tristan and Katherine were present throughout her illness, death, and burial. In Albania children are completely isolated from this process and are left confused by the disappearance of their loved ones. Her family members and friends were sad that they had to say goodbye to Lynette, but they were happy that Lynette was with the Lord, that she was finally home.

I miss Lynette very much, but I'm happy I have a friend that is living in the presence of God, interceding with Him for all of us. May her memory be eternal!

Gaye Buchanan ✥ *Best Friend*

Her Love of Beauty

I WAS FRIENDS WITH LYNETTE RAE HOLM HOPPE FOR TWENTY-eight years. We met at Moody Bible Institute as freshmen, living on the same floor in the dormitory. Ironically, her lifestyle as she started college at age eighteen was similar to the lifestyle she adopted throughout her struggle with cancer to the end of her life at age forty-six. Both times she jumped wholeheartedly into a health food/whole foods diet and exercise regimen. At age eighteen I thought she was a bit loony. At age forty-six I was eager for her to do whatever would help prolong her life. The years in between were filled with a smattering of diets, dreams, adventures, relationships, and thousands of wonderful, deep conversations together. I loved her and, thanks be to God, she loved me too: we were sisters.

We spent three years together at Moody, becoming better friends as each year passed. Directly after graduating, Lynette flew off to Africa for a short-term missions assignment teaching Christian Education in Mombasa, Kenya. I went to England to school, and we corresponded through that year and the next three or four as we finished up our undergrad degrees at separate colleges. We spent several school breaks together, visiting each other's families and sharing dreams, goals, and ideas. It wasn't until she moved to Wheaton College to attend grad school that we started rooming together. We lived one year in a basement apartment and then rented a house from some missionaries. We had two other girls who stuck with us for four years in that house. We were part of a great singles group at College Church in Wheaton during those years, and both of us grew a tremendous amount spiritually. Yet even then we were searching for something deeper. God kept pulling at us.

Lynette thought constantly about the mission field. Her degree at Wheaton was in missions, and she befriended many from other cultures and countries. Lynette grew up in Africa, the daughter of missionaries. My parents served as missionaries to Alaska. We both thought seriously about being missionaries. At one point in our friendship we decided to apply to a missions organization to work with the Kurds in Turkey. Lynette always had a heart for Middle Eastern and third-world peoples. She thought it easier to relate to them than to the average white American. So after we were accepted at candidate school, we drove to southern Pennsylvania for two weeks of training. At the end of this time, nervous about where they would send us, we each had an exit interview with the staff. They told us to "go home and get married, and then think about missions." Although highly offended, we dutifully went home, and in time we each married. Lynette became the missionary.

Nathan entered into our world during our time of studying and working at Wheaton College, shortly after our infamous Candidate School experience. God's wisdom certainly flowed through the missions center staff. Nathan became a terrific partner and anchor for Lynette. With Nathan, we first visited a little parish in Chicago that would change our lives. We were looking for depth in worship and theology and found a church that was searching too, only they were finding answers. So we stayed. Within a few years, Nathan and Lynette married and we were all chrismated Orthodox. What a journey!

Lynette and I loved Orthodoxy and the Eastern liturgy from the beginning. Lynette's artistic nature was drawn to the extraordinary beauty of the icons, the music, and the liturgy itself. She took a course in iconography and immersed herself in the prayers and spiritual dimension of the art. She thrived in producing art that opens a window into heaven.

Lynette was always producing some sort of art—either she would be painting signs for the dining hall, or sewing a dress for one of our parties, or fulfilling a pen-and-ink commission of a biblical character for someone, or cooking or baking for some event, or singing in church, or making huge textile banners for a professor's video series, or whatever came up. Life with her was never dull, always interesting, usually fun, and occasionally frustrating. She had a habit of not paying attention to the details of life. She focused on the matter at hand and other things would fade away. I cannot tell you how many times I followed along behind her picking up her purse from some store shelf so that no one else would take it. She never really seemed to care about it—she was busy with the matter at hand. I sense that this characteristic helped her focus on the people of Albania and not on her surroundings. She had a taste for things of importance. Yet a certain sense of practicality is always necessary in ministry. This is one of the reasons why she needed a husband.

Her love of beauty, her generosity, and her never-ending creativity meant that she always had some project in mind for the next free moment she had.

Some of my favorite times with Lynette were in the final year and a half of her life. We always had rich and deep conversations, but they took on a new dimension as she struggled to prepare her soul for death, if God should will it. She couldn't really see the incredible changes God wrought in her during those months, but her whole focus changed. Her humor changed. The earnestness of her conversation intensified. The direction of her gaze shifted toward heaven. There was a palpable taste of holiness or tranquility about her that I, and many others, found magnetic. I told her that her experience and transformation was the best argument for asking God for suffering that I had ever seen. If suffering produces the kinds of change that were wrought in her, then we should all be begging God for our own sufferings.

I learned from her that God really does not care as much about our circumstances—our bodies, our comfort, our work—as he does about our souls. These other things are completely dispensable, if the transforming of our soul and the souls around us requires it. For some, radical and profound transformation demand radical and profound suffering. Such was Lynette's battle with cancer. Thousands of us battled with her, suffered with her, and were profoundly changed because of her. It doesn't remove the pain of the loss of her presence, but it does give great beauty and value to her suffering. I am grateful to her for allowing us all to participate in it with her to the degree that we were able.

Lynette and I had many, many wonderful conversations. She was always questioning and yearning for understanding and information. One of her great joys in looking toward heaven was the realization that she would be able to participate fully in conversation with the men and women of great intellect from throughout history. Finally, she doesn't have to worry about being smart enough. I look forward with great anticipation to her next conversation with me, in heaven.

Sonila Dedja ✵ *Albanian Co-worker*

A Courageous and Noble Soul

IT IS NOT EASY TO WRITE ABOUT LYNETTE. HER LIFE OFFERS SO many rich and beautiful memories that when I am reminded that she is no longer among us, I deeply feel the loss.

I had the opportunity to meet the Hoppe family when they first came to Albania in 1998. I was a student at the Resurrection of Christ Theological Academy in St. Vlash-Durres. I remember our professors told us that an American couple was visiting the school and thinking about living in Albania as missionaries. They came to our class, and I was lucky enough to serve as their translator. I translated their initial impressions of Albania to my classmates. Although many years have passed and I can only recall a few things Nathan and Lynette shared, I will never forget the serene look on Lynette's face. From the very beginning, she tried to befriend everyone at the school. This was the beginning of my friendship with Lynette, which only grew stronger as the years passed. This bond especially increased during our Church's summer camp program. Lynette was a member of our staff, being responsible for the arts and crafts.

Everybody saw Lynette as a noble, devoted mother and wife, and a sincere example of one who truly loved Christ. We would talk about many things, including some very personal issues, and I remember how Lynette faced everything. She radiated a spirit that was guided by the light of Christ and the joy of the Holy Spirit.

Everyone felt terrible when we heard the news of her cancer. Our Albanian mentality and the way we face illnesses, especially something serious like cancer, made it very difficult for us to accept that a person such as Lynette could have such "bad luck." I come from a family that faced the loss of a very dear person from cancer. My father died on March 5, 1988, when I was only eight years old. During the final two months of my father's life, nobody, not even my mother, told us what was going on or what was going to happen. During that period our house was full of people—doctors, nurses, visitors, and family members—who were continuously crying. Only years later did my brother and younger sister discover that my father died of pancreatic cancer. Out of the three children in our family, only my eleven-year-old brother went to his funeral. I had to take care of my five-year-old sister. Everybody was terrified by the thought that my sister would ask about her father, and nobody wanted to tell her the truth. Even after my father's death, none of us had the courage to ask, "Where is Daddy?" even though we all lived in the same house and obviously noticed his absence.

My father had left this life, and we pray that God has embraced him in eternity. At the time of his death in 1988, though, nobody was allowed to mention the name of God or talk about such things as eternal life. We lived in Albania, the only country in the world which totally forbade any expression of religion since 1967. The communist regime banned God from our country. Although we didn't know anything about religion, we still wanted our mother to have the courage to tell us about our father, about her life with him, about his love for us, and other such memories that we could cherish. I remember very few things about my father, while my younger sister remembers even less.

Lynette was very surprised when I shared with her my experience with my father. She couldn't believe it. Lynette and Nathan, though, did the exact opposite of what my family did with us children. They had the courage to explain to their children about Lynette's sickness. They had the courage to face it together as a Christian family.

Lynette was always wondering whether her kids would remember her, and if so, what memories they would have of their mother.

Would they remember the times they played with her and had fun together? The only time I ever saw Lynette cry during her final months was when she asked these questions. She faced her cancer with an incredible strength, without complaint, always giving thanks to God for everything. I hoped that she would survive and live a long life. Thinking this way, though, made it hard for me to accept that she was slowly fading away. Every time I asked about her health she would say, "I am going to Christ, the One I am living for!"

I had the blessing to be with her during her final days. I didn't do much other than just sit next to her and talk with her relatives and all those visiting her home. Though tired and weak, she allowed visitors to come into her room and meet her. She had something special to say for everyone. I will never forget her last words to me and my fiancé Andrea just two days before she passed away. "Life is so beautiful but too short. We don't know what God's plan is for our life, so always be ready."

Lynette exemplified sacrificial love. Everyone admired the way she faced her death. Even weeks before her death, she offered a wonderful witness of Christ at the girls' camp. We will always remember the 2006 Camp Anthem—"Don't be overcome by evil but overcome evil with good." The memory of her creativity will always be with us.

I've only expressed a little of what I could say about my friendship with Lynette. I still have the impression she's abroad, and will be coming back soon. It is hard to accept the fact that she isn't returning to us and her family. Somehow I still see her joyful face during those last days, and I am reminded of the excitement she felt at joining her Lord.

Archbishop Ananstasios' eulogy aptly expressed what Lynette embodied: "She faced death . . . radiating love, conveying more faith, more peace, more love . . . thinking . . . 'Who is going to separate us from Christ's love?'"

Through her life we witnessed that even though alive we live as if we were dead, and even if we die we belong to God. Every time we talk about Lynette and remember her, I whisper deep down within my soul, knowing with a certainty that she is listening, "We miss you very much, Lynette!"

The Hands of God

AFTER LYNETTE'S DEATH, I REFLECTED ON ALL THE YEARS I'D known her. I tried to fix her in my mind's eye, to see her as a living being, a friend who hadn't really left but who would be a real presence in my life. From these reflections, an image emerged and stayed with me: Lynette's hands—like dancers—always active in creative movement. I remembered the many times I saw them balanced over a sheet of paper or a dessert or a bit of fabric, her fingers slightly moving as she considered how to execute the design in her mind. In my memory, I saw the fingers extended, the palm curved in, and I was reminded of Christ's hand in icons as he gives us a sign of blessing. Surely, Lynette's hands were a blessing to all of us, bringing beauty and grace to everything and everyone around her. What they produced was just the beginning of what she gave us. Their gifts emerged from her deep love of Christ and of all people, her desire to serve whenever possible, and her generosity of spirit, which she shared with us in so many ways.

I met Lynette in Chicago, when we were both learning about the Orthodox Church and found ourselves in the same parish. How many ways she touched and shaped my life, only God knows. She was a loving and patient friend who always accepted me where I was at but also gently encouraged me to stretch and grow. What I appreciated most were her quiet words: never judging, always understanding and relating to me from her own experiences.

Our friendship deepened and became even more important to me when I joined the Hoppes on the mission field in Albania in 2002. There, I consciously saw Lynette as a model of a wife and mother—as well as a model of a missionary—marveling at how she loved and cared for her family. In her marriage, I saw support for Nathan's ministry and honor for him as a person, and with her children I saw patience and gentleness that never seemed to falter. Two very special memories of how Lynette's hands touched my life and reflected the beauty of her spirit stand out.

Shortly after arriving in Albania, I met Panayiotis, who became my husband a year later. Lynette was a confidante and friend during our courtship and gave me such valuable advice and support. When we became engaged, Panayiotis and I asked the Hoppes to be our sponsors or *koumbari* for the wedding. A few hours before the sacrament, it started to rain heavily and the hairstylist couldn't meet me. Instead, Lynette stepped in with brush and pins and came up with an impromptu style. How dear that time was, as her hands worked away and she shared in my excitement and joy and celebrated it with me. Now married four years, I often think of her example and the things we discussed and the advice she gave. She deeply understood the role of helpmate and wife, and she shaped her own gifts and activities to be those that would encourage and support her husband. I know beyond a doubt that the things I learned from her have blessed our marriage.

A year later, Lynette participated in another important event in my life, when our first daughter Sophia was born. We were staying in Athens for the birth, and Lynette had business there for Archbishop Anastasios. Providentially, she arrived hours before we returned from the hospital and spent that time decorating our apartment with welcoming posters. Her calligraphy made everything special and beautiful, and the highlight was a "prayer for parents" that hung over Sophia's crib for more than a year. While I rested that afternoon, Lynette rocked Sophia to sleep and sang her lullabies, and again, I was so thankful to have her presence in our lives and to have our little baby receive that precious time with her.

Shortly after that visit, Lynette was diagnosed with cancer, and she fell asleep in the Lord only twenty months later. I remember her second trip to Athens when Sophia was a few weeks old, right before the Hoppes returned to the States for a full prognosis and cancer treatment. Lynette asked if she could take Sophia for a walk in the front pack, and the two set off on what remained a vivid memory for Lynette. She commented several times later on about that "sweet, special" time, and I imagine she found comfort in her own grief as she cuddled that new little life.

I also remember a story Lynette shared about her son Tristan shortly before her diagnosis. She was having a busy day and had lots to do, and he wanted to snuggle with her and read books. She said, "At first I wanted to say no, that I had too much to do, but then I thought of him growing up and not wanting to snuggle with his mommy much longer. I decided it was more important to seize the moment and spend that time with him." She was soon to find out that that time was even more precious and fleeting than she'd expected, and I remember that as I give hugs and kisses to my daughters. I looked forward to sharing motherhood with Lynette and the many challenges that were ahead for us as parents. I wanted to grow into this new role with her support and guidance, so now I gaze at her calligraphed Prayer for Parents and imagine her interceding for us in heaven.

The memories are precious and would be just as precious if life had continued its ordinary course, but losing Lynette has given them poignancy. And in all the memories, I see her hands, always working and creating and shaping. I wanted to write a poem about them and how they had blessed so many, but I didn't know how to find words that were sufficiently beautiful, graceful, elegant. Her hands themselves were the poetry.

Christine Pappas 🙢 *Co-missionary*

A Christlike Spirit

"But whosoever shall do and teach shall be called great." (Matthew 5:19)

"For not to ourselves alone should we be profitable, but to others also; since neither is the reward as great for him who guides himself aright, as for one who with himself adds also another." (St. John Chrysostom, Homilies 15 & 16 on Matthew 5)

OVER THE MANY YEARS I KNEW LYNETTE HOPPE, SHE WAS A friend, a mentor, a coworker, and a guide. When I first met her, her willingness to serve Christ as a missionary impressed me. Then her endless talents inspired me. Later, while seeing her work in Albania, her compassion to minister to so many impressed me. In the end, her closeness to our Lord awed me.

I was blessed to be in Albania during Lynette's final months on this earth. During those days, I so wanted to stay close to her, to serve her in any way, to make her more physically comfortable, to learn from her, to feel the grace surrounding her. We all wanted to be close to Lynette, to remain in the same room, to hear her speak— somehow it made us feel good inside, somehow it made us want to become better. It is difficult to explain why she had such an effect on us. She did not force her opinions and beliefs on others, but rather she radiated joy and inner peace.

During our time in Albania, my husband, Driko, and our two sons, Anthony & Kosta, grew very close to Nathan, Lynette, Tristan, and Katherine. We spent a great deal of time at each other's homes. The Hoppe family showed us a great deal of love and hospitality. Lynette made all guests feel welcome. She often told me that relationships were the most important thing. I didn't understand this at first, but learned through her example. Lynette contributed to the organized levels of ministry, but she also had a gift for touching people on a very personal level. She did this in so many ways: from sharing a cup of coffee with her crippled neighbor, to making a birthday cake for the Archbishop, to giving her extra flannel sheets to a new missionary, to ordering a special wedding cake for a young couple getting married, to hosting numerous small Christmas celebrations where she could give the children and needy families some special treats, to her famous St. Nicholas Day party for the mission kids, to making her special crepes for her kids and their friends only days before she passed away. Lynette showed Christlike love in all her gestures.

During the last days of her life, Lynette desperately wanted to finish some letters to leave behind for her children. She had put off writing them because of the emotional strain. As her health started failing very rapidly, time was of the essence to complete this important task. Although Lynette could no longer physically write the letters or type them on her computer, she asked me to type as she composed. Of course I wanted to do what I could to help, even though I knew how difficult it would be to listen to my friend write about special events in her children's future knowing that she would not be physically present. It saddened me to think of her not being able to raise her children. I kept reminding myself that God loved her children and would take care of them, while she would be watching over them in a different way.

Although very weak and on many medications, Lynette was strong and determined to finish these letters. She wanted to convey her love and some motherly advice to her beloved children. She overcame the difficult emotional and physical hurdles for the sake of her children. She wanted them to have letters from her at special events in their lives—their birthday, their graduation, their wedding day. She wanted to impart her love and encourage them to always put Christ first.

When I think of my dear friend, Lynette, I picture her beautiful smile. I feel certain that she is with our Lord and praying for us. St. John Chrysostom teaches us, "not to ourselves alone . . . but to others also." Lynette thought of others, did for others, and did it in Christ's name. She did that which the Lord asks. May her memory be eternal!

James M. Kushiner   Touchstone Editor

The Lord Provides

FROM 1991 THROUGH 1996, BEFORE GOING TO ALBANIA AS A MISsionary, Lynette Hoppe served as graphic design editor for *Touchstone* magazine. I was the editor. This quarterly journal was subtitled "A Journal of Ecumenical Orthodoxy" and provided a common meeting ground for evangelical, Catholic, and Orthodox Christians committed to what they saw as the common Christian heritage.

Touchstone was founded in the late 1980s to address issues in Christianity and modern culture through the lens of the historic Christian tradition, so it also naturally attracted a number of evangelical Christians who were on a pilgrimage toward the historic churches. Lynette and Nathan were two such pilgrims on this path when she began her work for *Touchstone*.

Lynette and Nathan became regular members of the same fellowship of Christians to which I belonged back then. We were all on a pilgrimage. Eventually, forty-nine of us joined the Orthodox Church in

1993 and formed All Saints Antiochian Orthodox Church in Chicago. The newly married Hoppes were chrismated a bit later, and All Saints remained their home parish from which they were sent to Albania.

That Lynette worked for *Touchstone* until 1996 was quite providential. We could not afford paid staff and needed someone to help with the layout and graphic design. Lynette volunteered. Her artistic and graphic skills were professional, and her contribution was generous. She took an amateur-looking magazine and redesigned it, a design that has remained the basis for subsequent minor revisions. I have no idea how I would have produced the magazine without her. We had a need, and the Lord provided Lynette.

During some of the time that Lynette served as design editor, she held a full-time job in Wheaton and would work on *Touchstone* after hours, sometimes late into the evening. She would patiently and painstakingly make alterations, corrections, and redesigns whenever needed. I do not recall her "losing her cool," even when, on at least one occasion, hours of work were lost when a computer crashed. With Lynette, I always knew the work would be competently completed, no matter what it took.

I have on file some forty of her original sketches, cartoons, and drawings, ranging from portraits of Orthodox theologian Georges Florovsky, Reformed theologian John W. Nevin, Pope John Paul II, and Baptist preacher Vance Havner, to caricatures of Charles Darwin and Carl Jung. My favorite was used for our spring 1996 cover: an exquisitely rendered portrait in pencil of an unnamed African Christian, a modern martyr silently bearing the cross—perhaps a reflection of Lynette's childhood experience among the suffering Christians of East Africa.

In 1995, when Nathan and Lynette were seeking to become Orthodox missionaries, they attended an ecumenical conference *Touchstone* was cosponsoring in Aiken, South Carolina. There they originally had planned to meet Archbishop Anastasios of Albania, who was a principal speaker, but he had to cancel at the last moment. They were able, however, to meet Bishop Kallistos Ware, one of our other speakers, as well as many other Orthodox Christians from around the country. Lynette worked at the conference as a volunteer and sold back issues and subscriptions at our table. The memorable conference proceedings were published in 1997 by InterVarsity Press as *Reclaiming the Great Tradition*.

Even in 1995, I knew our time with Lynette was sadly coming to an end, and it was not long afterwards that she and Nathan took their definitive steps toward Albania, the beginning of a new and fruitful ministry. I knew that the Orthodox Church in Albania was being rebuilt and that they could use someone with Lynette's skills to produce much-needed publications. Albania had needs, and the Lord provided both Nathan and Lynette.

Nine years later, on an early summer day in 2005, I walked into All Saints Orthodox Church in Chicago. At the back of the church there is an original icon of Christ written by Lynette. I venerated it and placed my hand gently on its surface. I prayed to the Lord for the healing of the one whose hands had written the very icon before which I prayed. I came away in peace, with a strong and unforgettable sense that Lynette was now entirely in the hands of the Lord who fashioned her and that all would be well.

Later that October, I had the privilege of driving the Hoppes from Chicago to Lynette's parents' home in Minnesota. They had just flown from Albania to Chicago, but their flight from Chicago to Minneapolis had been cancelled. I never forgot how Lynette had volunteered many hours to *Touchstone*, so I offered to chauffeur the Hoppes a few hundred miles to Minnesota. Lynette said it would be a lot more comfortable to sit and rest in the car rather than go back to the airport and negotiate all the lines. I was just happy to have the chance to spend the time with the family and make the trip more comfortable.

As we drove through the Wisconsin forests now turning to autumn, I told Lynette about the prayer before the icon. Somehow, I said, I knew "all would be well" and that the Lord had his hands upon her. To discover oneself to be fully in the hands of the Lord: that is a struggle of the Christian life. She spoke of her struggles, and talked about death and her acceptance of it, should that be the Lord's will. I never assumed that "all will be well" meant she would be healed of her cancer. In hindsight, it is clear that all is finally well, for she is now at home with the Lord. Lynette now had needs, and the Lord provided himself.

I primarily think of Lynette as a missionary to Albania, but in addition to the manifold fruits of her labors there, there is another fruit of her talent, also given to the Lord, that survives in a quiet way through the ministry of *Touchstone*, which has helped bring an awareness of the historic Christian tradition to many pilgrims. Lynette embraced this pilgrimage herself while she generously helped a struggling little magazine during its precarious and formative years.

So with heartfelt gratitude for the full life and labors of this dear servant of the Lord, I pray: May her memory be eternal!

Tressa Joanna & Friend from Chicago

An Icon of Christ

HE LOOKED UP AT HIS FATHER, AND THEN TO THE OBJECT SO tenderly venerated by him. It was an icon of Christ the Teacher which was adorning the stand as you first enter the nave of All Saints Orthodox Church in Chicago. He kissed it too, and they both gazed lovingly upon His face.

Eight-year-old Tristan Hoppe had been told only moments before that his mother had written this icon years ago. "This is a beautiful icon, Daddy. Mommy did this?" Tristan's voice was calm and it struck me how easy it was for him to talk about the mother he had lost to cancer only months before. He seemed delighted to see his mother's work. I fought hard to restrain my tears. It was as if she were there, calmly walking alongside as they made their way to the front of the nave to view another icon Lynette had written. "She did this one too? It's St. Nicholas! She did a wonderful job, Daddy!" His comments sounded so mature. There was a holy quiet in the nave. Soon Katherine, looking for her father, joined the two. What a picture. I thought perhaps I should leave them alone as they stood there together, but my feet felt glued to the floor. When the Hoppes are around, one wants to remain in their company.

So I stood and watched. I began to reflect upon an icon in our home that has a touch from Lynette. In the summer of 2005, I was to have my first opportunity to write an icon at a retreat in Wisconsin with iconographer Phil Zimmerman. Our group was working on the icon of Mary and the Christ Child, "Seeker of the Lost." Lynette and her family were back in the States where she could receive cancer treatment at the Mayo Clinic in Minnesota. Denise Reardon made a way for her to join us for a day. It was Phil who had directed her as she wrote her first icons, and it was a special reunion of sorts for her to be with him again. Nathan brought Lynette over midweek, and the spirit of the class took on a deeper dimension when they joined us.

Lynette, friendly and smiling, quietly studied what we were doing and spoke in quiet tones with her icon teacher, looking over his shoulder as he explained the next step to those gathered around. Everyone sensed that her presence was a gift. Our small group from All Saints purchased supplies for her so she could start the same icon. The supplies were placed in front of her, and she embarked upon completing as much as her strength would allow.

As we were painting, I was having trouble making Christ's hand look as it should. She was sitting next to me, so I leaned toward her, and interrupting her focused work, asked her to help me with His hand. "Lynette, if you help me, I promise I will pray for you each and every time I look at His hand."

I was a bit playful in my comment, but she took it seriously and responded quickly. She looked upon the icon and gently took my brush. She made a few strokes, explaining where the spaces needed to be for the knuckles and how to hold the brush just so for the fingertips. Soon I had the confidence to work up, layer by layer, to finish the hand from what she helped me begin. From that point on, the icon became an even more blessed work. No matter how it turned out, I would have the comfort of knowing she had a part in the hand of Christ that tenderly rested above the heart of the Theotokos.

At the end of the day, the Hoppes returned home. By the end of the week our group returned to Chicago. We had our icons blessed and were hard pressed to talk about our time with Lynette without breaking into tears. We each returned to our normal schedules, but our lives were not the same. For me, my return to the world included my job as a visiting nurse.

Before my retreat, I had told two of my patients that I would not be able to see them for a week. I promised that I would show them the icon I was going to write. Since both gentlemen were Roman Catholic and were suffering from terminal illnesses, they seemed more receptive to spiritual conversations. I took the icon I had completed to each of their homes at my next nursing visit. The first man offered money for the icon as he had beautiful artwork about his home.

The reaction of the second man was different, and especially touching. David studied the icon carefully and had tears in his eyes when I told him and his wife about Lynette's visit. I had earlier given his wife some of the writings from Lynette's journal about her journey with cancer. They were happy that Lynette was able to come to the retreat for a day. I recounted how I pressed her into helping me on my icon, promising to pray for her each and every time I looked at Christ's hand. At that moment David wrapped his arms around the icon and held it to his heart. He implored me to pray for him whenever I prayed for Lynette while looking upon the icon. The three of us wept. David went to the Lord four months later, and a copy of the icon remains with his wife. I cannot pass the icon in our home without venerating it, kissing the hand, and praying for the souls of Lynette and my two patients.

As I watch them in this holy place, I can only imagine how close Nathan and his children are to her as they look upon her icons that are in our church. O blessed Lord, as they look through the windows of heaven, may the love of his wife and their mother be amplified to them through the heavenly presence of Christ in His Spirit. To Him be glory forever and ever. Amen.

EPILOGUE

One Year Later ✌

"Therefore, since we are surrounded by so great a cloud of witnesses, let us also lay aside every weight, and sin which clings so closely, and let us run with perseverance the race that is set before us, looking to Jesus the pioneer and perfecter of our faith, who for the joy that was set before him endured the cross." (Hebrews 12:1, 2)

THIRTEEN MONTHS AGO, LYNETTE JOINED THAT GREAT CLOUD OF witnesses that stand at the throne of our Lord and cheer us on as we continue to run the race. I have been greatly blessed throughout these months knowing that I have a fan in the bleachers of heaven praying for me and cheering me on. The race has had many challenges and many joys. There have been times of great sadness and tears, but also a sense of healing and well-being.

The pace of life has been especially hectic and sometimes overwhelming in the last seven months. Just after Easter I resumed teaching at the Resurrection of Christ Theological Academy. It was a great joy to be back doing this work which I love, but it was also one more thing which pushed me beyond my capacity to fulfill all of my responsibilities well. I have felt torn in too many directions to be completely effective in any one of them. At times I have found myself completely overwhelmed by the magnitude of the tasks before me. It has been humbling to realize again how weak I am and how completely dependent I must be upon Him. It has been tempting many times in the past few years to feel like I had really come to understand the situations around me and that I had the answers for the problems which we face. These last months have taught me once again how little I know and how little I understand. His power is made perfect in weakness, and I have felt truly weak and inadequate. I need the prayers of many to help me find the wisdom and strength that come through our Lord.

Family Adjustments

Tristan and Katherine continue to be a great joy to me. They are best friends and spend endless hours playing happily together. They of course have the occasional sibling squabble, but ninety-nine percent of the time they're delighted with one another's company. I am amazed at their creativity in finding ways to play together.

Tristan is very sensitive and compassionate. He is often very enthusiastic, although he struggles with many fears and occasional depression. The last two months have been especially difficult for him. He has been visibly grieving the loss of Lynette for the first time. In these weeks, he has struggled with sadness, although not understanding why. He has cried often, while we have sat together, grieving our loss. I think it has been a very healthy process for him to acknowledge his grief and let go of Lynette. The season of grief seems to be passing, though I am sure it will return at different times and in various ways throughout his life.

His struggle with fear continues to be intense. He possesses great sensitivity and is affected much more deeply than the average child by the many perverse and diabolical things which the entertainment media makes part of children's entertainment. Things he has seen months earlier in the homes of friends continue to haunt him. One of the beautiful things during this challenging time has been the way he turns to Christ with his fear. He asks often that I pray with him, and he himself has said that his battle with fear has been good because it has made him turn to God. I pray that he will find his security and joy in our Lord Jesus and that all fear will be cast out by the love of our Savior and the security that is found in him.

Katherine is much more even-tempered. She approaches almost all of life with a bright smile and a laugh. Her smile is a bit jagged these days because her dentistry is in a state of flux. Many teeth have fallen out and some have been replaced. She has not quite grown into some of her adult teeth yet, making them look oversized. Nonetheless her winning smile makes everyone who looks at her smile back. Katherine enjoys school and is progressing well in reading and other subjects. She especially likes all sorts of arts and crafts, and has definitely inherited Lynette's artistic abilities. She has not yet experienced the seasons of deep grieving for Lynette. I am sure that they will come, but thus far she has accepted everything with good grace and a big smile.

The flexibility of both children has blessed me. Whether we fly a transatlantic trip, travel to Kosovo, or simply walk across Tirana, they travel with little complaint. They adapt to my ever-changing schedule and bless all whom they meet. They love playing with children, especially their fellow missionary kids. I have wonderful support in their care, which allows me tremendous flexibility in my schedule. I try to be home when they arrive from school and spend as much as possible of the weekends together. A highlight of our week is going out for Saturday morning breakfast together. The great bane of our life is homework. We all hate it, although I do my best to encourage and help. I don't like surrendering our precious time together to homework. Thank God their teachers have been very understanding and helpful.

One of my great ongoing challenges is balancing between quality time with the children and all of the things that pull me in different directions. One of the real concerns I had for this past summer was how I would care properly for the children during the time I needed to be in Kosovo for the children's camps that I lead there each summer. These are very stressful and demanding activities which my staff is very anxious for me to lead in person. The living conditions are quite difficult, with fifteen or more people sharing one bathroom and living in very close quarters. Therefore, it would not be easy either to take the children or to delegate the responsibility.

I used this necessary extended separation to provide the children with an opportunity to spend time with close friends and relatives in the United States. My mom came to Albania and returned to the States with the children on June 17. I completed the camps in Kosovo and met them in the US on July 15. The children used this time to renew friendships with their cousins and others whom they had missed very much. Of course, I felt the absence of the children, but I tried to call them fairly often. We spent a whirlwind two weeks in the States, during which we visited with many friends, family members, and supporters. Though they were tiring, I received great blessings and encouragement from those visits.

Key Lessons

As I have reflected on Lynette's illness and journey throughout this past year, I keep returning to several key lessons which I had learned, but which I continually need to relearn.

I've learned much about God's incredible love for us and his desire for our very best. Lynette and I spoke a number of times about the fact that God could use her illness for the salvation of us all. Though in itself her illness manifested the sin and brokenness of our creation, our loving God gave it to us as a tool that could draw us closer to Him and transform us more into His likeness. Lynette understood and accepted her cancer in this way, and allowed her journey through it to transform her. It was tempting to think that this was God's gift to her alone and that He was calling her to come home, while the rest of us would simply have to make the best of a difficult situation. In reality, though, God's love is for all of us, and Lynette's illness was for all of us. Just as God showed His goodness for Lynette by taking her home at this time, He also revealed His goodness for the children and me.

We received an incredible privilege in accompanying her to the gates of paradise, and this journey transformed me in many ways. I now have a much greater awareness of the temporary nature of this life, and much less fear of death. Having lived with someone dying over the course of many months imprinted the sense of mortality on my consciousness in a way that I do not think anything else could. In walking with her through her final days into the arms of death, I confronted death in a personal way which allowed me to experience its power and terror. It is a fearful thing that ripped away the life which vivified my dear wife and left her a dead body growing cold and eventually falling into decay. Death is a tragedy and a betrayal of the life which God intended. Death truly is our greatest enemy. Through the experience of Lynette's death, however, I encountered this terrible enemy and found it already defeated. Through Lynette's death I experienced the truth of the Apostle Paul's words, "O death, where *is* thy sting? O grave, where *is* thy victory?" By experiencing her death, I feel much more prepared to face my own. She truly did have "a Christian end to her life, painless, blameless and peaceful."

I have noticed several different responses to death over the past year. Many dear people search for the right words to say and express many things which are kind and beautiful, but I have noticed that their responses often fall into three categories. First, there is the emotional response to death, which points to desperation and despair. Death is the end of everything and an unexplained tragedy which provokes inconsolable grief, uncontrolled wailing, anger and alienation.

I describe the second response as secular. It accepts death as a natural part of life. Many books on grieving fall into this category. They explain death as a natural part of the life cycle. Seeds are planted, they grow, they age, and they die. Animals are born, they mature, they grow old, and they die. These books point to the normal cycle of life and say that we must simply accept death as a part of that cycle. People are born, they grow up, they grow old, and they die. Our loved ones grow old and die, and we will grow old and die. The sooner we accept this fact, the easier it will be on all of us. There is no inherent meaning to life or death, and the sooner we accept the fact of death, the less we will allow the fear of it to spoil the fun of life.

Finally, I saw the pseudo-religious approach to death. This view says that life in this fallen world is essentially evil, and we should gladly embrace death because it liberates us from this evil. Our real life begins after death. Life in this world only prepares us for the next life; thus death is not a tragedy, but a gift.

Although we may see elements of truth in all of these responses, I've realized that none of them are truly Christian. As Christians, we do not despair in the face of death, nor do we accept it as a normal part of life, nor do we embrace it as something good. Death is essentially abnormal. It is the destruction of what God intended. It is our great enemy, with which we must never make peace. The fact that we can be at peace in the face of death does not mean that we have made peace with it. We find peace with death because God has proven victorious over it. "Christ is risen from the dead, trampling down death by death, and upon those in the tombs bestowing life." This is the Christian approach.

Two qualities which we strove to cultivate throughout Lynette's illness were living life in the present and experiencing the joy of each moment. These, of course, go hand in hand. We grew in these and especially experienced them during her last days of life. I was able to experience this joy even on the day Lynette went home to the Lord.

Throughout the year since she died, I have reflected on that experience and realize how easily I have lost that joy. Logically, it would seem that if I can rejoice on the day of her death, then there is no day in which I will not rejoice. The reality, though, is that I face a daily challenge to live in joy. God gave me the gift of joy in the midst of a very difficult situation, but it is so easy to slip from this joy in the mundane struggles of each day's problems. I often find myself depressed, and annoyed and saddened by things of very small consequence. On one hand, I realize that this is part of the grieving process, yet on the other hand, I understand that I am surrendering the victory which is mine in Christ. I want to live each day in that gift of joy which Christ gives us.

I have found that it is possible to "rejoice in the Lord always," but it is also possible to forget the gift of joy. I think here lies one of the greatest tools which our enemy uses. He tempts us to slip from the daily, hourly, minute-by-minute experience of our Lord's joy, and gets us to face life as a struggle and drudgery. We should be filled with joy each day because we live the life of the resurrected Christ. "It is no longer I who live, but Christ who lives in me," and when we realize this, we comprehend that He loves us more than we can imagine. This is true every single day, regardless of what circumstances occur around us. This reality should sufficiently fill us with joy.

Flights from Tirana International Airport often leave very early in the morning, in order to connect with transatlantic flights and other European routes at the European hubs. This means that we often take off in the darkness just before daybreak. Many times it is rainy and cloudy as the airplane climbs to altitude, and then we experience a magical moment when we break through the clouds and see the rising sun. Each time I experience this, I think of it as a parable for our lives. We often live in the darkness under the rain and clouds, forgetting the true shape of reality. An obvious yet amazing truth is to remember that every day is sunny above the clouds. Every time we fly, we break out into amazing sunlight above the clouds. And the Son of righteousness shines forth every day despite the storms we feel around us. Each day, if we could only remember that above the clouds of life, the Son is shining, we have reason to live in His joy.

Lynette's Legacy

Lynette's memory continues to act as a shining witness here in Albania. The one-year memorial service, though poignant, was a joyful event celebrating her life and commitment to Christ. Archbishop Anastasios led the memorial service at the Annunciation Cathedral in Tirana and at the graveside in St. Vlash. A beautiful lunch hosted by the Archbishop followed in the seminary dining hall. During the lunch many people reflected on the life of Lynette and what her witness had meant to them.

I feel truly blessed by the years I spent with Lynette. I met her in the fall of 1988 as a 21-year-old college student. We grew together, finding our home in the Orthodox Church and our life's work in the Albanian mission. She blessed, challenged, and enriched my life in so many ways. I learned to see so much more of the color and joy of life by looking through her eyes. She challenged and inspired me to draw closer to our Savior by walking together on the journey of life. Together we received two of God's greatest gifts in our children, Tristan and Katherine, who continue to bless me.

The barrier between time and eternity has become a little more translucent since Lynette has crossed it. Though I still cannot see beyond, I have a much stronger sense of the reality of life on that side of the river. She is now part of that great cloud of witnesses which cheers us all on in our race. I feel strongly that God knew when

Lynette's race was finished and when it was time for her to go home.

I am tempted to view the remainder of my life as an epilogue, but I feel strongly that I am left here because there is still a race to run. I must embrace each new stage of the journey knowing that it is what God has prepared for me in His love for my salvation. I do not know what is in store for us on this road, or how long it will be, but I am striving to keep my eyes on Jesus. As I run, I strive each day to live in the joy of that day and in the present moment. It is this point at which time touches eternity and where we experience our Lord.

You've read her words—
now hear her voice!

ANCIENT FAITH RADIO
www.ancientfaithradio.com

A free download of Lynette's last talk, given just two weeks before she died, is available at the following link:

http://audio.ancientfaith.com/specials/endoflife_pc.mp3

The text of this moving talk about her own impending death is given on pages 187–193 of this book.

About the Editor

F R. LUKE A. VERONIS SERVED AS AN OCMC MISSIONARY FOR TWELVE years, more than ten of which were in Albania. During their final six years in the mission field, he and his family not only worked as co-missionaries, but became dearest of friends with the Hoppe Family. Fr. Luke presently pastors Ss. Constantine and Helen Greek Orthodox Church in Webster, Massachusetts, while teaching as an adjunct instructor at Holy Cross Greek Orthodox School of Theology and St. Vladimir's Seminary. He serves as a consultant for the Orthodox Christian Mission Center, and has authored the book *Missionaries, Monks and Martyrs: Making Disciples of All Nations.*